How to Avoid Getting Mugged in Rio de Janeiro by Singing Songs from Grease and Other Lesser Known Travel Tips.

By

Yeats

Copyright © 2023
All rights reserved.
No part of this book may be reproduced in any form or by any electronic or mechanical means including information storage and retrieval systems, without permission in writing from the author. The only exception is by a reviewer who may quote brief excerpts in a review. This book is a work of nonfiction. Names, places, and incidents are real except where the book notifies, they have not been changed because I have nothing of any value someone could sue me for.
Edited by Celie Verleysen de Nagy
Published at Amazon
ISBN: 979-8870611822

Table of Contents

Introduction	1
1	3
2	7
3	13
4	17
5	23
6	30
7	33
8	41
9	47
10	54
11	62
12	67
13	72
14	81
15	87
16	91
17	95
18	100
19	106
20	111
21	116
22	124
23	128
24	134
25	142
26	146
27	152
28	156
29	163
30	171
31	174
32	179

33	185
34	188
35	193
36	199
37	203
38	208
39	213
40	218
41	224
42	227
43	231
44	237

Introduction

Welcome to Book 2 in my travel memoir series where I will be giving readers some insights into the secretive life hacks on the best time of year to brew homemade tequila, ways for fathers to keep a straight face accompanying their 12-year-old daughters to a Taylor Swift concert, and how to purchase flooring for a second home in Majorca in the style you love, and the color you want, at a price that meets anyone's budget.

If new readers simply breezed past the fact that this is Book 2 in a vaguely linear series of memoir books, then I do not know exactly what to blame for the state of our education system. European colonialism? Global Warming? COVID?

Sure, any person can read Book 2 without having first opened a Book 1. But if that type of thing is to a person's liking, why not put this book down now and just go straight to Book 3? *How to Survive Making Yourself Look Silly While Dancing with the German Mafia at a Bavarian Nightclub, and Other Lesser Known Travel Tips.*

In fact, any such master of efficiency could also just skip past all the pages in *that* edition and head directly to the final page. The End. Boom. All done in time for dinner. But what will they miss if they do that? They will miss the nutty stuff. The offbeat. The mindlessly dumb. The hilariously stupid.

And enjoying life is all about *not* missing *that* stuff.

And this stuff also includes the times when I might have nearly been killed, almost shat my pants, or had to deal with my ex mother-in-law.

During my professional career in hospitals, I saw many dying people sadly arriving at their final page having skimmed through the moments of irreverence, craziness, and downright head scratching that should be a feature of anyone's life. I have done so much head scratching that I have worn parts of my hairline down to the skull.

Many people's lives peter out with the regret of having spent it chained to a desk staring at a screen all day, without ever having risked a single minute on an overseas adventure. You can see it in a person's eyes as they take their last breath. There are two types of people in this world. Those who diligently strove their entire lives to be productive for their boss and, as they expire, wish they had taken the opportunity to do something a little crazy. And those who hired a marching band to play *Wild Thing* by the Troggs as they quit their job before heading overseas to try their hand at professional wrestling in Mexico, and who regret nothing on their deathbed.

Readers should at least have some aspirations of the latter if they hope to appreciate the stories in this book.

But that is all set up in Book 1, which comprises stories in a poorly defined area of Oceania. This book deals with my continued misadventures in life while traveling through the Americas. North and South. Why is that geographic region featured in this book?

That is all set up in Book 1.

Will the stories contained in the following pages, about running around the globe with my pants perpetually on fire, be funny and interesting?

That is all set up in Book 1.

Will I ever coincidentally be reunited with the gorgeous French flight attendant, who I met for drinks in Delhi, before she broke my heart, and I was nearly pistol whipped by the police after a show by a disfigured stripper in the red-light district, even though all I wanted to do was go back to my hotel?

Read Book 1. Then read Book 2. Then read Book 3. Then wait for the movie to come out.

If you have already read Book 1 and are wondering, when am I going to get on with it? I apologize. Just had to stop and help those that have arrived at the party late.

Let us now have at it.

1

A Mexican magician tells the audience he will disappear on the count of three. He says, 'Uno, dos...' and poof! He disappears without a tres.

Like the Boston tea party held to save rich people from paying their fair share of taxes to the Crown, my experiences in the Americas started with a bang.

I spend my first night in the USA, in a downtown Los Angeles motel, wrapped in a wet blanket of fear, dismayed I have been dropped onto the set of a dystopian film. *The land of the free and the home of always needing to defend myself with a gun.* In November 1988, I was only 20. Timid and naïve, but taking life by the short and curlys, venturing to another country on my own. In a group, but by myself in that group. Everyone else on the university work exchange heads to the US that Northern Hemisphere winter/Southern Hemisphere summer with a companion. Except for one other guy in the 30 strong party, Dohers. I will get to him later. This is my coming-of-age experiment. I will have to dig deep inside me to find the character to survive three months in the US, or else I will turn tail and jump on the first plane home.

On that first night in the city of angels, a return flight was looking awfully tempting.

Our downtown motel looks like a block from Skid Row. I had never seen a homeless person before in my life. I naively thought that spending 20 minutes sitting on the sidewalk at the end of my parent's driveway when I ran away from home qualified as having been homeless for periods of my youth. Every time I venture out to go to the nearby diner to eat, I am evading homeless people pushing shopping carts like a game of *Frogger*.

Making the USA my first port of call as an independent overseas traveler, after just one week-long ski trip to Thredbo on the solo, is as nerve-wracking as being asked to fill in on lead guitar for *The Rolling Stones* after one guitar lesson.

"Hey kid. I heard you plucking on those strings, and you've got potential. I need you to fill in on the opening night of *The Stones' Voodoo Lounge Tour* in Springfield. Keith Richards has..."

"... Keith Richards has died?"

"Keith Richards. Dead? Fuck no. That bastard will still be kicking long after you are pushing up daisies, my friend. No, Keith wanted to be at the birth of his 76th illegitimate child, so he asked if I could find a replacement for him for the one night."

"Wow. Do you think I am up for it?"

"Not by a long shot. But Mick Jagger will get a kick out of watching you squirm."

In 1988, the USA still has the allure of the biggest, baddest hombre on the planet. ICBMs. Space Shuttles. The Cold War. While its cities are billed as gleaming Parthenons of its economic glory.

Downtown L.A. is not a concrete jungle. It is a concrete Redwood Forest. The massive skyscrapers towering overhead are 100 floors higher than anything I have seen in my life. Humans scurry along at street level in the shadows of the high-rises like ants on the rotting foliage of the forest floor. Sydney paled in comparison, and you know my thoughts about Sydney from Book 1. For those of you who do not, I will have to check with security as to how a novice made it this far into Book 2 without being apprehended.

L.A. is expansive, uncaring, and scary. I am not feeling the love for this city at all.

However, I fare slightly better on day two than on that restless first night. My first brush with death will not happen till day three. Dohers, the other loner on the tour, and I bond quickly. He and I are of the same age group of people at university. We attended different high schools in Brisbane and likely played against each other in inter-school sport. Without ever knowing who the other person was until now. The difference between us is that Dohers has more charisma than Wagner's 15-hour epic opera, *Der Ring des Nibelungen*, has musical notes. While I am a six-year-old at their first flute lesson.

But Dohers happily takes me under his wing, and we form our own little 2-man wolf pack. We then merge our wolf pack with a pair of guys traveling together who are a few years older than us, and we have a wolf herd. Safety in numbers, we all figure. On Day two, the wolf stampede takes a three-hour local bus ride down Wilshire Blvd. to the campus of UCLA. Which seems far enough away to be on the other side of the planet.

Traveling fifteen miles in Los Angeles' traffic takes as long as the opening of a Wagner opera. But we are rubbing shoulders with the Hollywood elite as we pass them on public transport and are starting to think we are invincible. The wolf brigade.

Riding public transport in L.A. provides a quick lesson in pre-planning when not in the familiar environs of my home city. The bus fare is exactly one dollar, but the driver does not give change. And he does not care if a person does not have the right amount. Each individual rider needs a one-dollar bill, or four quarters, or ten dimes, or five dimes and ten nickels, or 100 pennies. Or any other combination of the above. If I only have eight dimes, three nickels, and four pennies, then I am given a curt, "get off my damn bus!" If I only have a 20-dollar note, I get to ride the bus, but am a poorer man by exactly 19 dollars.

I have travelers' checks.

Ask an L.A. public bus driver if he accepts travelers' checks and he will give you a look like you are about to be shanked.

Thankfully, one of the members of the wolf colony has a wallet full of single ones.

That morning we found out from the motel receptionist that the Los Angeles Lakers and the Los Angeles Clippers are playing a professional basketball game in a stadium only a mile away from our motel. Superstars Magic Johnson and Kareem Abdul-Jabbar will be fronting up for the Lakers. This was too good to believe. The stars are aligning. My second night in L.A. and I have a chance to see sporting legends who would be recognized anywhere on the planet. Even though the Lakers are a huge draw, the

Clippers are so bad in 1988 that we understand there will be plenty of empty seats in the house.

Good enough reason to risk our lives again on L.A. public transport.

But this may also require me putting my complete lack of bartering skills to the test with trying to scalp some tickets.

That night, the wolf army ride the public bus straight down Flower St, one block over from the motel to Exposition Park. The site of the L.A. Coliseum featured in the 1984 Olympics. At night, the sense of invincibility we had that afternoon at UCLA has worn off. We are all on a knife edge. Every Hollywood movie about gangs, stabbings and shootings, showcasing the violence of American inner cities, seems to be set on a bus at night. So, a ten-minute downtown bus ride after sunset could equate to at least two murders.

2

Home is where you trust the toilet seat.

The first time a person travels somewhere new, they do not know what to expect.

My understanding of what went on in the world outside of Australia was primarily limited to the news and films I had watched. In movies set in Europe, the only people shooting and killing each other were secret agents in the mold of James Bond. In contrast, American movies were the Wild West. Even romantic comedies would feature at least half a dozen incidence of gang violence, or a female lead whose family had ties to the mafia.

Taking a simple bus ride at night feels like *Escape from New York.*

We arrive at the Los Angeles Memorial Sports Arena, beside the Coliseum, with all our body parts free from bullets. Now we must find the courage to buy tickets from the strange dark men standing on the side of the road dressed like pimps. It is all very nerve racking for a 20-year-old.

Thankfully, For Dohers, it is like a fireman coming to an elementary school class to talk to the kids about fire safety. And he is the fireman. The imposing figures hawking tickets out of their fur-fringed lined coats adore Dohers. They love him. He has them eating out of his hand in short order. We get our tickets for what seems like a bargain. Then take photos of the four of us and at least eight pimps. Surreal.

Some people have this innate ability to remain incredibly sociable, even when faced with a blood-thirsty mob. They can transcend cultural differences and knives brandished in front of their face with one hand tied behind their back. Mahatma Gandhi was like this. Nelson Mandela was another. Dohers is also one such person.

Then there is me. Apparently, people cannot pay for scalped sports tickets with travelers' checks either.

Travel tip. When feeling out of your depth overseas, always try to link up with someone who oozes confidence like it is sweat. Spend enough time with them. Some of that swagger will undoubtedly rub off on you.

Bonus travel tip. Make sure you hang out with people who carry cash.

The wolf regiment watches the game. The Clippers are in it until the starting tip off. Magic Johnson, Kareem, and the Lakers put on a clinic. What a night. What a start to a three-month trip. Can anything derail this adventure?

Sure.

Because now we must get back to the motel. And it is close to midnight.

Like clever little lemmings, the wolf horde makes their way back to the stop where we had gotten off the bus earlier when arriving at Exposition Park. It takes about 20 minutes, and the arrival of one bus, for us to work out that any bus from here will take us in the wrong direction. Flower Street is one way. When the motel receptionist gave us instructions on how to get to the arena, we did not think to ask how to get back.

It is always a capital idea to get directions on how to return home.

Getting lost while traveling is as much fun as a fractured skull.

Also, an even better idea is to remember the name of your motel and what street it is on.

There is a tanned gentleman with an inordinate amount of tattoos sitting on the bench at the bus stop, but he does not get on the bus when it arrives. Why would someone sit at a bus stop for over 20 minutes if they were not waiting to get on the bus? Perhaps he was homeless? Upper class homeless, because he had a bench.

One of the older members of the wolf gang decides to ask this man if he knows how we can get a bus back to downtown.

"Mate, do you know how we can get back to downtown?"

"No hablo Ingles," the stranger replies.

"What is he saying?" I ask.

This is my very first worldly interaction with a person who speaks a language that is not English. Also, the first time I have met someone with so many tattoos on his neck. The same goes for everyone else in the wolf battalion.

"He speaks Spanish," deduces Dohers.

The group's combined grasp of Spanish extends only as far as Arnold Schwarzenegger's line in *Terminator 2*. *Hasta la vista, baby*. At least we knew how to say goodbye confidently.

Except for one member of our tribe.

Dohers claims he has done some preparation for this exact scenario by learning some phrases in Spanish prior to the trip. His claim sounds legitimate. He has constantly been greeting everyone we met in Los Angeles with the line, "Que pasa, tio?" The translation in Doher's mind is, that he is asking *What is going on, mate*. Sure, when a person is talking to a person from Spain. *What is going on, uncle*, if talking with a person from any other Spanish-speaking country.

"You have to understand that there are masculine words and feminine words in Spanish. Nouns ending in the letter 'a' are feminine. Those ending in 'o' are masculine. Amigo, man. Amiga, female," Dohers lectures us.

"I'm already confused. Why do they do that?" I ask.

"It is derived from Latin," he says.

"Fucking Romans," hisses the drunkest member of the wolf group.

Dohers steps up to the man on the bus bench. "¿Que pasa, tio?"

"No soy tu tío," the man replies seriously. *I am not your uncle.*

"What did he say?" I ask.

"He said all is cool," Dohers answers me confidently. "Tio is slang for things being cool."

"That's good," I respond reassured, not wanting to get on anyone's bad side while standing on a deserted road in a rough-looking neighborhood of L.A. after midnight. Even if the person whose bad side I did not want to get on was homeless. And especially if he had lots of tattoos. He is probably not so homeless as to not own a gun.

Dohers turns back to the stranger. "Do you know how we can catch a bus back to downtown?"

I think nothing of the fact that Dohers has gone back to speaking to the man in English. My awareness of cultural differences is limited to the idea that we needed to speak Spanish just by way of introduction, after which both parties would carry on the conversation in English. Dohers is as confused as I am when the man looks at us like we are as stupid as a bag of rocks.

"No hablo Ingles," he repeats incredulously. "Habla Español?"

"He is asking if I speak Spanish," translates Dohers. This is somehow looked upon as success in this endeavor. "Si, habla Espanol. Do you know how we can catch a bus back to downtown?"

"Si."

"He said, yes. He knows where we need to catch the bus."

None of us are smart enough to understand that Dohers has inadvertently told the man that *the man* speaks Spanish. *Si habla Espanol* is a statement. Yes, you speak Spanish. The man replied, si. Yes. He had asked Dohers, *Habla Español? Do you speak Spanish?* But Dohers had not gotten far enough into his Spanish phrase book to learn that verbs need conjugating. As for the part of the sentence with the question about catching a bus? Well, the man likely did not understand. But we did not know that. We thought this conversation was going places.

"Where do we catch the bus?" the four of us ask in unison.

"Habla Español?" The man asks again.

"Si, habla Espanol," answers Dohers.

"Si," says the homeless man.

Blank stares between the five of us.

"I don't understand why he doesn't just tell us where to catch the bus," Dohers says.

"Fucking Romans," chimes in the drunkest wolf.

"Habla Espanol," Dohers tries again. "I am telling him I speak Spanish."

"Si. Hablo Español."

"Then the bus stop for downtown. Where is it?" Dohers implores.

A blank stare from the homeless man followed by a scowl.

"¿Qué pasa, tio?" Demands Dohers.

"No soy tu tio," the man yells angrily.

"This Roman is fucking with us," throws out the drunk wolf.

It occurs to me that if the UN cannot get shit done, then what chance do we have of sorting out this mess? A taxi is coming towards us down Flower St., and I flag it down.

"G'day mate. We are not sure where we want to go, but it is a motel in downtown. Near a diner. And there are lots of homeless people around it," I say to the man behind the wheel.

"I got you sorted," replies the driver.

"Get in," I call out to the others. The wolf rebellion jumps into the taxi. I am in the front passenger seat. "Hey guys, can someone give me some money to pay for the taxi? I only have travelers' checks." I turn to the driver, "you don't take travelers' checks, do you?"

The Latino driver laughs heartily.

"I'll take that as a no."

At least he understands English, or we would have been back to ten minutes of arguing whether the driver was insulted by Dohers referring to him as family.

The taxi is facing the wrong direction for downtown. This means we will waste valuable money going in a direction we do not want to go. But we are confident the driver will not drive too far south down Flower St. before turning around and heading north. He does. After a block and a half, Flower St. becomes Figueroa St. but the taxi goes at least six blocks south before making a U-turn and heading north on Figueroa. Figueroa then becomes one way all the way to downtown. Luckily our motel is on Figueroa and Dohers spots it.

If we had any directional sense, we could have just walked one block over from Flower St. to Figueroa and caught a bus there. But we did not know. That lack of knowledge, and our lack of common sense, cost us an extra $10 on top of what we would have paid in bus fare for the four of us.

Travel tip. If a person is traveling in a foreign-speaking country and expects to chat with the locals, they only have two options. Option number one is that they make a concerted effort to learn enough rudimentary words and phrases to converse with the locals in their language. Or option number two: insist that any person they speak with present them with a TOEFL certificate, signifying they have passed a test of English being their second language. If a person has TOEFL tattooed across their forehead, even better.

12

As our taxi pulls away from the curb, the drunkest member of our party leans out the window and shouts at the homeless man on the bench.

"Hasta la vista, Roman."

3

I want to die peacefully in my sleep, like my grandfather. Not screaming and yelling like the passengers in his car.

I can never forget the day that Roy Orbison died. It was a Wednesday. Or he died on the Tuesday night and the world woke up to this sad news the following morning. The same Wednesday that the wolf flock piles into an Oldsmobile courtesy of the National Rent-A-Car agency in downtown L.A., to drive to Steamboat Springs, Colorado.

The sedan is a horrible shade of tan, already the worst color imaginable. This car was destined to become a rental the moment it rolled off the production line. No one would ever buy it. I was not even comfortable renting it. I am about to have my introductory lesson driving on the right-hand side of the road during morning rush hour in the city that not only invented traffic jams but also perfected the concept.

I would rather give a rabid skunk a proctology exam in a locked closet than have to drive in Los Angeles traffic.

But this is where I am.

Pretty Woman is the first song we hear when we turn on the radio.

It is also the second and the third. And the tenth. And the hundred and sixth. And it does not stop. *Pretty Woman* is the song *du jour* on the multitude of radio stations of the L.A. Metroplex. Crikey, doesn't dead Roy have any other songs? It is hard enough coming to grips with having the steering wheel on the opposite side of the car that I am used to. Spending the entire drive to Las Vegas constantly reaching for the radio tuning knob with my right hand is requiring much of my concentration. *Pretty Woman* is everywhere. The entire wireless broadcast system was one endless stream of tributes to the man who wore sunglasses while he slept.

It is funny until it becomes psychologically distressing.

"Good morning, Los Angeles, this is KBIG radio bringing our listeners the sad news that Roy Orbison has passed away. Here is his classic, *Pretty Woman*..."

"What a beautiful morning it is to be waking up under the grace of our Lord and savior Jesus Christ on Cornerstone Christian Radio, but we have some sad news this morning: Roy Orbison has died. Let's listen to his classic *Pretty Woman*..."

"This is Go Country 105.1, country music non-stop 24 hours a day even when you can't stand another note of it, saying rise and shine to all our country music fans out there rolling out of bed. Sad news coming in off the wire. One of the greats, Roy Orbison, has passed away. You won't need any introduction to this classic. Here it is. *Pretty Woman*..."

"KROQ radio burning up the Southern California airwaves starting off this hard rocking Wednesday morning with a little tribute to Roy Orbison who as of today is no longer with us. *Pretty Woman* coming at you from the number one rock station on your FM dial..."

Even the Spanish language stations were all over it.

"Buenos días, amigos y amigas. Esta es Radio Salsa KLLI Cali 93.9 FM. La triste noticia para comenzar el día es que la leyenda de la música Roy Orbison falleció y no transmitiremos nada más que la canción *Pretty Woman* todo el día..."

Who knew that Spanish Christian Country radio stations could find enough listeners to sell advertising and avoid bankruptcy?

"Dios es grande. Dios es maravilloso. Vive alabando su nombre mientras escuchas Radio Nueva Vida. Esta mañana ha fallecido el gran Roy Orbison. Aquí está nuestra canción favorita de la gran cantante, *Pretty Woman*..."

Apart from learning that any song can become insufferable when heard too often, I discover that driving on the opposite side of the road on the freeways in downtown L.A. morning rush hour is not the scariest exercise in the world. Getting *to* the freeway on-ramp is the most terrifying.

Once a vehicle is settled into freeway traffic, its driver is an Atlantic salmon in a school of other salmon. They can simply follow the flow. Cars in front move, they move. Cars in front stop, they stop, and quickly try tuning to another radio station not playing *Pretty Woman*. However, making three right hand turns driving from the rental car lot onto the freeway on-ramp was a freaking nightmare.

The other members of the wolf swarm decide that I am the most boring, and therefore most responsible person in the group, so I am the first behind the wheel. Everyone else was drunker than I was last night at the basketball, as their friendship did not yet extend to loaning me money to buy beers because I only had travelers' checks. As hungover as the drunkest member from last night is this morning, I am surprised National rents him a car. Luckily they do, as he is the only one with both a credit card and a driver's license showing he is over 21.

As he is handed the keys by the rental agent, he immediately turns around and presses them into my hands. "Get us to Vegas."

In 1988, getting from downtown Los Angeles to Steamboat Springs, without the benefit of satellite GPS, took some planning and legwork. First night's stop was going to be Las Vegas. Another group of people that banded together from the work exchange were going to a different ski resort in Colorado. They had only rented their car as far as Vegas, thinking from there they would catch a bus. How naïve were they?

We were only naïve enough to think we could do it without a map. Surely there would be signs telling us which way to go for the entire journey. None of us had any real concept of how large the US was. Or how many freeways there were that go in every direction between north and south. But every journey of a thousand miles starts with that first step.

The first step was getting on the freeway. Easy enough to say.

But saying and doing are two entirely different matters.

The National Rent-A-Car employee responsible for inspecting our vehicle prior to us leaving the lot tells me how to get it done with easy, clear instructions.

"It is going to be simple. Drive out of the lot, turn right. Turn right again at the second light and make a third right at the next street and after one block, there will be a freeway on-ramp to your right."

"Beautiful mate, that sounds like a piece of cake. Three right hand turns, on-ramp to my right," I repeat back confidently.

"Three right hand turns, yep. Just don't turn the wrong way down the one-way street after the first right-hand turn. Go two blocks, then second right. You cannot screw it up."

"Perfect. And then once on the freeway. How do I get to Vegas?" My final question.

Now the National Rent-A-Car employee speaks an unfamiliar language.

"Once up the on-ramp, you will be on the 110. Take that to the 101. From there, it is a quick change to get on the 10. Stay on the 10 for quite a while until you get to the 15 and that will take you to Vegas."

"Mate, I don't follow you at all."

"There will be signs for Vegas. Follow those."

"And double checking with getting on the freeway," I recap. "Three right hand turns. Don't drive the wrong way up a one-way street, and on-ramp on my right."

"Simple," he nods.

Simple.

For this National Rent-A-Car employee most things in life are simple. Losing a limb. Beating cancer. Dealing with rejection from French flight attendants. But, less than half a kilometer of inner city driving ends up being a more lethal endeavor than the video games *Frogger*, *Grand Theft Auto,* and *Call of Duty* combined.

At least my *Frogger* skills have been honed to a laser sharp point while making my way to the diner over the last few days.

4

It's not the fall that kills you. It's the sudden stop at the end.

If the motel we had been staying in was *close* to Skid Row, then the lot for National-Car-Rental is Skid Row's living room. While I am fretting over learning to solve the Sudoku of highway numbering to make it to Vegas, the other members of the wolf litter start chatting to a prostitute named Marcia, who is just hanging out in the rental lot. Marcia is originally from Detroit, so I will come to realize later that L.A.'s Skid Row is a step up for her in terms of living standards.

The others inform me that Marcia is a lovely soul, and is willing to accompany us on our trip to Colorado for the right price and a return airline ticket. And they have been seriously discussing this. It is left to me to shoot down the idea. I go from being laughed at for trying to pay for everything with travelers' checks, to being despised as Commissioner Gordon of the fun police.

"I am sure Marcia is a sweet soul, but no."

I must get this show on the road and keep it there.

Take four naïve, 20-year-oldish Australians. Cram them into a tacky, oversized American-made car with luggage and drop them in the heart of the seedy underbelly of one of the world's most populous cities.

What do you get?

Apart from tactful negotiations with hookers.

What we come up with is the phrase, "Jesus, get us out of here. Don't stop for red lights!"

And that is exactly what I do.

Dohers, apart from his mastery of Spanish, has come armed with the knowledge that US drivers enjoy the luxury of legally being allowed to make a right-hand turn at a red light if traffic is clear. In downtown L.A., I extend that rule into justified clearance to proceed in any direction at a red light, in any amount of traffic.

The Yeats' Law is in full effect.

We first learn that Roy Orbison has died as I gingerly back the car out of the rental space. The pervading sense of melancholy in the car seems appropriate, knowing that we all might be dead soon ourselves, what with my driving. A few feet away from the car, Marcia's pimp is starting to get agitated in his conversation with her, presumably over something relating to us, and he opens his coat to display a gun in his waistband.

Say no more.

My foot rams the accelerator to the floor. The Oldsmobile's wheels spin in the gravel and we speed down the line of parked cars in reverse. I quickly throw the car into drive and head straight out the exit and onto the street. I turn right without checking for oncoming traffic, narrowly missing a policeman who is arresting a drug dealer on the sidewalk.

All I care about is, *right-hand turn. Then stay on the right side of the street. You need to drive on the right-hand side of the street.*

Dohers yells out the window, "the pimp has a gun."

But the police officer probably hears that line so often that he does not even bother looking up.

Before our car makes it the two blocks, past the one-way street and leading up to the all-important second right-hand turn, we are passed by three police cars with their sirens wailing. These patrol cruisers are responding to a call for backup from an officer performing a traffic stop just around my second right-hand turn.

This is unique to Los Angeles. Whenever a patrol car makes even a simple traffic stop for a broken taillight, dozens of other police vehicles show up. Hundreds, if they are close enough. Any police officer in the city, who is not otherwise involved in solving a high-profile case like the Nicole Brown Simpson murder, or on traffic detail at a location movie shoot, descends on the location.

It must be intimidating for the criminal.

It is intimidating for me, and I have nothing at all to do with whatever the offender has done. The police officers always make a point of parking their patrol vehicles in the most haphazard way possible, impeding traffic. It is frustrating as a law-abiding citizen. Nothing is orderly and precise. Like the way some wankers chaotically throw dice when playing Monopoly. They can never keep them on the playing board. *Ahh fuck it, I am throwing the dice against the wall. My turn, fuck it, I am going to hit the cat on this throw.*

This police practice must be adding immensely to the disarray and congestion that is Los Angeles traffic. Police cars snarl traffic to educate an unknowing driver on how bad driving can cause traffic congestion. I have barely completed two-thirds of my assigned right hand turns and I am corralled in the police car version of Yahtzee.

I cautiously drive around the patrol cars parked randomly across the street. At the next right-hand turn, I hesitate briefly as two fire engines barrel down the road I am turning onto. This is all the time it takes for a vagrant dealer standing on the curb to proposition the two wolf members in the back seat to buy drugs. I inch the car forward to signal our lack of interest to the vendor. The front of the vehicle comes within a meter of a bag lady pushing her shopping trolley across the intersection.

The lady with the shopping trolley stands in front of the car and screams at me.

Everything she is saying is incoherent, and I can barely understand a word of it. Worthy inspiration for any number of Eddie Vedder crooned *Pearl Jam* songs.

"What! Y'all get up all in my... Who you think you... Jesus... Don't be looking like... I'ma punch you in the... Damn Jesus... in the face... You be smiling... Out your damn ass... And they called, and I said that I want what I said... And then I called out again."

It seems bag ladies have personal space issues. It would have been nice if the National Car-Rental guy had dropped that nugget of intel on me as well.

"If you come within a few feet of a homeless person and their shopping trolley with the car, they will attack you. Your insurance will not cover this."

The woman stomps up to the grill with the shopping cart and rams it against the front bumper. I am in tears. I have no idea what to do. What does the law allow me to do? If right hand turns are permissible at red lights, is running over a psycho, homeless woman damaging my rental car for no reason given a thumbs up, as well?

The drug dealer reappears at the back window.

Roy Orbison is wailing, *pretty woman, walking down the street. Pretty woman, the kind I like to meet.* I am one more right-hand turn away from the promised land, two if you include the deviation to get on the on-ramp. My breathing becomes short and rapid. The USA is a land of firsts. My first time driving on the right-hand side of the road. My first time being attacked by a homeless person. And my first panic attack.

I hate downtown Los Angeles, country/pop music, and the indigent with a burning passion.

I wish I had never left home.

The enraged homeless woman starts coming around the car towards me on the driver's side.

I am petrified. But I now have an opening.

Say no more.

I press my foot to the floor. We accelerate around the corner. The car bumps the shopping trolley out of the way as we push past it, and it rolls into the gutter. This unleashes more unintelligible ranting from the bag lady.

"I see them... Round the front way, yeah... And I know and I know, I don't want to stay... Make me cry."

The last right-hand turn is now in the bag. The slight move to the right to curl onto the freeway is nothing compared to what I have just been through. It is an on ramp. They do not award a Nobel Prize for people who can negotiate an on-ramp.

However, the genius of traffic in Los Angeles is that on-ramps have stoplights in an attempt to control the flow of vehicles. This is to curtail the backlog of cars caused by a population of drivers who have no idea how to merge into moving traffic. No one coming into the main flow of traffic seems understands how to accelerate, or slow down, in order to squeeze into a gap.

The prevailing approach of the Los Angelenos, in incoming cars on the on-ramp, is to drive at the exact same pace as the traffic on the freeway and expect the drivers already on it will create a gap to let them in. This bypasses the need to learn the whole concept of merging into traffic.

The irony is that these lights appear to create as much of a problem as they attempt to solve. Cars stop at the lights on the ramp, waiting till they get a green light to proceed forward into the merging lane. This causes a backup of traffic at the lights. Vehicles then proceed along the entire length of the merging lane, waiting for someone to allow them into the procession of cars. If they are unsuccessful, they must stop at the end of the lane and aggressively edge their way into the first lane of traffic. This invariably causes drivers to stop and let them in.

Bingo, now there is a traffic jam. The drivers in the first lane then try to move over into the wider lanes, but they do not know how to merge either. So this creates the same mess across the entire freeway.

The end result? Traffic snarls are unending in Los Angeles at all hours of the day and night. Because they have the best traffic mediation system in the world. It is more ironic, more satirical, and more indicative of why human beings should not live in cities the size of Los Angeles than anything.

On the day the wolf mob drives out of L.A., and Roy Orbison became the late Roy Orbison, we hear on the radio that a judge for the city has been involved in a road rage incident.

"Welcome back to KPRR, L.A.s hippest radio channel. With all the new music straight to your ears. If you hadn't heard already, Roy Orbison is dead. Roy Orbison is dead. Oh, this just in. A judge got irate after another driver cut him off on the Ventura freeway, jumped out of his car and shot the other driver dead. Now back to the sad news of the passing of Roy Orbison. Let's all enjoy *Pretty Woman* one more time this morning."

Wow. Hollywood is not just the Wild West in the movies. This was the sole piece of news deemed worthy enough to compete with the demise of Roy Orbison. A gun wielding judge! Not a troubled ex-marine or a trigger happy former con. A member of society held in such high esteem as to be granted the right to pass judgment over our actions. Here he is blowing away a fellow motorist for failing to indicate. Wow. Driving on the freeway in Los Angeles is like nowhere else in the world. It is likely to contain more gunfire than a Clint Eastwood spaghetti western.

Thankfully, when I learned to drive, I was taught how to merge into traffic. Find a gap and go for it. The Oldsmobile makes it safely onto the freeway. All I have to do now is act like an Atlantic salmon. Unless getting onto another freeway demands it, I will not try to change lanes for the next 5 hours. It is my responsibility not only to get us to our destination, but to avoid getting us fatally shot. I yell at the two in the back seat to stop complaining about having no room for the prostitute and to keep an eye out for any cars on the road with gang members, members of the judiciary, or Lee Van Cleef.

Then I settle into driving. Thankfully, there are plenty of signs for Las Vegas on the freeway. All roads lead to Sin City, it seems.

5

Two Wi-Fi engineers got married. The reception was fantastic.

I have never heard of any life-defining travel experience that was perfect. I had one *trip* that was close to perfect. It only lasted a weekend, but did not do anything to test my character. But there were plenty of trips that were far from perfect, and they all influenced me. But never one that was bang on perfect. It does not matter if the trip is a weekend camping trip with the lads, a sports team tour, or a month-long excursion through Europe with a sister stricken with ALS. Whatever it is, there is no chance it will go perfectly. And if it did, you would probably be bored.

But therein lies the beauty of travel.

Give me a far from perfect day of traveling over a month of perfection while sitting at home any day of the week.

My trip to Steamboat in 1988 was life defining for me in so many ways. First time being on my own out of Australia. Overcoming that paralyzing fear. First time standing up on a snowboard. Overcoming my natural uncoordinated self while being too poor to pay for lessons. First time having my newly purchased snowboard stolen. Overcoming grief and anger. First time falling in love. First time having my heart crushed, then stepped on, then thrown in a blender. First time having an UZI in my face.

There was no time in my life more memorable than the three months I spent in Colorado during the winter of 1988. I was a raw lump of clay, and this small northern Colorado ski town was the pottery wheel. It was a huge, tense step up in life. And I learned that facing up to uncertainty will open the unlimited possibilities of the world to me.

Steamboat Springs, often shortened to Steamboat or even The Boat, lives up to its billing as a ski town with a cowboy spirit. Ten-gallon hats and boots are a common sight along the main drag of Lincoln Avenue. The world-famous cowboy downhill runs every January, coinciding with the National Western Stock Show in Denver. Up to 100 professional rodeo riders descend on the town, to show off their complete inability to ski. The Hindenburg landed in a more graceful fashion than these cowpokes after they hit the slopes.

The town's name derives from the abundance of natural, hot mineral springs in the area. Early trappers to the Yampa Valley mistakenly believed that the chugging sound emanating from the hot springs was a steamboat coming down the river. I wonder how many times trappers went off tramping to find animal pelts into the untamed wilderness at an elevation of 7000 feet and stumbled across a steamboat navigating a shallow mountain creek?

Ever since I was in high school, the US sports culture had fascinated me. Americans spend 56 billion dollars a year attending sports events. This is almost the entire GDP of Australia. During winter, no other sport dominates like American Football. And Denver has a team. The Broncos.

Getting to see the legendary Lakers play, by masquerading as Clippers fans, taught me a valuable lesson about taking in sporting events while traveling. Everyone wants to support a team when they are winning. Ticket availability and cost are therefore always at a premium. So, I realized that it is far more cost effective to only ever go and watch a sports team play when they suck.

The 1988 Denver Broncos fit the bill perfectly. The team was having a shithouse season.

Like me, Dohers dreamed of going to a professional football game while in the States. He hatched a plan for us to drive to Denver to watch the last game of the season at Mile High Stadium after the Broncos got eliminated from playoff contention. He would arrange tickets. He would arrange transportation. I just needed to be a passenger.

Wow, could we do this?

It seemed like, for Dohers, anything in life was a possibility. He ate charisma for breakfast and shit personality. His persuasive charms would convince a die-hard, liberal progressive voter to work on Trump's re-election campaign, before having them start a petition for less gun control. He had no issues with traveling to the USA by himself. He was perfectly self-assured. It was almost inevitable that I would follow him around like a lost puppy.

His proposal was simple. Get up early on a Sunday morning, drive four hours to Denver to watch a sport that has 11 minutes of action in its three hours of game time, and then drive four hours back to Steamboat. Child's play. I was wide eyed enough to be 100% enthusiastic but naïve enough to have no consideration of black ice, mountain switchbacks, and poor wheel alignment. A week before the last Denver home game of the season, the cogs of this plan turn into motion.

To attend the game, we first had to buy tickets. There was no internet in 1988. Stubhub.com did not exist. Lastminutetickets.com did not exist. Life as a sports fan was a nightmare in the 80's. But somehow, we all survived. Everything in the 80's was paper tickets and Ticketmaster charging an arm, leg, and kidney for doing nothing more than keeping tickets in an envelope at Will Call. Dohers locates a person in Denver, reselling his season ticket seats for the last home game in the newspaper. He phones the man up to let him know we will drive down on Sunday morning before the game to buy them.

The golden rule of scalping tickets is that the first person in with the cash gets the prize. A bird in the hand is worth two in the bush is the hard doctrine for people in this line of work. Without paying him upfront, Dohers somehow convinces the man to hold the tickets for us till Sunday morning.

I have never been charged with buying anything greater than a movie ticket before. I did not know what the process of scalping a ticket was before I landed in L.A. I still do not, because Dohers handled it all with the pimps. But along with all these new experiences, I am adding street credibility to my resume. Learning new ways to approach life. If there was a way to get things done, then I set the goal to find that way.

Within a week of arrival in Steamboat, the wolf commune had purchased a car. It cost us the grand total of $400. One hundred per person. I do not know if we registered the vehicle, do not know if we had insurance on it. My only role in the transaction was coughing up my split of the price. The one thing I remember is the other members of the wolf team tersely telling me to find a bank to cash a traveler's check, as they would not accept it.

The car was a 1974 Subaru 4WD sedan. It was blood red, and we nicknamed it *The Death Trap* because we could not get the vehicle to drive in a straight line. There was an issue with a tire being bald, or the wheel alignment was off, or the suspension was shot. After outlaying the considerable sum of $400, we were not about to throw more good money after bad to have it assessed by a mechanic. Driving down any street, the car would suddenly deviate two meters to the right.

Dohers and I thought it was a prudent idea to use *The Death Trap* to take us 156 miles and over mountain passes to Denver. There were two routes we had the option of taking. One had a single section of mountain road, Rabbit Ears Pass, and the rest was flat and easy to navigate. Rabbit Ears pass was straightforward. No switchbacks, just elevation gain to 9420 feet. The other route required traversing Rabbit Ears Pass *and* the far more treacherous Berthoud Pass at 11,300 feet. This pass had more switchbacks than Keith Richards has illegitimate children. There were sections of road on both sides of the pass at a white knuckle steep 6.3% grade. Berthoud Pass had been described to us as being jaw dropping in its scenery. When driven in a car with a two-meter margin of error, jaw clenching would be more appropriate.

Because, of course, Dohers and I took the route with the two mountain passes.

It looked slightly less driving distance on a map.

Thank God for that snowbank on one hairpin turn.

But the forging of lifelong friendships happens in those uncertain moments when travelers turn to each other in tears and embrace.

"Didn't you see how far down that cliff is?"

"Well, it is not like I meant to drive towards it."

After a four-and-a-half-hour odyssey, that bumps Hannibal's crossing of the Alps from the top spot of ill-conceived mountain traverses, Dohers and I rejoicingly make it to the flat street grid of Denver. The house we must get the tickets from is out in the eastern suburbs. Denver has a unique way of naming its streets. The East-West avenues follow the simple first, second, third numbering system. The North-South streets have names, and they go alphabetically. Two streets per letter. Lansing Street, then Lima Street, then

Macon Street, then Moline. Of course, some letters get three streets: Jamacia Street, Jamacia Court, Joliet Street, then Kenton, Kingston, and Kramer.

Why?

Because city planners are a pack of arsehats.

Dohers and I get lost in the U, V, W, section of town.

Google maps do not exist in 1988, so we are following handwritten directions Dohers had penned down on a paper napkin.

We find the address with barely 40 minutes left to kickoff.

This is our first experience of suburbia in America. Apart from *Nightmare on Elm Street*, *Scarface*, and *Streets of Fire*. The rows of houses look peaceful, just like they always do in the movies right before a S.W.A.T. team shows up and raids a house. That is a uniquely American experience in which I am not interested. I do not even think we have S.W.A.T. teams in Australia.

Dohers parks the car outside the address. "Go up to the house and get the tickets," he says.

"Why me?" I reply.

"I was the one who drove here."

"You almost killed us on that last pass," I shoot back. "Why does that make it my responsibility to go up to the house alone?"

"It just does," he retorts. "Those are the rules." Dohers had all these secret regulations mandating human behavior that he needed to teach me.

"Why can't we go up together?" I ask.

"One of us has to stay in the car and keep the engine running."

Nothing like a comment hinting that we may need to make a quick getaway to inspire confidence.

I wonder how safe is it in America to walk up to a stranger's home and knock on the door? Extremely safe, moderately safe, or John Lennon safe? Dohers pushes me out the door. "Stop being a pussy." He is making me do this as a favor, he announces.

I tentatively walk up the path to the house. Suddenly, the cold air of a Colorado winter felt even more chilly.

Tapping on the front door, all I can think about are the news stories of American gun violence I saw on television in Australia. Firearms, the second amendment, and vigilante justice are as American as apple pie, 4th of July, and Jerry Springer. The cliché, if it bleeds it leads, does not refer to restaurant customers who order a raw steak getting served their meal first. The media fuels the American fascination with people being shot, or protesting for the people's rights to shoot people, or protesting against the people's right to shoot back when they are shot.

At 20, my underdeveloped brain does not have an opinion on guns either way. I do not like guns but am not averse to bad guys being taken down. Standing outside the house, I am just scared. The homeowner may answer the door with a rain of bullets. While it is highly unlikely that I come face to face with Freddy Kruger, I am not 100% certain that it is completely unlikely either.

I lightly tap on the door again. I feel an impending panic attack, waiting for a response. Opening the door is an African American man dressed in a bright orange suit. He did not seem to be uncomfortable, as if he were wearing the suit because he lost a bet. But he is surprised to find a nervous white kid standing on his doorstep. I stutter I am here to scalp football tickets for him. He bursts out laughing. "You aren't scalping, boy. I am doing the scalping." The introductions out of the way, he grabs me by the arm and pulls me into his living room.

Everything in the house is orange and blue. The carpet, the sofa, the wallpaper. All in the official colors of the Denver Broncos team.

The man has never met an Australian before, so he finds me intriguing. Thankfully, a few notches below Jeffrey Dahmer level intrigued. He wants to know all about my country. I have never met an American black man before. The bulk of my knowledge of African Americans came from watching the urban drama movie *The Warriors* as a teenager. As young minds do, I assume every black man in America was a member of the Riffs gang when he was a teenager. My knees tremble at the pace of a flamenco dancer's castanets.

But the man shows a genuine interest in the land Down Under. And standing in the sea of orange of his living room, before a man in an orange suit, I feel strangely empowered. Bold statements are the theme of the day. So, I grow in confidence. I explain everything I know about Australia as best I can. Starting at the beginning. Aboriginal dreamtime. I then move onto Captain Cook sailing up the East Coast in 1770 and naming the Glasshouse Mountains because they reminded him of the huge glass furnaces in his native Yorkshire.

As I am regaling him with the story of Prime Minister Harold Holt's disappearance while swimming in the surf in 1967, and the likelihood that he was really a Communist spy, I am interrupted by a frantic pounding on the door. It is a panic-stricken Dohers.

"Hey, you left me out there in the car by myself," he chastises me.

I point out that I did not leave him as much as he chose to stay.

"Did you get the tickets?" he asks. "We still need to find the stadium."

I suddenly realized that, as enjoyable as reviewing Australian history with an American who does not know that I do not know what I am talking about was, I had a game to get to. I quickly summarized: The First Fleet; how stealing a handkerchief sentenced convicts to a life in Australia; Bushrangers; the Eureka Stockade; Gallipoli; Gough Whitlam getting sacked as Prime Minister for being a dick; the 1982 America's Cup, and Olivia Newton John being cast in *Grease* as the high-points of my cultural heritage.

Then, tickets in hand, Dohers and I bid our farewell.

My conviction to only pay to watch sports teams that suck, after obtaining game tickets for face value from a die-hard fan whose house interior was decorated in team colors, now solidified.

We head off in search of Mile High Stadium. So named because the city of Denver is at a mile altitude above sea level. This puts the entire city 250 meters higher than the base elevation of Australia's premier ski resort, Thredbo, for those keeping score.

6

Two men walk into a bar. You would think one of them would have ducked.

There are certain experiences people will have overseas that they would never try at home. Plenty of non-drug users visit a coffee shop in Amsterdam to smoke pot for the first time. Plenty of people who would normally play it safe walking across their living room strap themselves into a harness and brave the plank walk on Mt. Huashan in China.

This is a walk alongside a sheer cliff face where hikers tread on narrow strips of wood, nailed into the cliff face on a 7000-foot peak, which creates a ledge 30 cm wide. Adventurers must wear a safety harness attached to the safety line, which allows the bravest to lean out over the drop for the obligatory photo. Then these same people go home and spend their money on buying a vehicle with 14 airbags to keep them safe while driving around the corner to the shops.

After the movie release of *The Beach*, starring Leonardo DiCaprio, drinking snake blood became the new cool thing to do when in South-East Asia. Who would do something that insane at home? If they did, drinking snake blood would be popular in Queensland where I grew up. We have all the snakes a person could want. For snake blood aficionados it would be like living in the Heineken Brewery.

Most of these experiences are risky, if not outright dumb. Running with the bulls in Pamplona is as inherently dangerous as stepping out into traffic. But when a person gets injured in Pamplona, no one questions why they stepped in front of a bull.

"Fractured my leg. Ruptured my spleen. And dislocated my shoulder."

"That's terrible."

"While in Pamplona, running with the bulls."

"That's awesome."

Most of the time, the motivation behind participating in these activities is a pissing contest.

"I bet you don't have the balls to do XYZ," is the most underrated incentivizer in human history. Say this to any man and you can get them to do most anything.

"I bet you don't have the balls to go hang-gliding in Rio?"

"I bet you don't have the balls to do the world's highest bungee jump in South Africa?"

"I bet you don't have the balls to go on the teacups in Disneyland."

I am not a big fan of risky activities, nor am I am also not one for engaging in pissing contests with my mates.

However.

While overseas by myself for the first time in Steamboat Springs, I am susceptible to the feeling that I should be more daring and try anything. No matter how stupid the idea sounds.

That is how people think when they travel.

"Oh, I am on holiday in France. Let me try frog legs."

"Oh, I am on holiday in Japan. Let me go to the fish market and watch vendors eat live eel straight out of the barrel."

"Oh, I am on holiday in South Africa. Let me swim with Great Whites."

And few things in life are more certain than this: it is always a stupid idea to enter a who-can-eat-the-most competition because another person goaded you into it.

And, in no particular order, those more certain items are: politicians will promise voters anything to get elected and then do nothing; *The Bachelor* will wind up being secretly in the love with the runner-up; and once a person moves to an apartment right on the ocean, they will end up going to the beach less often than when they lived miles away.

Ever since the famous egg eating scene in *Cool Hand Luke*, it has somehow become a manly endeavor to eat a greater amount of food than is humanly possible. Paul Newman announces he can consume 50 hard-boiled eggs in an hour. And this ten-minute movie scene has now evolved into international competition. The USA has a professional eating league with rankings even. The MLE, Major League Eating, features heroes such as Joey Chestnut, bad boy Max Suzuki, and Richard 'The Locust' LeFevre. Names with accomplishments that every employee at *Golden Corral's* endless buffet franchises knows by heart.

Eating competitions are thoughtless enough when professionals do it. They should be considered criminal when attempted by untrained amateurs. There is never a good time, never a good reason. No matter the circumstances. Especially when a person is drunk, which is 99.8% of the times these things happen.

I had foolishly accepted an eating challenge once before. At a party, to prove myself to the cooler kids who were there. To gain acceptance.

"I bet you don't have the balls to do it?" my mate Shane cried. I did not, but I still said okay.

The challenge seemed simple. Consume two Weet-Bix in under two minutes at an Australia Day BBQ. Easy to do, most people would think. I thought the same thing. Basic math. One Weet-Bix per minute.

However, there is a reason the Bachelor always goes back to the number two girl he initially passed over. Humans do not always make smart choices when given limited information and are under pressure. I regretted accepting the eating challenge within the first two seconds. The first bite into the Weet-Bix and the flaky bran components of the cereal sucked my mouth dry. It was impossible to chew. I failed the challenge atrociously. It was a humiliating moment in front of my peers at the BBQ.

Never again, I said.

Then what happens? I travel overseas. And suddenly it is easy to forget that there was a reason I did not try stupid things back home.

7

Build a man a fire, and he'll be warm for a day. Set a man on fire, and he'll be warm for the rest of his life.

My job, arranged through the work exchange program, had originally been to work in a coffee shop at the Steamboat ski resort. Selling pastries and liquid morning consciousness. Before this, I did not know how to make a basic cup of coffee. Let alone an espresso. My lack of worldly experience had me wondering why people, before they had their morning coffee, would come to the coffee shop window acting strung out from a heroin detox.

The two older members of the wolf posse were given far more preferable, and lucrative, jobs that involved selling alcohol. Dohers and I, being under 21, were not allowed. He started work as a room service attendant at the Sheraton Hotel.

But Dohers was a man who had the moxie to dream of bigger things while on his first solo overseas trip. He applied for a job on the mountain as a lift operator. My ultimate dream job from when I was a young man. At night, as the wolf pod worked out the nightly sleeping arrangements in the one-bedroom apartment we had rented, I listened breathlessly to his tales of the attention his Australian accent got him while working at his lift. His accent was a novelty and a huge draw.

And Dohers had been stationed on the kiddie lift. He got to act like a fireman coming to give a talk at school every single day.

Wouldn't it be outstanding if I got to do something like that too?

Did I dare to chase after my dreams?

Well, my dreams were certainly not going to chase after me.

In a rash move - completely out of character for me - I quit my job in the coffee shop. I applied at the mountain for a job as a lifty. The winter gods smiled down on me and imparted their blessing, and I was rewarded for following my dream. I was offered a position as the fourth most senior lift operator for the Burgess Creek lift, located halfway up Steamboat Mountain.

I was starting at the bottom of the totem pole. There were three others ahead of me in line for promotion up the corporate ladder at my specific lift. But I had done it. I had achieved one of my life's aspirations.

Nothing in the world can ever take that moment away.

I could not be happier going to work every single day. Even though the operators on the Burgess Creek lift had to be the first ones on the mountain in the morning. This meant I had to be on that 7am gondola ride when the diesel winch was initially cranked up for the day. An early start in the middle of summer, let alone the dead of winter. None of the other guys I worked with seemed to share anything close to my enthusiasm for going to work as a lift operator.

"What is wrong with you?" was their normal greeting, when they saw my excitable, beaming face at 7am when we lined up to walk into the gondola station.

Maybe their life's dream was to be a coffee shop attendant?

Well, I knew of an open position.

There was such a disparity between how I felt about going to this job, and how they looked at it. To them, it was work. To me, it was heaven.

Choose an occupation that you love, and you will never work a day in your life.

The others on my lift all had to get high at 6.55am before they got on the gondola.

I did not need to take a toke; I was high enough on life already. There are no other words for it. And I have stayed high for the 35 years since I did something as basic as going to work in a minimum wage job in another country. I did not know at the time how an experience like this was going to be so priceless.

Dohers was having the same revelation I was. He did not puff either. Dohers certainly did not need to get high on anything. He bristled with happiness, excitement, and energy while brushing his teeth. God help the world if he did toke. The other two members of the wolf regime got high every night after work and never left the apartment.

I assume this is why Dohers asked me to go with him when he wanted to do something stupid.

One Tuesday, there is a call for me on the mountain phone from the kiddie lift. Dohers' excited voice pummels me over the line, "let's go for Taco Tuesday happy hour at the Holiday Inn after work. I am famished."

He did not need to push me. I was starving as well. We were always hungry. The four members of the wolf drove never seemed to be organized enough to go food shopping. Dohers was always leading me off to the pub to teach me how to be sociable. The other two would always remain on the couch in a haze of smoke. The only food item we ever had in the apartment was ice cubes.

But the budget constrained ski lift operators of Steamboat Springs revered the Holiday Inn for its daily happy hour. Every day between four and six, the hotel bar laid out a table with piles of delicious nourishment. The Holiday Inn always had quite the spread. To eat at this buffet, all you had to do was purchase a beer. This made it a magnet for Dohers and I. A few stale tortilla chips and runny salsa was a veritable royal feast compared to a tray of ice.

But up until now, we had always eaten just enough to feel satisfied.

Dohers had to go turn it into a pissing competition. Look away now if you do not want to know the outcome.

"I can eat at least ten tacos," says Dohers. "Maybe 15."

"Great," I answered. "Don't make yourself sick."

"How many tacos do you think you can eat?" he shoots back.

"I don't know. Don't care to find out."

"I bet I could eat more than you."

"Probably. And I am happy for you," I say, avoiding what I fear is coming.

"I bet you don't have the balls to find out."

Ah, the magic words. His taunt ignites the fire in my belly. My fighting spirit is awakened.

"Oh, I have the balls."

"You think you can eat more than me?" He challenges.

"I could try."

"You want to try?"

There is dead space on the line while I think about this for a moment. *Go on Simon, you are overseas. Who is ever going to know if you make a fool of yourself?*

"Yeah, I want to try." I say, my top lip firming.

"Do ya?" Dohers questions.

"Yeah!"

"Yeah?"

"Yeah! Really!" I repeat.

"Yeah? Really?"

"I am sure."

"You are sure, you're sure?"

"I have never been more sure of anything in my life!" I spurt.

This is classic pissing competition banter.

"Let's do it then!" Dohers throws down the gauntlet. He chuckles. "You accepted my challenge. Taco Tuesday happy hour. As many tacos as either of us can eat in the two hours."

"Do I have to drink a beer?" I ask.

"Were you dropped on your head as a child? Of course, you must drink a beer," he scolds.

Dohers is one of those people who would single out a lonely person at a party and chat with them just to make them feel welcome. Then just as likely to ask, let us see who can eat the most slices of pizza?

That is how ridiculously easy it was to propel me into the half-witted situation of testing the elastic limits of my stomach lining. How could I have been so stupid as to fall for the oldest two tricks in the book? Playing on my hubris and playing on the thrill of having food in my stomach. Man's two greatest follies. I assign most of the blame to the weakness of my feeble, hunger possessed mind. And once the challenge had been accepted, I could not back out.

"There is a code of behavior," Dohers informs me. "Once you give your word, you can't break it."

Well, it was official then. I was well and truly roped in.

Rather than pistols at dawn, it was tacos at twilight.

And Dohers was taking this competition as serious as a person could. I arrive at the Holiday Inn to find he has enlisted the help of a guy we had met at a ski rental shop on our first day in Steamboat to act as a match official. In case I try to cheat. I am not sure how a person can cheat in an eating contest apart from throwing the food on the ground then claiming it did not come from their plate. But Dohers is not taking any chances.

This idiotic undertaking is about to unfold like Benny Hill starring in *Cool Hand Luke,* dressed in après ski wear.

I arrived a half hour after the start of Happy Hour, so we will not have full use of the entire 120 minutes of unrestricted eating. Fine with me. As well as being the first lifties on the mountain in the morning, my lift is also the last to close. We must wait for the ski patrol to do their final sweep of the trails. Dohers has an easy run of it at his lift. They shut down promptly at 3.30pm every day.

"Alright kids. Lift is done for the day. Piss off back to your parents."

Dohers already has a beer waiting for me on the table at the Holiday Inn bar. I take a small sip.

"Pussy," he exclaims, watching me touch the beer's head timidly to my lips.

"Gentlemen, let us establish the rules of engagement," booms our judge, Jim, relishing his role in this stupidity. "Each man will collect five tacos on his plate, come back to the table, and devour them. Both of you must then return to the serving table together. A competitor cannot go to refresh his plate alone. This makes it easier to keep track of rounds and the number of tacos consumed."

I do not know how a friendly bet over who can eat the most tacos has elevated me to the status of being 'a competitor,' but here we are.

Hopefully one, or both of us, can only eat six or seven tacos in total and this entire debacle will be over in ten minutes. The rules have been established, so that is it. Now is the time to stop talking and get down to business.

I take another light sip of my beer.

"Pussy."

That was Jim, our esteemed referee, talking.

Now this contest is starting to get under my skin. I am not going to sit back and be the slow starter in this tortoise and hare race. I am going to come out of the blocks showing both, I mean business.

When a person has that mindset at the start of an all-you-can-eat contest, spectators can be certain that things have already started to go downhill.

Dohers and I fill our plates with five tacos for the initial round. My opponent is not overly generous when filling his hard shells with meat, fixings, and condiments. Taco night in my childhood home meant I loaded my tacos with as much mince, chopped lettuce, cheese, tomato, sour cream, and guacamole as I can fit in the thing. I had to compete with two sisters and a brother. So, I am not skimping on the free food, even if eating it in a competitive format.

Besides, I have some extra incentive that Dohers does not have. Wednesday night's Happy Hour features prawns, and I am horribly allergic. After tonight's feed, I will have to survive on ice cubes till Thursday.

The first round ends. We both clear our plates of the five tacos.

The second round ends. Neither of us is willing to give an inch.

The third round ends. I am hanging tough. I had thought this would have been long finished already. The smack talking from both sides has finished. Any movement of the mouth other than the act of chewing is a waste of valuable energy.

The fourth round ends. Dohers complains that I left a sliver of lettuce on my plate. Jim threatens to disqualify me unless I eat the lettuce. I eat it. The contest resumes.

The fifth round ends. Dohers is sweating. I sense a chance for victory. Then he burps and carries on. No injury timeout.

The sixth round ends. I am not sure if I am getting full or have gas.

The seventh round ends. I definitely have gas.

The eighth round ends. Both of us look at each other as if we are begging the other to put a stop to this madness.

The ninth round ends. The contest should have ended in the eighth round with a double default, but Jim, the referee, is pushing us both to keep going. He tells us our personal pride is at stake. Not only that, there is a chance of making the Guinness Book of World Records for mindless stupidity.

The tenth round ends. We are both out on our feet.

The time is 5.58pm. The stage is set for a nail-biting finish.

Dohers is on his third beer, while I am still happy with my first. Sipping it only to keep my palate moist. Right on the hour of six, the hotel servers appear from the kitchen to clear the table of the remaining food. Dohers and I jump up and quickly load a final five hard shells with fillings onto our plates.

Jump is a bit of an exaggeration. How do sloths move?

We have both consumed 50 tacos a piece. We feel bloated. Like a pair of dead seagulls lying on a beach, their stomachs filled with non-biodegradable plastic. The serving table is now empty and there is no going back for Dohers or me.

I valiantly hung in this fight with my more heavily vaunted opponent. But I knew before standing up to refill my plate for the last time that I had come too far not to be the last man standing. Or at least the last man hunched over the toilet bowl.

Dohers and I start eating the last set of tacos on our plates. We both polish off the first taco. We both slowly get through the second taco. There is no quarter asked or given. I watch the last of the buffet spread being taken back to the kitchen and afford myself a chuckle.

My competitor laughs back. "Don't know what you are laughing about. This is heading to a draw," Dohers says.

"No. I've won," I say, smiling through the mince and cheese.

"How can you have won? We are dead even."

"Yes, we are. But I will eat more tacos than you." I proclaim quietly. "That was the bet."

"How do you think you will do that if we both finish our plate?" Dohers questions.

I pause to take as deep a breath as I can. My stomach does not allow for much. "Easy. I put six tacos on my plate during the last visit to the table. You only put five." I spread my hands wide to show four crispy Mexican delights sitting on my plate to the three that Dohers has on his. "Doesn't matter what you do now. We can both stay here till midnight to finish. You can't eat more tacos than me," I explain.

Dohers looks at his plate and expels a deep sigh, "thank fucking god." He stands up and runs outside to the parking lot. I finish another half taco to seal my victory, then join him. My chest swells with pride as much as my stomach bulges with corn tortillas.

Dohers should never have brought a knife to a gunfight.

The excruciating pain in my stomach tempers the thrill of my victory. Women often say that men do not understand what it is like to carry around a baby for nine months. Well, if a woman has never eaten 52 and a half tacos in one sitting, she would not know whether or not we do, now would she? It feels like I am carrying full term triplets.

But I have taken on the world and beaten it. Not since my under six soccer team won the grand final have I felt so accomplished. That momentous sporting victory was built on the back of a long season of hard work and dedication at training. My victory tonight was built not on my athletic prowess, but on using my brains.

Travel tip. For people traveling and finding themselves involved in a pissing contest that they would have avoided if they were at home. Work smarter, not harder.

After what I considered - and what will go down in history as - the finest hour of my life, I have an overwhelming desire to say that victory tasted sweet. But it tasted decidedly more like salsa.

8

Before you criticize someone, walk a mile in their shoes. That way, when you criticize them, you will be a mile away and have their shoes.

On the way home from the US, I spend a few days by myself in Los Angeles. As during the drive back from Steamboat to L.A., I separate from my mate Shane and one of the older wolf team, and end up in Austin, Texas for a few days.

If readers are confused as to how my high school mate Shane, the same one who convinced me to eat two Weet-Bix at the party in Australia, appeared in Colorado when he had nothing to do with the work exchange and did not even know I was there, rest easy. It was simply a mind-blowing coincidence. You can read about it in *My SECOND Life*, or you can just accept that no matter how big you think this world is. It is not really that big.

Also, if readers are confused as to how I can wind up in Austin, when a straight line from Colorado to California does not come within 900 miles of Texas, I can explain that in two words. A girl.

If a person is dumb enough to eat 52 and a half tacos, because someone asked them to, then they are dumb enough to fly off to Austin on a whim because a cute girl on a ski trip said, "come visit me in Texas, sometime."

Dohers is partly to blame for me having the confidence to do something as crazy as that. Team Wolf woke up one morning to find Dohers and all his clothes gone from the corner couch where he slept every night. He left us a note. *Headed off to see what Vancouver, Canada is like. See ya round.*

And just like that he was gone.

Before I left Shane at Reno airport to fly to Austin, we arranged to meet up again at LAX on the date of my flight back there. But I end up arriving three days early. Thankfully, out of 15 million people living in the greater Los Angeles area, I know one. Ryan and I had played rugby at my club in Brisbane. I somehow had his number in my address book, and I gave him a call on the off chance he remembered me.

Ryan is happy for me to stay with him at his parents' home in Palos Verdes, an affluent suburb covering an entire headland rising above the south bay beaches. He will come pick me up from my motel near LAX the next morning and I can watch him play a rugby game. Then I can join in the post-match festivities with the club.

The only problem is, Ryan has a date planned for later that evening.

Should he cancel? He asks.

Now, I am never going to deny a mate his chance at finding true love because I arrived on his doorstep unannounced. I can look after myself. I just survived three days in a motel on the outskirts of Austin after arriving at the door of a girl who asked me to visit her.

"Why did you come here?" She questioned.

"You asked me to come visit you," I reminded her.

"You should have known I did not mean it."

"You were on the phone with me, giving directions from the airport to your house before I booked my flight!"

Attraction between two people who are away from home is *always* a short-lived, fickle thing. Tacos and women, two things I now do my best to tread carefully with.

Unless they are French. Then I just throw the rule book away.

What will I do while Ryan is off on his date? Go back to his parents' house? Be an annoying third wheel? It is quickly decided that I will hang out with his rugby team that night, then get myself back to his house.

That afternoon after the match, all the players retire to the home team's bar for post-game drinks. One player on each team had unfortunately split their head open during play. Luckily, both teams have a doctor who plays with them. In true rugby fashion, the injured players are laid side by side on the pool table. The doctors were challenged to scull a beer, then race to see who could stitch up their player first.

A pissing competition at its finest.

Ryan leaves me at the bar to go on his date. His teammates take me to a luxurious three-story townhouse owned by a player who is away for the weekend and missed the game. Left his teammates high and dry. One guy knows where he keeps the spare key hidden. So, we sort of break and enter the apartment. The captain uses the missing player's Pay-per-View account to purchase the Mike Tyson-Frank Bruno heavyweight fight.

Why not? He had the perfect large screen TV for everyone to watch it on.

He will not be so quick to miss a match in the future, I am told.

Who needs an ex-wife with friends like this?

Tyson scores a TKO in the fifth, and the team departs for a nightclub in Hermosa Beach. I had only met the guys that afternoon, but they were all friendly and welcoming. It is only after I visit the nightclub's bathroom that I suddenly realize I do not remember what anyone I came with looks like. Matters are not improved with the fact that, eight years after I was willing to take a cricket ball to the testicles during a match rather than wear glasses to see it, I still choose not to wear spectacles even though I need to.

I wander around the nightclub, inserting myself into any large group of people, asking if someone recognizes me. No one does. The guys I came with forgot what I looked like as well. This is a bummer. Out of options inside the bar, I walk out to the street. I pull out my wallet to see what I have. There is a five-dollar note and a travelers' check. Not enough for a taxi to get me back to Ryan's house in Palos Verdes.

What are my options?

Apparently, I did not learn my lesson from the tacos' incident. I decided it is a prudent idea to hitchhike to Palos Verdes. Los Angeles may be a large city, but surely it is filled with friendly people willing to give me a lift. It is not like I am hitching a ride in Skid Row. This is the suburbs. I wonder how eager I might have been to thumb a ride if *Pulp Fiction* had been released in 1988.

In life, good judgment is derived from experience, but experiences are derived from moments of shitty judgment. Within a minute of sticking out my thumb, a car pulls over. The City of Angels must have the most welcoming citizens in the world. The driver courteously asks where I want to go.

"If you would be so kind as to take me as close as you can to the big hill called Palos Verdes at the bottom of Redondo Beach," I tell him.

The driver pulls back into traffic from the edge of the major road I was standing beside. I now have improved my sense of direction, and am paying attention while in the city. Knowing this ability would have saved me $10 in unnecessary cab fare back when I was first in L.A. We are headed south. The correct direction for Palos Verdes. We are on a main thoroughfare, that I assume is the same one Ryan drove me on this morning after he picked me up. To get to his house, he turned right off this road onto another with Palos Verdes in the title. Then right onto another street with Palos Verdes in the title. The gated entrance to his subdivision was just on the left after a short drive.

Not too shabby for a kid who, only 87 days prior, wanted to turn tail and jump on a flight back to the comforting familiarity of Brisbane.

Suddenly, the driver turns off the main road we are on. He negotiates his way through side streets until he arrives at a parking lot at the oceanfront on Redondo Beach. The car engine is turned off.

Hello? Did he get lost?

Me thinks not.

"What do you think about gay sex?" Are his polite, but not-too subtle, first words.

"If I am being honest. Not my cup of tea," I reply. "If I am being really honest. Fuck no."

"So why are you out hitchhiking on the side of the road in L.A.?" he questions. "Why else would you do that?"

"Do you know what a travelers' check is?"

"Of course."

"Well then, you would know they are useless," I state. "I do not have enough money for a taxi."

"You wouldn't be interested to try if I asked you?" He asks. "Have you ever had gay sex?"

"Mate, I am sure the experience is just as novel as eating 52 tacos. And I have already done *that* once, so it is a hard no for the rest of my life."

"Have you ever tried it?" He persists.

"Mate, I am not gay. I know all my friends call me a pussy, but I am still not thinking about becoming gay. I apologize if all the ads about how convenient American Express travelers' checks are turned out to be a flat out lie. But I just hitchhiked because I did not have any other options. I do not like wearing glasses because I don't think any girls will find me attractive. Even when they seem to, they don't appear to have any trouble inviting me to fly 1000 miles only to dump me on their doorstep. It has been a long few days for me. I would just like to get back to my mate's house and go to sleep."

"Well, I'm not interested in driving you there anymore."

"I was hitchhiking. You picked me up. You have to."

"It doesn't work like that," he says, shaking his head.

"Sure, it does. There is a code," I respond.

"What code?"

"A code of behavior. My mate, Dohers told me. You gave your word to give me a lift, implied by the action of opening the car door to let me in."

"I picked you up with the expectation for more than that."

"Well," I say in a sympathetic tone. "Let's not have the night end with *both* of us being disappointed."

"I don't think so. Would you mind getting out?" He retorts.

"Who does that?"

"It is my car."

"No. What type of person agrees to me buying a plane ticket and tells me how to get to their house from the airport on the bus? Then, when I knock on the door, they tell me to get lost. What type of person does that?"

"Someone here? In L.A.?"

"In Texas! I flew all the way to Texas."

I unload on him the circumstances of the trip to Austin.

"I'm sorry," he offers. "That is terrible she did that."

After my heartbreaking story, the driver relents and drives me as far as a service station on Palos Verdes Dr. West. The man behind the plexiglass safety window is gracious enough to call me a cab. When the taxi arrives, I get in the front seat, as is customary in Australia.

"Where do you want to go?" The cabbie asks.

"Drive this way," I say, indicating for the taxi to continue in a westerly direction. "Take me as far as $5 will get me, then just drop me on the side of the road. I will walk the rest."

"Are you sure?" He queries.

"Yep. Not unless you are willing to take a traveler's check?"

The taxi driver was nice enough to take me all the way to the entrance gate to Ryan's private community. I knew L.A. had to have more sweet souls, like the prostitute hanging out at the National-Car-Rental lot. Marcia could not have been the only one out of 15 million people.

9

My girlfriend and I got into a fight because she complained I never listen to her, or something like that.

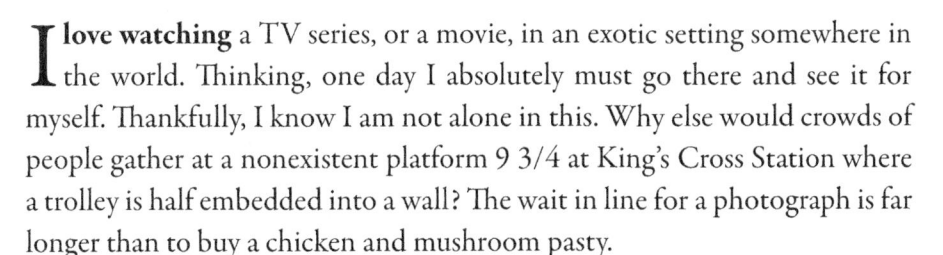

I love watching a TV series, or a movie, in an exotic setting somewhere in the world. Thinking, one day I absolutely must go there and see it for myself. Thankfully, I know I am not alone in this. Why else would crowds of people gather at a nonexistent platform 9 3/4 at King's Cross Station where a trolley is half embedded into a wall? The wait in line for a photograph is far longer than to buy a chicken and mushroom pasty.

Although I was more interested in the pasty shop at King's Cross as I had seen a lifetime's worth of trolleys on L.A.'s skid row. Almost had one embedded in my rental car radiator.

There are so many places in this world to keep adding to a bucket list. The waterfall shown in the television miniseries *Twin Peaks*. The Italian landscapes featured in *Under the Tuscan Sun*. The limestone atoll on James Bond Island, which makes an appearance in *The Man with the Golden Gun*. Indelible images that should tempt anyone to blindly throw in the towel with their employer and go visit.

Then there are places that I consider low brow but still hold a curious attraction, inspired by a leaflet handed out on a street corner, a billboard advertisement for a tobacco company, or a television commercial. During the late 80's early 90's, there was an advert for Jack Daniel's Whiskey that ran on Australian television that, I am not embarrassed to say, held me captive.

The ad was nothing more than old men sitting under trees, or on porches, whittling wood. That was it. There was nothing super striking about the scenery. There were no celebrities featured. But there was something hypnotically alluring about grown men taking their sweet time doing nothing at all. Lynchburg, Tennessee. This township, for me, became ground zero as a focal point for exploring the known universe.

If, aside from sweet Tennessee whiskey, this municipality happened to have batting cages, a drive-in movie theater, and a Walmart, I might consider setting down roots there.

But I knew in my heart I had to see this whittling Mecca for myself.

In November 1991, at the age of 23, I was finished with university study. Before I applied for a job, before I settled on a safe mutual fund company for my retirement, before I spent a moment thinking about the banal work that was going to occupy much of the rest of my life, I made plans to go to Lynchburg.

I made the trip in the company of a young lady friend. For reasons I am not at liberty to divulge, the relationship ended very soon after the trip. As in after the wheels touched down and before the plane parked at the gate. The writing was on the wall the moment they checked our passports at Australian departure control as we left.

Traveling together is the acid test for any couple. It will make or break them. If you are in doubt, stay home. The odds are something like 95 to 5. Even 96 to 4, in favor of couples breaking up after a trip. And this is for couples who are merely dating. For married couples, the odds are worse. At best they stay together for the sake of the kids afterwards.

Bob Marley once said, everyone in life is going to hurt you. You must just figure out which people are worth the pain. Figuring out someone is not, while you are both 15,000 miles from home, is never fun.

However, this should never deter a person from rolling the dice and asking their partner if they would like to embark on a Hawaiian cruise, visit the museums of Europe, or take a crack at the plank walk on Mt. Huashan in China. Even a one in 100 chance of finding that perfect travel partner will open doors to far more enjoyment in life. Apparently. I would not know. I have had some shocking trips with companions. While my perfect travel partner stormed away from the table in Delhi in a huff and still chooses not to return my phone calls.

To my credit, I have forgotten all about her.

My trip to the USA with Bec in 1991 was my first ham-fisted attempt at combining the thrill of travel and the satisfaction of true love. Bec and I flew into Memphis from Las Vegas and rented a car. First stop, Graceland. Another fabled attraction on this earth that draws people in, then ensnares them like a Venus flytrap. There is nothing I can say about Graceland that pilgrims of Elvis have not already put into writing a thousand times over in magazines, newspapers, and in reams of Greek literature by the poet Homer.

Graceland is a landmark. It is history. It is legend. It is essentially a big house.

But it is the second most visited residence in the USA, after The Bunny Ranch. No, I am kidding. Second after the Presidential abode. The White House. From the casual fan to the obsessive Elvis enthusiast, Graceland is a must see for anyone looking for garish interior design involving shag carpet. It even has its own cemetery.

I grew up a massive Elvis fan. I know exactly where I was on Saturday, August 20, 1977. This was the day the announcer on ABC radio reported that Elvis had passed on while lying in his bathtub upholding his meticulous hygiene standards. I was seated in the backseat of the family car. Dad was driving the tribe to a Rotary Club family barbecue at the beach. Elvis had died four days earlier on August 16, from what the coroner officially listed as a heart attack. But in 1977, it took several days for any news of a celebrity death to reach Australia. Then another day or so to make it to Townsville.

Buddy Holly's 1959 plane crash was reported in 1966. While Jim Morrison's heart failure made the news in 1975, four years after he was laid to rest in Paris. Everyone in North Queensland currently lives under the impression that Whitney Houston is still alive and touring.

As taken as I was with the life and times of the King of Rock and roll, I pale in comparison to a family I once saw featured in a TV program. A father and son team takes turns watching 12-hour shifts of television to document every time Elvis's name gets a mention. As ridiculous as this may sound, I think these two would shy away from seeing how many tacos they could eat in one sitting.

I am not sure what the point is of their efforts, but I am certain it makes them minor celebrities in their trailer park. My only thought is, who monitors the television if they must take a bathroom break while the other one is sleeping? My reverence of Elvis is what made me an early devotee of Tennessee whiskey, before I switched to gin. The King would often wash down a handful of pills with a straight shot of Kentucky Straight Bourbon Whiskey. The amalgamation of Elvis, alcohol, and whittling, was my absurd justification for the rabid level of enthusiasm I felt driving to the Jack Daniel's distillery in Lynchburg. My lady friend couldn't give a shit. She was simply along for the ride.

Lynchburg has a population of less than 500 people. No batting cages, no drive-in movie theater. The town is so small that just locating the town is more of a challenge than finding the Jack Daniel distillery once you are there. The township is in Moore County, which is one of several dry counties in Tennessee. A dry county means that even though it is permissible to *make* whiskey here, it is not legal to *buy* it.

No. No. I am not making that up.

There is nothing more ridiculous in this world than some of the laws that politicians and lawyers keep on the books. In Florida, it is illegal to fish while in the act of driving over a bridge. In one town in Georgia, it is against the law to tie a giraffe to a lamppost and all citizens are required to own a rake. Anywhere in Alaska, it is a civil offense to push a live moose out of an airplane.

Laws are often there to protect us from ourselves. And to protect the moose population. However, it still is not illegal to eat your own body weight in Mexican food while in Colorado. Go figure.

Moore county's convoluted rule dates to when the state prohibition laws were passed in the early 20th century. When the US federal government repealed the 18th amendment in 1933, ending prohibition, no one thought to send a memo to the far-flung parts of Tennessee. I wonder if the residents of Lynchburg are waiting for Al Capone to ride into town and have a showdown with Kevin Costner, so they may buy a beer.

These are the deep innermost thoughts of a 23-year-old while driving through the back country of Tennessee with a traveling companion who stopped talking to me in Vegas.

Bec and I arrive at the distillery in plenty of time for the 12.30 tour. We have driven up from Huntsville, Alabama this morning after visiting Wheeler dam. This impressive piece of engineering stretches 6,342 feet across the

Tennessee River. My dad is a civil engineer, and it would thrill him to know that his son went to see the widest dam in Alabama. A man never grows out of wanting to make his father proud.

My soon to be ex-girlfriend did not show the same enthusiasm for the construction as I did. This had become something of a friction point in our relationship. Me wanting to marvel at things made of concrete; her wanting to shop. We arrived at the distillery on a Saturday. We are confronted with the usual increased weekend visitor traffic of Midwesterners with horrible dress sense. This could make spots on the already limited number of distillery tours scarce.

Thankfully, we were okay.

We purchase tickets and wait for our tour to fill up with other visitors. The attire of some people is spectacular. Sleeveless plaid shirts, sandals with socks, tight Lycra leggings slipped on legs with more rolls than a bakery. I respect every bold fashion statement I see.

And then I spy them.

A group of tour guides, clad in denim overalls, sitting on rocking chairs and whittling away at pieces of wood. Just like in the commercial. Except far better. This was actual life right in front of my eyes. I cried.

Being present, while slivers of wood peeled away by whittling knives fell to the floor, exceeded the heights of my expectations. This is not always the case with travel. My satisfaction from being in Lynchburg sits in stark contrast with the deflation most tourists experience when they finally see the little mermaid in Copenhagen, arrive to Four Corners in New Mexico, or stop by the 'tree that owns itself' in Athens, Georgia. However, The Jack Daniel's Distillery is already everything it could be and more.

Simple, simple things.

Bec and I must have looked like the least fashion challenged people there, as a manager approached us with an offer. Or maybe it was because we were the quietest people there, as the only couple not talking to each other.

"Would you two like to attend a lunch at Miss Mary Bobo's Boarding House?" The manager asks us.

Bec shows the first glimmer of excitement I have seen in days, but I am very reluctant. Firstly, I am not comfortable in a room full of strangers my girlfriend can complain about me with. And secondly, having attended boarding school for several years of my life, I am all too familiar with the glaring similarities between boarding house food and prison food. Greasy meals served with healthy portions of disdain by overly plump women who apply way too much mascara.

So, I am not exactly jumping at the chance to relive the horrors of the day I asked Pearl, a kitchen lady at school, for an extra helping of porridge and her fake eyelash fall into my bowl as she dished it out.

The manager senses my feeling of horror. "Don't worry. Miss Mary's serves the finest dishes in all the county."

"Can I get a beer there?"

"Ah, no!"

Disappointing, but his description of Miss Mary Bobo's Boarding House is not what I envisioned. "It has been a venerable institution in the town of Lynchburg since 1913. It is an old inn that serves up Southern hospitality, tradition, and warm charm to visitors and locals alike," the manager tells us.

"And the kitchen ladies?"

"Lovely young women of the town."

The history of the restaurant is overwhelmingly small-town Americana. Jack and Mary Bobo had been neighbors and classmates as kids, then became lovers and business partners as adults. They took over the inn, known as the Grand Central Hotel, from its proprietor Dr. E.Y. Salmon and renamed it the Bobo Hotel. Remarkably, the good people of the South continued frequenting the place despite its uninspiring name.

Jack attempted to branch out into other business ventures, all of which failed. A line of children's' toys, the Bobo Yo-Yo and the Bobo pogo. Then a disastrous gamble trying to run a nightclub in downtown Lynchburg, the Bobo go-go. Jack died in 1948, a bitter, disillusioned man. But Mary continued to run the inn and dining room for 25 years, now exclusively tailored to feed the distillery's invited guests.

After her death, just a few weeks before she hit 102, the distillery bought the building to maintain the town's heritage. Its standing firmly established, dining at Miss Mary Bobo's Boarding House has since become the hottest culinary ticket in the Midwest. Reservations must be made well in advance. Getting a seat on a normal weekend is near impossible. To get even a look in for a seat at Saturday's midday meal between Thanksgiving and New Year's, a person must be a State Senator, a Clinton, or well connected to the Chicago Mob.

The manager hands me a brochure which describes the ambience at the restaurant as very old-fashioned. The place runs on tradition. A bell rings to alert guests that the mealtime is about to begin. Then a table hostess reads out the names of the diners to direct them to their seats at one of the table. The hostesses are the young ladies of the town who may have been unsuitable for marriage. It is their job during mealtime to keep the plates full and the conversation flowing. The tables seat 11 people, including the hostess, and as is the Southern custom, diners must pass the food around the table from right to left.

On this Saturday, there had been two very last-minute cancellations. As a diner's aunt had suddenly passed on. A cancellation at Miss Mary's is as rare as rocking horse droppings. No one passes up a reservation unless it is for a very good reason. The couple who ended up cancelling, had still tried to make it to the lunch after Nan had unfortunately passed on. After the funeral home had picked up the body, they rushed to the car only to find they had a flat tire and no spare. This meant two chairs at one of the dining tables would be empty. And because of the Southern etiquette for passing around food, two empty seats meant a lot of food would end up on the floor. That, or it would stop circulating around the table. Because heaven forbid folks living in the grand ol' South reach across a chair to get it.

Bec's stare makes it clear that she wants to go without her needing to tell me. And if she goes, I *have* to go. Her glare makes it official. I am roped in.

10

I never knew what happiness was until I got married – and then it was too late.

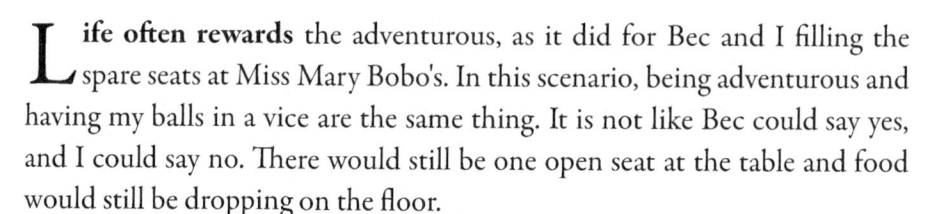

Life often rewards the adventurous, as it did for Bec and I filling the spare seats at Miss Mary Bobo's. In this scenario, being adventurous and having my balls in a vice are the same thing. It is not like Bec could say yes, and I could say no. There would still be one open seat at the table and food would still be dropping on the floor.

My soon to be ex would have been more than happy to leave me at the Jack Daniel's distillery. Alone with all the fine portly women in Spandex fighting for my attention. But traveling with another person, who is almost at the point of openly expressing their desire for me to crawl into a hole and die, is a marvelous way to learn diplomacy. I did as her glare commanded: I agreed to go to Miss Mary Bobo's.

Besides, Bec had the keys to the rental car in her purse and could leave me behind if she wanted to.

Again.

The manager tells us there will be no cost to our meal as a token of gratitude for our participation. Why did he not say that to begin with? I will pass the Brussels sprouts as enthusiastically as any man if it gets me a free meal. The distillery will reserve two spots for us on a later afternoon tour. This creates a small hiccup in my timeline for getting to our next sightseeing location, Mammoth Caves National Park by way of Nashville, but I think I can still pull it off. I had lied to Bec and said there was a large shopping mall adjoining the caves. I will deal with the fallout from that when we get there.

The manager urges us to hurry to Miss Mary Bobo's as the lunch bell is about to ring. All guests must be on time to be seated at the tables. Sounds very much like Miss Mary learned her restaurant management skills from the Gestapo. Thankfully, the inn is only four blocks away from the distillery visitor's center. Straight down Main Street Lynchburg.

The tables at the restaurant comfortably seat eleven. I will spend the next hour with a lunch group of four other young couples, a hostess, and a girlfriend next to whom I must sleep with one eye open. That table is an eclectic assortment of characters. One couple is an oddity, hailing from the Lone Star State of Texas. The other six are a group of friends from Tennessee, three couples.

The delightful young hostess, Lilith, first gives an informative talk on the history of the building and the extraordinary life of Mary Bobo. The business failures of her husband Jack get pushed to the side and ignored. Lilith explains that after Mary's death, there was great concern that the restaurant would close its doors. It could have been sold and ended up as a Starbuck's or demolished to make way for a Walmart parking lot.

I wonder how the descendants of Jack and Mary could be that business challenged. They must have inherited their entrepreneurial genes from Jack. They could have simply licensed the restaurant out to a national chain, and still cash in on their famous name. The Mary Bobo El Pollo Loco would be a huge draw, while opening the town's tourism trade up to a whole new market: Mexico.

At the hostess' request, everyone at the lunch table introduces themselves. That is part of the draw and charm of the restaurant. The table chatter. Guests must associate with each other in keeping with the Southern ambiance. Everyone must leave their pretense or snobbery at the door. Long before the existence of cell phones, people were already having difficulty interacting with others. However, the enjoyment of good southern food demands that there be good company.

Things start awkwardly when I discover that I must explain to everyone at the table where on the planet Australia is. In 1991, most of the world is still quite naïve regarding foreign cultures and countries that do not border their own. So, I make a world map. A gravy boat is used to represent Australia. The salt and pepper shakers are the two islands of New Zealand, and the USA is a large pitcher of homemade iced tea. The other guests do not give me a single sign of comprehension. It was like Oklahoma was the edge of the known world.

"Is it further than Denver?" One guest asks.

"Yes, further than that."

"So, closer to Salt Lake City, then."

"They are from another country," assists Lilith. "Australia is not a part of the US."

The looks of surprise on the faces at the table were slightly unnerving. While Bob from Texas was visibly sullen. He had unquestionably come to Mary Bobo's for lunch, not a geography lesson.

Thankfully, the staff at Mary Bobo's are well coached in bringing out the best in people, so that everyone enjoys their experience. Judging from Bob's early reactions, I can tell he will be the hardest nut to crack. Question is, was Lilith up to the task? The fact that the curtains are open and entrancing sunlight illuminates the spotless décor helps the mood in our dining room. The diners do not feel uncomfortable wedged into tight, dark booths with less stomach space than an economy class airline seat with the tray table down.

If that had been the case, the limited space would have made Bob a nonstarter.

The food is first class and there is as much of it as I desire. This is not the type of restaurant where diners order off a menu. The chef sets the meal dishes a day in advance. Pork medallions in a pepper sauce, seasoned fried chicken, steaming scalloped potatoes, fried okra, catfish casserole, and Miss Bobo's special macaroni and cheese from her own private recipe. The hostess adds to the mystique of the mac and cheese when she tells us never to speak a word to the outside world about eating this famous dish. It is Miss Bobo's secret.

To me, it tastes just like every other mac and cheese I have eaten in my life. However, all the other diners proclaim that Miss Bobo truly unearthed the secret of perfecting the dish. Including Bec. I could just envision her lawyer addressing the judge at our divorce proceedings.

"Your honor, this man ate the world's most delicious mac and cheese, which my client absolutely loved, and thought it was ordinary. Their differences are irreconcilable."

Some people are easily convinced by a fancy dash of propaganda. While I try not to be overly influenced by young female hostesses in long, flowing white frocks that made them look like they just walked off the set of *Little House on the Prairie*.

I do not mind that the menu was set in advance. My meal is free. However, there will always be one person in a group who complains, no matter what. In this group, that person is Bob from Texas. Bob wants ribs for lunch. He has probably had ribs for lunch every day of his life. Miss Mary Bobo's trying to change his eating schedule had him melting down like Dustin Hoffman in *Rain Main* when he cannot watch Judge Wapner.

Bob also has the disconcerting habit of implying with every sentence that things are better in Texas.

"How can gas in Tennessee be 97 cents a gallon? In Texas it is 89 cents."

"What do you mean it snows in Alaska? The weather is always warm in Houston."

"Well, in Texas, we barbecue our ribs with plenty of sauce."

The notion that people might travel to other places to experience things differently from the way they are back home is completely lost on Bob. Everyone at the table secretly wishes for Lilith to lean across the table and smack Bob across the face with the ladle from the fried okra. No one else cares that ribs are not on the menu. If Bob wants ribs so badly, someone tell him to walk across the street and erect his own restaurant, and name it *Bob's house of Texas ribs*.

Despite Lilith's explanation regarding the set menu, Bob just cannot take the hint. He wants a serving of ribs, or the governor of Tennessee will hear about it. Bob must think he has a lot of sway outside of his home state. He has an arrogant air about him, like a petulant child who does not get its way with the toys at kindergarten. I am not 100% convinced that he is not a Klansman. He has a way of coming across playfully racist. Or maybe racism is a just a part-time hobby.

The strangest couple at the table is sitting directly opposite from me, both quietly spoken and unassuming. Too quiet. They have all the trademark signs of fervent religious folk, or serial killers. The wife is the personification of timid. Most of the time, she looks overwhelmed by the social context of this group setting. She nervously shivers every time someone asks her a direct question.

It makes me wonder what she was expecting after reading the advertising pamphlet for lunch at Miss Mary's. An intimate dining experience for couples devoid of all other human contact? Perhaps this is the way her friends decided to help expose her to the world. By making her have lunch with five strangers.

The husband is not as shy, but still has a long way to go if his dream is to have the charisma of a professional wrestler. He has the slightly annoying habit of describing everything he is doing, as he is doing it.

"I am now sitting down at the table."

"I am pulling the chair in."

"I am picking up my napkin, now laying it out on my lap."

It is like he is giving himself personal commentary on every moment of his life. The most animated I see him is when the hostess asks if anyone would like to say grace. Both he and Bec raise their hands.

Bec volunteers for me to say grace in Latin. This is one of the useless skills I learned from the boardinghouse dining room. Her father once asked me to say grace at family Sunday dinner, and she knew how mortified it made me. Even in front of her family. So, she puts my name up and Lilith chooses me to say grace over the quiet, religious husband.

"I really can't," I say.

"Yes, he will," Bec loudly proclaims to the table.

This girl loves sticking knives in my back. I always thought I might be able to use this unusual skill to earn kudos while dining with the landed gentry in England. Before settling in to watch the men's single's final at Wimbledon from a VIP suite. Instead, I will be using it to subtly force some class into Bob from Texas because Lilith seems reluctant to make a go for the ladle in the fried okra.

Everyone at the table bows their heads.

"Benedic, benedicat. Creatum christum dominum nostrum," I utter solemnly.

Bob bursts out in incredulous laughter. "Ha ha, we don't say it that way down in Texas." His comment makes me feel small, but everyone else at the table offers me a dutifully impressed smile. Except for the couple directly opposite. They both give me a prolonged, over-thoughtful glare. The way soap opera actors dramatically stare into space at the end of every scene. Then the pair turn to each other and start whispering their own prayer among themselves. According to them, having it done in a foreign language does not count.

Everyone else at the table must now respectfully wait for them to finish. Their private grace carries on much longer than we all expect. Lilith calmly holds up her open palm for us to wait and will not step in to speed along proceedings.

I can barely make out what they say are saying in their fervent hush.

"Thank you, God, for this bountiful meal. Thank you for the mashed potatoes. Thank you for the mac and cheese. Thank you for the flavored ice-tea. Praise JESUS! Thank you for the bread rolls. Thank you for the butter with which to butter those bread rolls. Praise JESUS!"

The volume change from everything else they were saying to the part where they say the word 'Jesus' is dramatic. It goes from a baby whisper on the 'praise' part, to a full-throat, willing a 40-1 long-shot past the winner's post at the Kentucky Derby roar on the 'Jesus.'

When I attended church as a young boy, everyone always pronounced the savior's name with a hushed voice. Like they were commentating golf.

"On the green in two after a great approach shot from the rough beside the bunker. Jesus has what looks like a four-foot putt to make par."

Everything I took for granted about the world changed at that moment. This pair cried out to Jesus the same way I would if an alligator grabbed me by the leg. Jesus Christ! Then straight back to whispered murmurs. "Thank you for the catfish in the casserole. Thank you for the pepper used to make the pepper sauce. Thank you for the okra in the fried okra. Praise JESUS!"

Finally, Lilith has to say something to wind it up.

"Okay and thank you. That was lovely."

If she had remained silent, we might have been 20 minutes in and still waiting on this pair to give thanks to each individual herb and spice used in the seasoned chicken. But I have now learned something extra about the American Deep South. Religion there is like duck hunting. When praising their Lord and savior they like to go at it with both barrels.

How much fun would attending church be in the South? Parishioners get to yell at the top of their lungs.

"Can I get an AMEN?"

"AMEN!"

"God can't hear you."

"AMEN!"

"He still can't hear you! God is sleeping. Let's wake him up with a freshly brewed cup of AMEN."

"AMEN!"

"That's better."

In the Anglican Church, I was not permitted to raise my voice in the chapel even with a hallelujah.

To add dramatic effect, sometimes a Southern Pastor adds in a pause when saying the Lord's name. JE... SUS! As in, by the power of JE... SUS! I absolve you of all your sins, in the name of JE... SUS! I like this version far better than the way priests taught me to pray as a child. The way I was taught was so groveling. This way allowed me to say the Lord's name with more authority. Like how Bruce Buffer introduces UFC fighters into the octagon.

'IT'S TIME! Weighing in at 160 pounds, the great white hope. Trained as a carpenter until he found his true calling inside the ring. He will admonish you for your sins and make you beg for forgiveness. His signature move is the crucifix. Fighting out of Nazareth in the holy land... JEEEEEEEE... SUSSSSSSSSS!"

These are the nonsensical, irreverent thoughts filling my mind as a 23-year-old, sitting through 10 minutes of a couple expressing their gratitude for the molecular structure of matter before I could have my first taste of something called fried okra, while my supposed girlfriend kicks me under the table because she thinks I am staring at the young lady sitting opposite me because I find her interesting, rather than out of disbelief, while attending lunch at Miss Mary Bobo's Boarding House in Lynchburg, Tennessee.

11

What is the difference between an outlaw and an in-law? Outlaws are wanted.

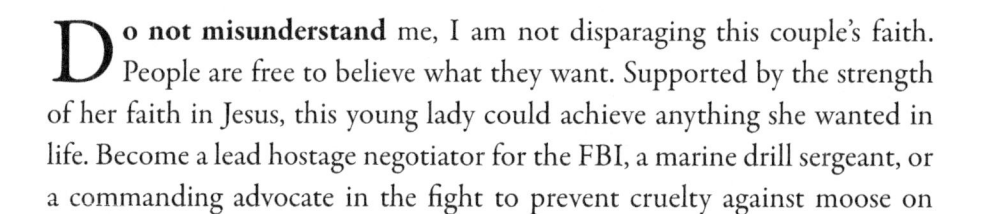

Do not misunderstand me, I am not disparaging this couple's faith. People are free to believe what they want. Supported by the strength of her faith in Jesus, this young lady could achieve anything she wanted in life. Become a lead hostage negotiator for the FBI, a marine drill sergeant, or a commanding advocate in the fight to prevent cruelty against moose on airplanes.

And good for her if she does. Many times, I wondered if my lack of conviction in myself, before I started to travel, held me back.

During table chatter, the young religious couple admits to their unwavering belief in disgraced TV evangelist Jim Bakker. Even now, three years after his conviction for fraud. Bob from Texas finds that news hilarious. He puts in a few shots at Jim and Tammy, while helping himself to another portion of the fried okra.

"Did you hear what happened after they took off all of Tammy-Faye's makeup?" Bob jokes. "They found Jimmy Hoffa."

I am not a big fan of Bob's jokes, or the fried okra. Which I do not touch again after my first mouthful. Fried mush might be one way to describe it, except mush has more taste. Bob thinks anyone at the table is fair game for a good roasting. This is the Texas way. Builds character. I have to wonder. If God did not intend for people to take the mickey out of each other, he would not have invented New Zealand and jokes about having sex with sheep.

All the guests at our table excel at the one important skill we need to make lunch a success. We all unquestioningly pass the food around the table from left to right. Bob would often ask for something just off to his right-hand side. And it would dutifully circumnavigate the entire table before being handed to him. The religious husband would give us his play-by-play account.

"I am passing along the buttered squash."

Bob would place the food item back exactly where it had been without touching it. Then let out a great big belly laugh. What an arsehat.

If there was ever a lull in conversation, Lilith would step in and fill in the blank with some history on the house. Or about the man Jack Daniel. Or regarding the town of Lynchburg. And everyone would offer their polite amazement. Except for Bob. I learn more about Texas than I do about anything else.

The most interesting tidbit about the Jack Daniel story is how he died. The oft-told legend is that he died of septicemia, or blood poisoning as it was once called. The myth is that Jack developed an infection in his big toe after kicking his safe when he could not remember the combination to open it. This begs the question, who put him in charge?

Jack did not have the best memory for numbers. And he often forgot the combination. According to Bob, in Texas they would refer to him as being a retard. However, Mr. Daniel's modern-day biographer states that this incident, as the likely cause of his sepsis, is simply a myth. Bob offers the most interesting take on Jack's demise.

"Down in Texas, retards don't go around killing themselves by kicking stuff and getting infections in their blood. They blow their own heads off with a gun."

Prior to the lunch, I knew next to nothing about Jack Daniel. I learned a great deal while dutifully passing food dishes around the table to keep Bob amused. I did not know anything about Texas either, except that sitting in a motel in Austin for 3 days waiting for a flight to L.A. is more than enough time for self-reflection. Thanks to Bob, I am now an expert in the Lone Star State.

However, the story of Jack dying after kicking his safe was featured in one of the television commercials I had seen in Australia. Lilith tells the story again at Miss Bobo's. Later in the afternoon, on our tour of the distillery, the story is repeated. The same version of events told three times by three separate sources. I do not know how much more confirmation a person needs to pronounce this story as verified and true. The religious pair sitting across from me at lunch believed it.

"That poor man. That safe was the devil, come to earth to lead Jack from knowing Jesus's love."

"But he is happy with our heavenly Father now."

Whether the stories a person hears while on the road exploring the world are true or not, they are always worth repeating. They are what make conversations at lunchtime so worthwhile. Remember, we spend one-third of the time we spend eating, eating at lunch. Without richly woven tales of people and places, the world would just be facts, facts, facts.

This story is an integral part of Jack Daniel's legend. Take away this fable and there is no marketing. No marketing, no sales. No sales, Jack Daniel has no distillery. No distillery and there are no dozens of storage buildings filled with aging casks of Tennessee whiskey dotting the hillside of Moore County. There is no economy in Lynchburg. The IRS does not get an eight million dollar check handed to them every two weeks to pay the company's taxes. Without those taxes, the USA has no money to pay for Medicare for its elderly citizens' healthcare. There is no annual budget for the military to protect the country from Iran's nuclear threat. Take away the story of Jack Daniel kicking his safe only to die of sepsis and they may as well take away the entire American way of life.

The table makes it all the way to dessert with nary a word spoken about politics, abortion, or gun control. Bob desperately wanted to unload his views on the current government in Washington, but Lilith always expertly deviated the conversation in another direction every time he broached the subject. Bob would come charging like a bull with some incendiary statement, but the hostess would expertly twist the narrative like a matador swirling their cape. The discussion would turn from the jackasses in the Senate to the joys of needlepoint within seconds.

I liked our hostess. Lilith deserved to find herself a good man. I hoped that next Saturday her table would be filled with ten handsome bachelors all vying for her attention. I even considered it could be a million-dollar idea for a reality TV series. *The Bachelorette*. Every week Lilith could notify one unlucky gentleman that his amorous advances were no longer required on the show by serving the spurned suitor a bowl of fried okra.

For the last course of the afternoon, the restaurant serves up baked apples coated in Jack Daniel's *special sauce*. The unwitting use of the phrase 'special sauce' has me pass on the tasty-looking treat. Uncomfortable memories from boarding school. Everyone at the table agrees that the baked apples are the most amazing item they have tasted today, with Jack's special sauce being the kicker. The two opposite me quickly offer a prayer.

"Thank you, Lord, for Jack Daniel's special sauce. Praise JESUS!"

Stifling a chuckle, I decide I should leave a little explanatory note for Miss Mary Bobo's marketing department when I sign the guest registry.

Upon conclusion of the meal, Lilith encourages us all to go to the registry and leave remarks before we depart. As we crowd around the registry book, the table members start a conversation about how difficult it had been to get a reservation for the day's meal. Especially on this first Saturday after Thanksgiving. The religious husband takes the pen first.

"I am signing the guest book," is his color analysis.

Bob from Texas secured the booking for himself and his wife at Easter time, on the recommendation of a friend. Presumably, another Texan who shamefully had not forewarned Bob about the likelihood of ribs not being on the menu. The group of six had been on a waiting list since the previous Thanksgiving, then finally secured their booking in January. I shudder at the thought of being on a waiting list for over a year. For lunch.

The hair at the back of my neck stood up knowing how it would crush them to know myself and Bec had just rocked up at the distillery that morning and been handed an invitation. *Do not say a word.*

"And what about you?" One of the six asks Bec.

"How did you hear about Miss Mary's where you live?" Adds Bob.

I shoot Bec a look. Do not answer. I need some time to formulate a response. A half-baked, but semi-believable story, something like that I have been waiting half my life to try Jack's special sauce. It is called diplomacy, and after 13 days of traveling with someone who despises me, I now knew more about diplomacy than UN Secretary General Boutros Boutros-Ghali.

Bec and I had not spoken, or even looked at each other, for the entire meal. She now tosses me a cynical smile that screams; *I am so angry at you.* She turns to Bob to answer his question.

JESUS, please don't.

Bec speaks before I can grab a ladle and fill her mouth with fried okra.

"We had never even heard of the place," she says. "We arrived at the distillery this morning for a tour, and they told us they needed someone to fill in two empty places from a cancellation."

She did not realize what she was doing. Or this was her way of getting back at me for making her drive six hours to see a dam. All I know is that, after a delicious lunch, suddenly there were now an additional eight people in the room who deeply resented me.

12

My teachers told me I would never amount to much because I procrastinate so much. I told them, "Just you wait."

To offset the disappointment of having to accept adulthood and get my first professional job, I left Australia to work in America in 1992. Combining the thrill of travel with the soul sucking reality of work seemed like a smart move.

In 1992, there were plenty of hoops to jump through to work overseas. I shudder to think how big those hoops are now with the advent of computer technology. Things being simple in the 90's had its curses and blessings. It took me four days to cross the border from Canada into the US in early 1992, when we still had the paper visa system. When asked in the same year by the US medical system for a detailed account of my university degree, I photocopied the university handbook. That sufficed. I recently had to contact my alma mater about my university files, and they do not know where they are because I attended before they had computer records of attendance.

For me to work in the USA in 1992, I had to be accepted by the professional fraternity of my medical specialty. That meant taking a test. As I was working near Tampa, Florida, Jacksonville was the closest city I could take the national certifying exam for Physical Therapists. The distance from Tampa to Jacksonville is half the state of Florida. Florida is a long state. Conservatively, it should take three and a half hours to drive there. With my luck, and Yeats' Law, I estimate it would take five.

It ends up being seven.

The trip starts with a full tank of petrol and my head full of anticipation. My AMC Eagle Kammback, the COVID-19 of 80's automobiles, has performed solidly during the one kilometer drive I do each morning to work while on a temporary professional license. The car only cost me $1000, but the tradeoff is it barely averages about ten miles to the gallon. Time to see how large a carbon footprint this beast can make heading across and upstate.

For over half of the journey, everything goes smoothly. But that half was on a freeway. A mile past Ocala, which is a sketchy little town in the middle of Florida's grassy central plateau, I exit the freeway for two-lane back roads.

The road I needed to take has several designations: the Sid Martin Highway; North Main St; and Highways 301 and 200. The Florida Department of Transportation expects drivers to have a PhD. in mathematics, while I am naively looking for a sign with a big white arrow and the word *Jacksonville*. America has the greatest highway system in the world. Driving on it is a fantastic, uniquely American experience. But once a driver leaves the freeways for the smaller state roads, he is thrust into a disorientating universe not unlike the narrow alleyways of Cairo.

Ten minutes after getting off the freeway, I am worried that I am lost. I pull my car to the side of the road in front of a house and distract a few locals from their banjo playing exploits on the front porch to ask directions. Thankfully, one of them claims to know the way to Jacksonville.

"Just keep on the way you is headed," he twangs. "You is on the right road."

I hope his directions are better than his subject-verb agreement.

The Sid Martin Highway gets its name from a former member of the Florida House of Representatives. Sid also has a Biotechnology Incubator at the University of Florida named in his honor. When I die, I would love the honor of having a Biotechnology Incubator named after me. As for a section of bitumen that traverses through a few boondock counties, I think I can leave it.

I am happy to be back on my way. Briefly.

Somewhere between thinking, I have not seen a house in a while, and what sort of person would live in a house out here? The Kammback's engine starts to give off smoke. Foolishly thinking that if my car engine is on fire, the faster I drive the quicker the wind through the motor will put out the blaze, I speed up. The smoke gets worse, not better.

Shit, this is not good. I am in the middle of nowhere. No cars. No houses. Not even the sound of banjos.

I am caught between a rock and a hard place. The travelers lament. If I drive faster, there is more smoke. But I will get somewhere faster before my engine explodes. If I drive slower, there is less smoke. But it will take me longer to get somewhere and hopefully get this problem fixed.

My mind is a fretful game of Pong.

Go faster.

No, go slower.

No, go faster.

Slower is better.

The engine situation remains dire as the car speeds, then limps its way into the town of Waldo, Florida.

It is fortuitous that I choose to enter town by inching along the road. The formerly unknown settlement of Waldo was recently ranked #3 for 'Worst Speed Trap Cities' in North America. I have no idea whether it was nationally rated on the day in 1992 when I drove into town. It might have been in the embryonic stages of developing its traffic citation money spinner.

The Florida Department of Law Enforcement opened an investigation which resulted in the entire Waldo Police force being disbanded. This led to Waldo zooming up the rankings of small towns in the USA plagued by illegal gambling, crystal-meth manufacturing, and prostitution. But in 1992, I believe there is nowhere on earth I will find more honest help than in a small American town.

Along with aggressive law enforcement, Waldo thankfully has a mechanic. The mechanic did not have a shop, per se. He conducted business out of the shed beside his house. That is okay, I thought. Apple started off in a garage in Palo Alto. Waldo's car repair specialist pops the bonnet of the car and looks inside. Americans say, 'hood,' instead of, 'bonnet.' They also say, 'trunk,' instead of, 'boot.' This creates some confusion between me and the mechanic.

Our respective accents do not help matters. His southern drawl is as heavy set as a Sumo wrestler at a Las Vegas buffet, my Aussie brogue as lavishly thick as Tom Selleck's chest hair.

I finally manage to explain the situation with the smoke.

The mechanic takes all of three minutes to find the problem. There is an oil leak from a ruptured gasket dripping onto the hot engine, causing smoke. It is lucky I did not continue driving, and fell in love with the homespun authenticity of the town of Waldo. The engine would have drained of oil and seized. This is the good news. The bad news is, where am I going to find another gasket for a 1986 AMC Eagle Kammback in Waldo, Florida?

If the travel gods of Mt. Olympus ever wanted to show love to one of their followers, they choose this day to do it. After only one phone call, the mechanic locates another local who has a junked AMC Eagle in his possession, and he has a replacement seal for me. The miracle of Waldo! And if the travel gods have a sense of humor, they also choose this day to show it. The guy cannot bring the seal to the mechanic for a few hours. He has banjo practice. Followed by a long overdue moonshine still cleaning. Then more banjo practice.

When the part finally arrives, tucked into the owner's overall pocket, it takes all of 60 seconds to install. Relief washes over me like a soapy loofah in a Turkish bathhouse. Now it brings us to the matter of the bill. I am not expecting an itemized bill, and I am prepared to pay a reasonable amount to cover the cost of a phone call, a rubber seal, three quarts of oil, and four total minutes of the mechanic's valuable time.

"How much will that be?" I ask.

"How much ya got?"

"How much time do I have?" I query back, uncertain of his meaning. "Not much, unfortunately. I really need to get to Jacksonville, and your mate's second banjo practice went on longer than I expected."

"Not how much time ya got, twinkle toes," he winks as he speaks.

"I don't understand then. How much what?"

"How much money ya got in your wallet?" He persists.

It is a shakedown. What else did I expect? I am a naïve foreigner in need. No one is required to help me. Sympathy costs money in most parts of the world. And I am being extorted by the Waldo version of the Mafioso.

"I have $100."

"That'll do it," the mechanic says.

The extent of my experience of this type of situation, which is none, tells me to shut up and do as I am told.

"Excellent," I gush, "I am so sorry I cannot pay you more. An absolute pleasure doing business with you, sir."

I tremble as I hand him the cash and suffer the indignity of watching him count the $20 bills several times, as if I were the one trying to cheat him.

The descending sun gives its final peek above the tree tops as the day resigns itself to dusk. My AMC Eagle Kammback roars up the Sid Martin memorial thoroughfare while I quickly push my experience in Waldo back into the furthest reaches of my mind. At eight the next morning, I am due to take my board exams to allow me to fully practice my profession in the States. If I fail the exam, I will have to return home to the reality of life.

Having the opportunity to live overseas is like a dream. Occasionally a nightmare in places like Waldo. But for the most part a dream.

I have 120 kilometers to go to Jacksonville. I now have no money for a hotel and no money for the petrol to return home. What had I learned from going to Steamboat Springs three and a half years ago for the work exchange?

Do not carry travelers' checks, always have cash. And look how that worked out for me.

But I mean, apart from that. I learned to live without excuses and travel with without regrets. Worse comes to worse I could prostitute myself for gay sex to make some money.

13

It takes a lot of balls to golf the way I do.

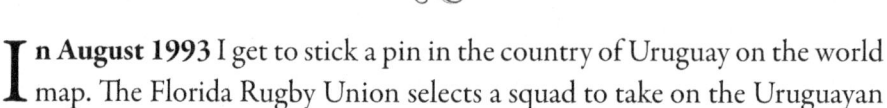

In **August 1993** I get to stick a pin in the country of Uruguay on the world map. The Florida Rugby Union selects a squad to take on the Uruguayan national side in Montevideo. Due to poor planning and minimal fundraising efforts, several members of the team are unable to afford travel. So, they opened the tour up to anyone who played rugby in Florida and who could afford the plane fare.

I will do whatever it takes to come up with the money. I had never been good enough to get selected for a rugby tour in my life. Now there is an opportunity to bribe my way onto one. I will somehow find the cash. Even if it means I must sell my beloved AMC Eagle Kammback. The hunchback of automobiles.

Further poor planning by the tour administrators means that the game against Uruguay will occur the day after we arrive. Fourteen hours of travel. No sleep. Then a game of rugby in life-threatening conditions. That will be more fun than a reunion with my ex-girlfriend Bec.

I decide to get in on the poor planning myself. Just to fit in. While I do make the effort to change money into Uruguayan pesos, I neglect to obtain an entry visa for Uruguay. I also fail to get a visa for Argentina, needed for the return flight home and the dramatic airport change we will need to make in Buenos Aires.

All those issues will pale in comparison to the mess I find myself in at Miami airport when we get back.

The night of our departure from Miami International, the entire team waits for me at the airline check-in desk as I pace the sidewalk outside praying for my passport to be delivered by the Uruguayan embassy attaché. Good thing I went to Miss Mary Bobo's and learned how to properly get the attention of the Lord.

"JESUS, are you listening? Please get my passport here on time. Are you hearing me, JESUS?"

The attaché arrives with barely anytime left. With passport in hand, the entire squad and I sprint through the airport to get to the departure gate. Thank God this was prior to the existence of the TSA and the need for pre-boarding X-rays.

South America is the last continent on earth I thought I would visit, let alone go on a rugby tour to. I am beyond excited. All I want to do on the flight is sleep, while the rest of the team wants to drink.

"Pussy," is the response of the guy sitting next to me when I decline his offer for a beer. I then make the mistake of opening my wallet and he sees the picture of the girl I had started dating since living in the US.

"Nice photo," he says.

"That is my girlfriend," I say proudly.

"What is her name?"

"Brandi," I reply.

"With a y?"

"With an i."

"An i? As in Candi with an i? Is she a stripper?"

"No. Not at all," I say. "She is actually quite religious. She gave me this photo to keep in my wallet to remind me of her while I am away."

"Wow. You really are a pussy."

The team flight connects to Montevideo through Asuncion in Paraguay. Even though we never leave the airport, I fully intend to put a pin for Paraguay on my world map. This is in violation of the standing requirement of the international court in The Hague that a traveler must have spent the night in the city to claim it as a visited destination. They can take me to court to get me to remove the pin.

There is the mandatory South American delay with our flight from Asuncion to Uruguay. There is a trivial issue, they announce over the speakers. They cannot locate the connecting aircraft. Who misplaces an entire plane? At least the airline is honest with their passengers about the reason for the flight delay. Unlike in the US, where it is normal to sit and wait for hours with no idea what the problem is. In South America, they take a far more pragmatic approach.

"There is a delay with the flight because the engine has caught fire."

"There is a delay with the flight as the arriving aircraft has been hijacked."

"There is a delay with the flight because the pilot has shown up for work drunk out of his mind and we are just brewing the coffee."

We finally land in Montevideo a few hours later than expected. Less time for sleep before the big game.

Our lodgings are the Uruguayan version of the hotel in *The Shining*. Nestled on the city's waterfront, the hotel is a classic Gothic style construction riddled with high arches and echoing rooms. The once majestic crown jewel of accommodation options in the capital city. A towering flagpole, proudly waving the light blue and white flag of the nation, adorns a small front lawn.

The main lobby is poorly staffed, but cavernous. While the hallways on the floors are narrow and shadowy. The linen in the rooms is threadbare. My mother has thrown out dishrags that are less frayed than the towel I am expected to dry myself with. The team shares three people to a room.

As luck would have it, we arrive at the same time as a yearly massive storm that parks itself off the Uruguayan coast and drenches the nation for two weeks. We get to our rooms to find several windows have blown out. The eerie resonances of the wind howling through the hotel only add to its character.

Let's Go South America labels Uruguay as the most boring country on the continent. Judging by our quick stopover at the Asuncion airport, most of the team consider Paraguay to be at least as boring. The team eats dinner at a small bar across the road from our hotel.

In the bar, we all discover how difficult it is to communicate in a country that speaks only Spanish. And by only, I mean there have been more separated couples with restraining orders against their spouse who reunited after an overseas trip than people in Uruguay who speak a word of English. But it is also in the bar that we unexpectedly discover the chivito. This is

Uruguay's national sandwich and there is not a finer example of a delicious, unique dish that could make a nation more proud.

The French have crème brûlée.

The Moroccans have couscous.

India has tikka masala with lamb on a bed of white jasmine rice.

But the chivito is king. It rules all other foods with an iron fist.

All the guys on the tour who speak only English, which is all but one, use the chivito as their starting base to learn Spanish.

"Un chivito, por favor." *May I have one chivito, please?*

"Dos chivitoes, por favor." *May I have two chivitoes, please?*

"Tres chivitoes, por favor." *May I have three chivitoes, please?*

"Oye, quita tus malditas manos de mi chivito." *Hey, get your god damn hands off my chivito.*

When I pull out my wallet to pay for dinner, I notice that the photo of Brandi is gone. Did it fall out on the plane? In Asuncion? In the hotel? In the bar? I have no way of knowing. This starts my trip off on a sad note.

I really must be a pussy.

The next morning, the day of the game against the national team, there is a deluge of rain over the city of Montevideo. The squad gathers in the dining room for breakfast, a team talk, and the ceremonial presentation of the jerseys. I am famished and eager for an à la carte option of cereals, omelets, and fruits. But when I open the menu, I am greeted with a photocopy of the picture I had lost. Below her picture is the caption, 'Donde esta Brandi?' *Where is Brandi?*

Every other menu in the hotel restaurant opens to the same page. The entire room laughs heartily at my expense. My teammates revel in the prank. My position on the tour is now cemented as the Aussie pussy that brought a picture of his girlfriend on a rugby trip. None of us realize that this meal is akin to our last supper.

The stadium field is underwater. We could have used it as a rice paddy. A quagmire would have been preferable. Coming from a late Florida summer, the air temperature too is several degrees below comfortable. I am miserable. And that is before the final score of 78-5 against my team gets recorded. Two players are treated for incidental drowning.

During the post-match function, several members of the Uruguayan team come up to me and asked, "Donde esta Brandi?" Not sure I enjoy being famous. After the meal, several teammates and I catch a taxi back to the hotel. The mundane drive to the waterfront is a *Gone in 60 Seconds* audition for our driver. He takes every turn 30 miles an hour faster than the signposted limit. The instant the light turns green at a stoplight, our driver immediately leans on the horn to provoke the car in front to move. His reaction time is instantaneous. Green light, horn.

It is quite an alarming experience.

As is the rest of the week in Uruguay, because the photocopied page with Brandi's photo on it turns up everywhere I go. At restaurants. At the mall. At the famous landmarks we visit in the city: The Palacio Legislativo, The Catedral Matriz, and the Plaza Independencia. Every single night we go to the bar across the road for chivitoes. There is a photocopy of Brandi on the door of the bathroom.

Brandi was fast becoming a minor celebrity in this South American country.

I had been the recipient of pranks before with rugby mates. The diving on me in bed after I had broken my ribs prank. The breaking into my house and drinking all my beer prank. The stripping me naked, tying me to a goal post, then burning my clothes prank. But none of those could match this one in size and scope.

As we check out of the hotel on the last day, I locate the original photo. It is under a weighty, glass tabletop in the hotel lobby. It takes five of us to slide the thick glass covering off its wooden base to retrieve it. This could have been a $2000 mistake in the making. Five of us can barely hold the weight of the glass top to lift it, and the other four nearly drop it when I let go to snatch the picture.

A prank of this magnitude is deserving of some grandiose faux outrage. "You are all a bunch of cun…" I state loudly in the hotel lobby.

"… Hey. Hey, careful with your language," a teammate interrupts me.

"No one here speaks English. They do not know what the word cunt means."

A man in a business suit standing at the hotel counter turns to us and says in a heavily accented tone. "I understand what it means."

"One person. One person knows what it means," I defend myself. "And he is checking out, anyway."

"I am checking in," the businessman informs me.

"Well, we are checking out. So, you will enjoy a cunt free stay while you are here, mate."

Our return flight to Miami is via Buenos Aires, Argentina. In a masterstroke of travel planning, the rugby team must not only change planes, but we must also change airports. And we only have an hour's worth of time in which to do this. I had made a midweek dash to the Argentinian Embassy in Montevideo to obtain a stamp for my travel document.

On my return to the hotel, the taxi driver wanted to drop me off at a bordello.

"Many beautiful girls for you."

"No thanks, mate."

"You go for just a few minutes. See the girls."

"I don't need to see the girls."

"They waiting for you."

"Mate, it is not even noon. I doubt any of them are even awake."

The team gets from Montevideo to Buenos Aires without incident, and rush outside to get taxis to the other airport. The taxi drivers in Argentina made the ones in Uruguay appear as relaxed as cooked spaghetti. The transfer from the domestic to the international airport was happening at rush hour. The cross-city roads are choked with vehicles. We are concerned we will not make it in time. But the taxi drivers were not.

When we end up stuck in traffic molasses, the taxis simply leave the road and drive in convoy across the lawn of a city park. They drive on the sidewalks. One taxi drives over a person's front yard. Unlike in Montevideo, the use of the horn is considered passé in Argentina. The taxi drivers merely scream obscenities out the window at slower vehicles.

We make our flight home without losing a single combatant.

With South America behind us, our flight touches down in Miami at 5am. Apart from the five-hour drive back to the Tampa area, I feel like I am home. Everyone is fatigued at the end of the trip. The team solemnly trudges through the arrival lounge to the immigration check. I must stand in a separate line as I am the sole person on the squad without an American passport or green card. I step forward to the immigration official to present my passport and the piece of paper that proves my legality to work in the US. The immigration official shakes his head.

"Where is your entry visa?" He asks grimly .

"My what?"

"Your entry visa."

"It is that piece of paper, isn't it? That allows me to work in the USA," I ask hopefully.

"Yes, that allows you to work once you enter the country. But first you need to enter the country, and to do that, you need an entry visa!"

Is this the same as the law in Tennessee that allows people to make whiskey but does not allow them to sell it? I thought the point of an entry visa was to allow people to enter if they were *not* allowed to work.

Because it is 5.30am and I am exhausted, I completely forget all the details of the drama that kept me from entering the US for four days from Canada 18 months prior. The official shakes his head. "I can't let you in." I am shell shocked.

"Can you please follow me, sir," he commands as he climbs out of his booth. I walk behind the official as he leads me past the surprised looks on the rest of the touring party. He takes me to a small room with one other occupant. I sit down and wait quietly and respectfully. This is always a person's best option when body cavity searches might be introduced at any point.

The other person in trouble is older than me, but not as patient. He has yet to learn some crucial rules regarding travel. Somehow, he has arrived in Miami from Chile without a passport. Even first-time travelers understand they need a passport. Even Bob from Texas would have known that he needed a passport to fly to Europe to note with disgust how different everything was from his home state.

However, the Chilean man's failure to pass the first basic test of international travel does not deter him in the slightest from feeling entitled. He loudly demands to be let into the country. He verbally abuses the immigration officials with the Latin flair of an Argentinian taxi driver. The official who is dealing with him is certainly in no mood to be generous.

"You will be held here and put on the first available flight back to Santiago."

"You Americans think you are so smart and important," the Chilean man spits out. "Let me go. I have the right to come here."

The Chilean man is certainly pushing his luck. I know how tough the immigration procedure is in the USA. My experience of needing four days to get from Vancouver to Seattle had taught me that. A person never wants to be a jerk in this kind of situation. With his attitude, I am expecting him to be stripped naked at any moment by a husky customs agent with hairy arms and a latex glove allergy, then searched for drugs and the meaning of life well past his anus.

Hopefully not right in front of me.

After dealing with the increasingly aggressive Chilean man for ten minutes, the official turns to me. "You don't have an entry visa," he informs me for the second time. "We are going to have to send you back to the airport where you boarded your plane."

"I am so sorry. I thought the paper I had was the right thing. That is what I showed when I first came over from Australia."

"You're a nice kid. Ill-informed, but nice," the official states. "I am sorry."

Then, the man from Chile comes to my rescue.

"You stupid dogs in your uniforms," the man curses. "You think this is a game, don't you? It is an outrage. You are all stupid pigs."

The official sighs, then looks me straight in the eyes. "If you give me $100, I'll let you go."

"Of course," I blurt. I open my wallet. I have 10 Uruguayan pesos on me. JESUS! What I would not do for a travelers' check. "Oh no. I do not have $100."

The official sighs again. Deeper this time. He looks over at the Chilean man, who is still muttering abuse. "I'll get someone to take you out to the ATM at the airport's front entrance."

I do not know if any of this is legal, or standard homeland security procedure, or the normal way immigration and customs officials let all the drug runners into South Florida. The year is 1993, so the US does not have homeland security yet. Now that they do, I hope they improved their system to allow a person to pay this bribe with a traveler's check or by Visa.

But I feel as if I am the luckiest man on the planet. So, I do not push my luck by asking what bank the ATM is affiliated with. As I normally dislike having to pay the exorbitant fee to use another bank's ATM. Today I will swallow the $2.50 and be happy.

The immigration official gets two men, both armed with weapons, to escort me out to the ATM in the airport's main lobby. Several of the guys I went to Uruguay with are still hanging around at the airport lobby. Including the two I am supposed to drive back to Tampa with.

"Look at this pussy," they chuckle as I am marched up to the ATM.

So much for the experience giving me some street credibility.

I empty my bank account with the withdrawal of $100. Liberty comes at a price. The men escort me back to the area of the immigration booths. I hand over the money. The official returns my passport. I walk through to collect my luggage and exit the airport a free man.

"I will not be going back to South America again," I tell myself.

Famous last words.

14

What do you get when you cross a polar bear with a seal? A polar bear.

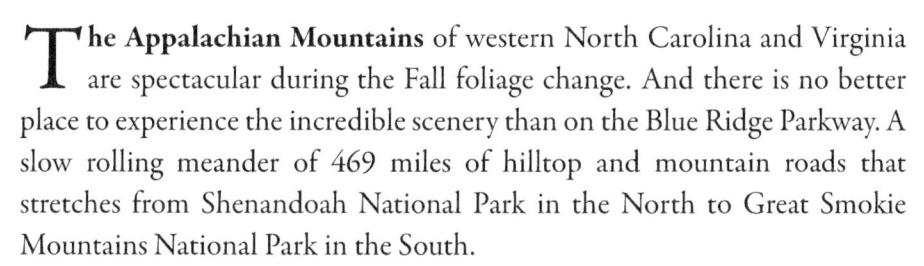

The **Appalachian Mountains** of western North Carolina and Virginia are spectacular during the Fall foliage change. And there is no better place to experience the incredible scenery than on the Blue Ridge Parkway. A slow rolling meander of 469 miles of hilltop and mountain roads that stretches from Shenandoah National Park in the North to Great Smokie Mountains National Park in the South.

I am driving from Tampa to Boston in a 3-cylinder Chevy Sprint. The Verne Troyer of 80's automobiles. The reluctant upgrade in vehicles, from my AMC Eagle Kammback, was forced on me after the Eagle developed a water pump leak. It cost me less to buy another car than it did to replace the water pump.

Following behind me in her Isuzu Amigo imitation sport utility is Brandi. Not only did we move in together, we are also moving together. From Florida to New Hampshire.

The Blue Ridge Parkway is not the quickest road to get to the northeast states from Atlanta. However, my father had never been afraid to deviate from the major roads for his family to experience an unfamiliar sight. Our trip down the treacherous Skipper's Canyon in New Zealand in a non-4WD vehicle being the most obvious example. So, I veer off the I-85 freeway at Greenville and head towards Asheville, so I can join up with the southernmost part of the Parkway.

Driving what is the world's most famous back road through the hills of the Appalachian Mountains is a tick off the bucket list. The Fall colors had reached their peak. This is getting back to the bare-knuckle roots of humanity. There is no Walmart in this neck of the woods. No 24-hour pharmacies. No all-night diners. None of the modern amenities and services that my life in America has me overly relying on. This is pure, unadulterated nature.

After an hour and a half of driving through rolling hills, in the middle of nowhere, there are only trees for company. Our two-car convoy is miles from any sign of civilization. All three of the cylinders in the Chevy Sprint are really working their arses off to get me up and down the inclines.

Then my oil light comes on.

Probably should have been prepared for that eventuality before we left the main road.

A few days before Christmas 1993, Brandi and I sit in the Jax Jr. Cinema, a longtime anchor business on Littleton's Main Street. Littleton is a quaint town in the far north of New Hampshire with two exits off the I-93. The freeway that dissects the state through Concord and Manchester.

This is where we have moved, and I have a temporary job at the hospital there. We are 20 days into a winter that saw temperatures plummet to 40 degrees below zero. Whether the -40 whether is Fahrenheit or Celsius, that is cold. Coming from Florida, which is slightly warmer than the surface of the sun, it is bitterly cold.

That is the greatest challenge of going on a vacation. Most everyone is traveling from one end of the climate spectrum to the other. In the dead of winter, everyone heads to warmer climes. Everyone who lives where it does not snow wants to go skiing. So whatever clothes are comfortable to wear going to the airport at the start of the trip will not be suitable for the conditions on the ground where you land. A person will be either be overdressed or underdressed.

Do not ask me for the solution. I have not worked it out, either.

I arrived in Littleton in shorts in November, and within two hours, word had spread around every business in town that some dumb southerner from

Dixie was seen wearing shorts that close to Thanksgiving. It did not matter that it was a hot day.

Someone told me the mayor even mentioned it in a city council meeting.

As I was buying tickets for Brandi and me at Jax Jr. Cinemas, the young girl behind the counter makes a comment. "You're that guy that was wearing shorts right before Thanksgiving, ain't ya?"

"It was a hot enough day that I was sweating. You know about that?"

"I never heard anything like it," she said incredulously.

"Has nothing else newsworthy happened in this town for the last thirty days that will stop people from talking about that??"

"I'ma tell all my girlfriends that I met you."

I love the informality and friendliness of small towns anywhere in the world. America has some of its finest citizens living in rural areas. Small town gossip is a little off-putting, though. I am concerned that at some point I will be driving down Main St. and notice the town has erected a statue in my honor. It will undoubtedly be in cargo shorts, fists raised above its head, Rocky style.

Tonight's offering at this tiny movieplex with two screening rooms is *Wayne's World II*. The sequel to the classic *Wayne's World*. We are both excited. When a person finds themselves in a small rural town, with limited entertainment options, and the temperature is cold enough to freeze pure antifreeze in a car's radiator, a night out at the movies is a high-level distraction.

The theater fills with townsfolk, young and old. Grandparents, middle-aged couples, and teenagers. The lights in the cinema dim. But when the pre-screening commercials are over, strangely, the lights come back on. A man walks down the center aisle to the front of the room below the screen.

"Listen up. I am the owner of this business and I just want to warn all of you young folks about creating a disturbance during the movie," the man bellows. "I won't have it."

There are some sniggers among a group of teenagers on the left, and the man turns his attention directly to them.

"You want to giggle? Well, let me tell you that the highest number of people I have thrown out of my theater in one night is four. Four! And I am just itching to break my record. Just itching," he sneered. Then he steps up close to the largest group of teenagers. "So, try me."

The sniggers stop. The adults in the room are trembling. This is the most persuasive *do not disturb the showing of the movie* warning any of us have ever heard.

The man stomps back up the aisle, goes back to the projector room, and lowers the lights again. This is what life is like in small town America. I love it. It was the quietest cinema I have even been to.

I have always wondered how many adolescent movie-goers that man has killed since the advent of cell phones.

Two months after the movie experience, I am driving North up the New Jersey turnpike in the Chevy Sprint. It is after midnight. My relationship with Brandi fell apart in January, and she moved to Delaware. I am still caught up in the magic of a romance forged in the fire of two people from different countries and backgrounds finding each other captivating. Because I do not listen to my own advice about romances established while people are away from home being fragile.

They are poison.

But this weekend I have driven from New Hampshire to Dover, Delaware, to try and keep the flame burning.

The outside temperature is still hovering around the -35 range. My ticket for driving on this road blew out the window, almost immediately after I collected it at the toll booth, because I was slow at winding up my window as I accelerated down the road. This means I must pay the full fare of driving the length of the turnpike even though I am not. How annoying.

Then my oil light comes on.

Probably should have been prepared for that eventuality before I got on the turnpike.

It is early May 1994, and I am driving up the 91 Interstate in Vermont on my way back to Littleton. I had been living, working, and freezing my butt off in Littleton for five months. Brandi had left me. Then we reunited. Then we broke up again. Then we got back together.

Long-distance relationships fall into the same category as agitated hippopotamus, the bison in Yellowstone N.P., and cars driving off a cliff as things a person does not want to pursue in their life.

To get my thoughts together, I had gone back to Australia to see my family and visit my almost two-year-old niece for the first time. I have returned to a new temporary job working in Lebanon, New Hampshire, for a month. After that, who knows? As the lyrics in my favorite *Cold Chisel* song go, *I am trying to find a place to settle down where my mixed-up life can mend.*

It is approaching 5pm on a Friday. I left work early so I can get to Littleton before sundown to collect all the worldly possessions I had left behind with a coworker from the job there. The old coworker is heading off camping in the mountains with some friends over the weekend, and I do not want to hold her up. I will collect my things, then head back to Lebanon and relax.

Every year, three motorists die hitting a moose on the roads of New England. They end up being crushed. It is not the impact with the animal that is the problem. The moose is so tall that the vehicles only run into their legs. But the body of the moose falls on the roof of the car, squashing its occupants. As far as deaths go, this way is slightly better than dying of boredom.

As I round a bend in the freeway at 65 miles/hr...

... My oil light comes on.

I am still driving the Chevy Sprint. The same beast of a car that got me through the nightmare of running out of oil on the Blue Ridge Parkway and the New Jersey turnpike. If there had been a moose on the road, as you all thought, I could not have been in a safer car for that scenario. The vehicle is the size of a matchbox and would have easily fit under the moose and passed between its legs.

The oil light coming on is not too problematic. Me and the car have been here before. In the middle of nowhere. No extra oil to top up the engine. There are about 50 miles to go to Littleton. I will grab a few quarts of oil at the gas station, and that will sort everything out.

I take a deep, relaxed breath and continue admiring the glorious spectacle of Vermont mountains, rivers, and forests, all waking up from their winter induced coma. It is so peaceful outside. Life is renewing in the Spring.

Then the engine of my car explodes.

Probably should have been prepared for that eventuality before I started the drive to get my stuff.

Travel tip. If a person is going on a road trip to enjoy the wonderful expanses of landscape outside of the cities, trust me. They do not want to get into car trouble while in the mountains, on a turnpike late at night, or in the middle of nowhere in moose infected territory.

15

I can tell when people are being judgmental just by looking at them.

If I were to throw out a date, June 17, 1994, nobody would have a clue what I was talking about. If I was to throw out an event, the night OJ Simpson led police on a freeway chase, that rivaled Dohers and I for speed as we moved through the Holiday Inn parking lot after we consumed 50 tacos each, everybody will remember that moment in time.

But I can guarantee that no one else had the same experience I did while watching the events of that day unfold.

For me, the memory could not be any clearer. I am now living and working in Boston. The home of America's famous insurrection against the British, and the reason I cannot get a decent cup of tea for breakfast at a diner in the USA. Beantown is the city of missed opportunity. For me. I lived here for seven months and the list of fun things that I did not experience while being here is long and distinguished. I did not watch the Head of the Charles rowing regatta. I did not go drinking at a bar near Harvard. I did not watch the Boston Marathon. I did not go to *Cheers*. I did not go whale watching off Cape Cod. I did not go to historic Fenway Park to watch the Boston Red Sox fail to advance to a Baseball World Series. I did not visit Martha's Vineyard on Nantucket.

I spent my entire time there pining over Brandi.

And my roommate Phil found it hilarious.

And somewhat disturbing.

Phil and I had met at my residential college at university in Brisbane. Phil came over for one year to study on an exchange from his Alma mater, the

University of Massachusetts. He probably regrets it, but he stayed in contact with several of his friends from that time and every single one of them availed himself of his couch over the following years.

I drove down from Littleton one weekend to go drinking with Phil. Sharing the floor with me was Gav, who was headed back to Australia after a year spent exploring Africa, and Shields, a girl from our sister college. She was on her way to London. We also met up with Jeremy, but he was rich enough to afford a hotel room.

That infamous Friday afternoon, I came home from work and had a pine for Brandi. Phil was not at home. He was out on a date. Or he had made that up as an excuse to get away from my incessant pining. After I cleaned up my area (I slept on a mattress in the living room) I had another pine, then turned on the television. The car chase had just begun.

The only television we had in the house was a small portable television device that doubled as a radio. The screen was four by four inches. Even by 1994's Blockbuster Video standards this relic was antiquated. This thing had a built-in antenna to pick up the analog television signals still used by the three major stations. It was serviceable. Tonight, it sat on the kitchen counter, enabling me to watch the Ford Bronco crawl down the freeway as I prepared my dinner of spaghetti.

Phil and I lived on the top floor of a two-story duplex in Watertown. Every house in the neighborhood was the same. Sound traveled up and down from the other apartments clearly, as well as across the backyard fences. OJ Simpson's vehicle had just past the 605 while westbound on the 91 freeway, when I heard the voices of my back neighbors getting into an argument.

"Get out of here. Get out of here, you pig."

This was not that unusual. This pair went at it at least once a week. Sometimes it was just an argument of a few words.

"You pig."

"You bitch."

And then silence.

Sometimes the spat lasted a few minutes. Occasionally, if I was lucky, it might go on for the entire ten minutes I was in the kitchen making my dinner. But tonight, with the vitriol in the screaming, I had the sense that they were going to serve up something special.

But the OJ car chase was being shown live on TV.

Ahh, but I had it on a portable television.

I quickly strained my spaghetti and poured my sauce over the top. No time to grate Parmesan. With my plate of spaghetti in one hand and the portable TV under the other arm, I scurried out to the back porch. I set the TV up on a small table and sat down in a chair to watch the two dramas unfold. I am not normally the type of person who intervenes in a crisis, but I am happy to spectate.

Out in L.A., OJ and Al Cowlings could not be doing any less to make their criminal activity duller. The car chase was painfully slow. Al was indicating when making turns. Looking both ways before crossing an intersection. Meanwhile, in Boston, the neighbors were making a public disturbance the way it should be done.

"You son of a fucking bitch. I don't give a shit you have nowhere to go. Get out!"

"You slut. You fucking slut. You fucking slut, slut. Slut. Fucking slut."

The man had really reached deep into his dictionary to prepare his argument for tonight's debate.

This exchange of slurs goes back and forth for approximately ten minutes. OJ is still on the 405. When suddenly a gunshot goes off at the house behind me where the argument is coming from. Oh, my God. Who shot who? The screaming continues.

"You fucking pig."

"You fucking slut."

It does not sound like anyone is hit by a bullet. If someone in the house had been injured, I would have expected to hear something like, "you shot me, you fucking pig," or, "you shot me, you fucking slut."

But my attention is now 100% on the house behind mine. Sorry OJ, you need to step up your game a little if you want to keep your viewership.

Then the police arrive. The police cars surround the house as haphazardly as the L.A. police making a traffic stop. Officers are out of the cars with their guns drawn. A megaphone is brought in.

"Put down the weapon and leave the house quietly," booms across the neighborhood. "Put down the weapon or we will not hesitate to return fire."

Meanwhile, yawn, back in L.A. the police have OJ on the line.

"Hi OJ, how you doing? I'm a big fan. Listen if you wouldn't mind doing us all a huge favor and just put down the gun and step out of the car. I promise it will all be okay. We have some Jamba Juice here if you are thirsty."

The standoff happening live in front of me is winning the ratings battle hands down. I want to know who has the gun, the pig or the slut. Because, unlike many, I am not so sexist as to believe that women do not have an equal opportunity to create mayhem. OJ would have needed to pull out a grenade launcher or lob a Molotov cocktail at the police to have me regain interest.

The neighbors were barricaded in the house for an hour. One holding the other hostage. I finished my spaghetti, and it was a big plate, with enough drawn-out drama remaining for me to have a large bowl of chocolate Bear Claw ice-cream for dessert before the woman finally turned herself in.

Ring one up for the feminist movement. Another glass ceiling shattered.

Yep, the day that OJ held the eyes of the world captive, except for one pair, was quite an evening.

16

Two fish are in a tank. One says, "How do you drive this thing?"

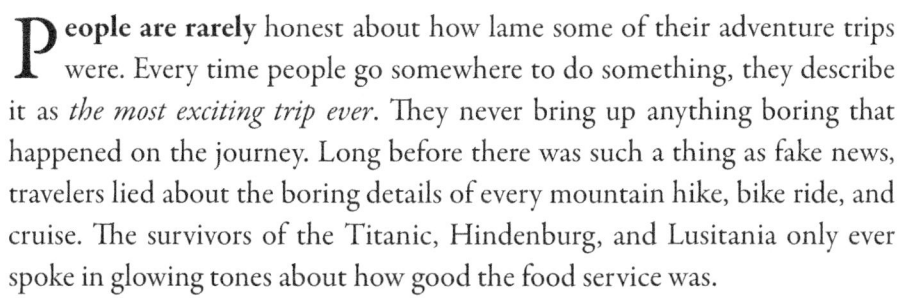

People are rarely honest about how lame some of their adventure trips were. Every time people go somewhere to do something, they describe it as *the most exciting trip ever*. They never bring up anything boring that happened on the journey. Long before there was such a thing as fake news, travelers lied about the boring details of every mountain hike, bike ride, and cruise. The survivors of the Titanic, Hindenburg, and Lusitania only ever spoke in glowing tones about how good the food service was.

A highlight of the year I spent living in San Antonio in 1994 was the time I spent getting out of San Antonio. San Antonio is a fabulous city. It has the Alamo and the Riverwalk. A person can either see the Alamo first then go to the Riverwalk. Or do the Riverwalk first and then see the Alamo. Plenty to do. The options are more limited outside the city limits, as there is only open scrub and sagebrush in all four directions of the compass. However, when a person is desperate enough, they will bear five hours of driving and seeing nothing just to have an adventure.

This is the case with my drive to Big Bend National Park out in the isolated western part of Texas. There is nothing in this corner of the world except for this National Park. Nada. Zip. Zero. Tourism wise, the area could undoubtedly benefit from the addition of an Alamo or two. Maybe a shuttle launch site for NASA. Perhaps even a gigantic theme park called Desert World, where visitors can take selfies standing beside a giant cactus.

I am going to Big Bend with Brandi. She is the reason I am in San Antonio. She moved there from Delaware. Yep, we ended up getting back together. It only took me jumping in my car in Boston and driving for a solid three days to say, "Let's just give it one more chance."

If, now, I do not get some satisfaction from writing about how stupid I was chasing after Brandi, then what was the point?

As we spend a long evening driving westward toward the setting sun, the expansive horizon of Texas spreads out before us. The countryside in much of West Texas is devoid of greenery. Bland and uninviting. If this is so called God's country, then the man upstairs has little in the way of imagination. Is this why the Holy Land is a desert, too?

The fading day gives way to an evil dark sky, peppered with shimmering stars that appear several light-years closer than I have ever seen before. The night brings a fresh perspective of the vastness of the land. The countryside of West Texas looks a great deal more inviting when I cannot see it. Despite hours of driving, we come up short of reaching the entrance to the park. We make it as far as the town of Alpine, 60 miles from our destination. At least I think it is Alpine. It could have been a ghost town. This municipality makes an abandoned shipping container on the roadside feel like Ancient Rome during its heyday.

I pull into a motel, ask for a room, and make small talk with the young lass behind the counter.

"So how long will it take us to get to Big Bend?" I ask.

"To where?" The receptionist replies.

"Big Bend," I state. "The National Park."

"The National Park?" She replies, dumbfounded. "And where is that?"

I am seldom floored by the lack of knowledge of people, but this is one of those times. There is no other sane reason for anyone to pass the town of Alpine unless they are heading to, or coming from, Big Bend National Park. Yet somehow, in all her 18 years of life, this young woman has remained completely oblivious to the only reason for civilization to exist where she lives. Someone throwing a brick at my skull would give me less of a headache than discussing world events with this girl.

Then I get worried. Maybe the reason she does not know anything is that she is not the real receptionist? This woman is a serial killer who was in the middle of robbing this motel when we unexpectedly drove up. The dead body of the receptionist is hidden behind the counter, or in a closet, while she feigns being an employee to give her more time to commit the crime.

These are the deep innermost thoughts of a 27-year-old as I hand over my credit card to a person whose true identity I have no way of knowing, other than that she is standing behind a motel check-in desk in Alpine, TX, therefore she must be the receptionist at a motel in Alpine, TX.

The next morning, Brandi and I arrive at the barren rock expanse of Big Bend. It is 9am. Already the sun scorches whatever life may have survived the bitterly cold overnight temperatures. Boiling hot during the day and freezing at night. Deserts are the unwanted, bipolar stepchildren of the topographical world. And apparently God's favorite. While they serve no worthwhile purpose for humanity apart from acting as a backdrop to Clint Eastwood spaghetti westerns, allowing the activities at Burning Man to occur far out of sight, and conserving water that is better distributed to sustain lush tropical islands.

Unless I was a scorpion, a rattlesnake, or David Attenborough, there would be no good reason for me to be wandering around in a desert.

Brandi and I struggle for an hour to erect our tent at the Maverick Ranch RV Park. The camp site is solid rock. I would have been more successful hammering my tent pegs into the middle lane of the George Washington Bridge. However, humans less resourceful than me have survived living in these conditions. The entire population of Alpine, for instance. Tent pegs are a luxury for the privileged 1%. One good lightning strike, flash flood, or starving mountain lion, and whether my ground sheet is securely fixed to the soil will be the least of my concerns.

After weighting our tent to the ground, by using large boulders placed in every corner, we go for a drive to survey the lay of the land. Barren rock greets us at every turn. Visiting Big Bend National Park is like being on Mars. Except Mars might be slightly more habitable.

This is the largest area of Chihuahuan Desert topography in the USA. With an elevation change within the park of over 6,000 feet. However, it does not rain down in the low part of the desert and it does not rain up in the high part either. The Rio Grande River delineates the park's southernmost border over a 240-mile stretch. At three places along its course in the National Park, the river cuts into an elevated plateau, forming spectacular sheer walled canyons. It was the sight of one of these canyons in a travel magazine that drew me to this place. The odds would be stacked against me to venture here at all if I did not live in San Antonio. And if I did not get my fill of going to the Riverwalk and the Alamo on my first weekend there.

The travel magazine advertised the whitewater rafting trip on the Rio Grande as a breathless, white-knuckle ride on one of the world's iconic rivers. Brandi and I have a booking for this whitewater extravaganza on the Santa Elena Canyon section the next day.

17

I went to buy some camo pants but could not find any.

The next morning, we are up before the sun. Brandi and I must be at the pickup spot early for a pre-raft briefing. Despite being a desert, this is still America, which means there are a hundred legal disclaimers to be filled out before the guide will hand a person a paddle. Once everything gets filled out in triplicate, they take a nose swab, then a blood sample, then they encourage us to sign up for indemnity insurance.

Only now can our guide drive us to the river access point.

At the access spot for the Rio Grande the river is unhurried, wide, and shallow enough that it could be traversed easily from the Mexico side on an inflatable Lilo. According to our guide, the population of the Mexican village on the other side cross the river daily. To crack down on illegal immigration into the USA, surely the Department of Homeland Security could track inflatable Lilo sales in the cross-border region of Texas.

I thought the motel receptionist in Alpine had been a little lost, but our whitewater guide was on another level. He is a wiry, athletic man in his late forties, originally from Baltimore. He could have been a teenager for all I knew, because the brutal desert sun had obviously taken its toll on his skin. Tanned leather has a more youthful complexion. The scraggly beard on his face may have been hiding a few more years, or even a family of woodpeckers. My physical description of him does not do the man's character justice. It is his paranoia that makes him so compelling.

The man fears that an overreaching American government will come to take away his guns. It was this strong apprehension that forced him to move to the desert several years ago. It was only in the farthest reaches of the unforgiving Texas desert that he felt he was able to maintain his liberty. The guide and his guns settled down in a cozy two-bedroom cottage and they hope to raise a family of pistols one day. I imagine that most of the living space in his house is filled with stacks of emergency canned goods. Rows and rows of tinned baked beans aging quietly, waiting for insurrection day.

Our river guide lives his life in a constant state of DEFON 5. Anytime someone mentions the word *government*, his top lip gets taught and his eyes squint. Out here, among the sagebrush and cactus, he will only speak in whispers. The Feds can still listen in on us. It seems a few Americans make some strange choices to maintain their gun rights. If he is afraid of his guns being taken, why did he not choose from any number of weapon friendly locations in the USA? Any one of them would be more hospitable to live in than the Chihuahuan Desert. NRA headquarters, the entire state of New Hampshire, or apartment 104 of the Fish Creek Condominiums in Steamboat Springs.

The occupant of apartment 104 had stuck a sub-machine gun in my face on New Year's Eve 1988. That story is told in the memoir, *My SECOND Life*.

Thirteen miles into the paddle, we enter Santa Elena Canyon. The water flow so far has been as gentle as the Nile. Super lethargic and benign. But, as far as I know, no one claims that sitting in an inflatable raft floating past the pyramids of Giza on the Nile is white-knuckle excitement.

For the next seven miles, there are only the three of us, our raft, and the government listening in. The vertical walls of canyon rock rise directly out of the water on either side and soar to over 1,500 feet. It is as spectacular as it is formidable. I realize that someone would need to be a little bit cuckoo to want to live here in this uncompromisingly, harsh environment.

Thirty years later, I wonder if that guide is still taking raft tours, warning travelers about the ever-expanding government. I heard the other day that President Biden wants to take away people's guns. The river guide was right. Only 30 dry, sun-bleached years too early.

Even the water flow inside the canyon is sedate and passive. This is not a thrill-a-minute mountain whitewater ride pummeling down the slopes of the western Sierras. This is the lazy river ride at *Universal Studios Orlando*. Albeit one without an easily accessible funnel cake stall.

I allow myself to slide gently over the edge of the raft into the Rio Grande's cool refreshment. The width from canyon wall to canyon wall is only 30 meters. I freestyle over and touch the Mexico side. Then I pretend to flee a reprisal from the Sinaloa drug cartel and swim back to the safety of the American side. There I turn and flee from the tyrannical US government back to the raft. Illegal immigration is easy even without a Lilo.

A few miles into the canyon, we beach the raft on a rocky outcrop so the guide can survey the rapids of a stretch of water known as *The Rock Slide*. Fantastic! We have finally made it to the rapids.

"I need to scope out how the river is running before we risk it. One false move and it could be curtains. I need to know the danger," the guide spouts.

Luckily, I have a previous white-water rafting experience. The Tully River in North Queensland, Australia, is a solid Class IV River. Now, I do not proclaim to possess the technical skill to navigate the dangling gates on an Olympic kayak course, but I know what danger on a river looks like.

We climb up some rocks so we can get a look at the rapids. The whitewater that the guide has spent the last three kilometers building up as being Niagara Falls Part Deux is a single, un-deceptively tame half foot drop. After the excitement the guide has been drumming up for an hour, I feel deflated. *The Rock Slide* rapid is as docile as an asthmatic redneck the morning after the *Daytona 500* weekend.

While everything is big in Texas, it seems that the biggest thing is the hyperbole. It felt like the guide had wanted to prank us. But he remained deadly serious.

"See that rock near the drop?" He points out earnestly. "There could be a whirlpool right there."

Travel tip. Learn not to trust authority sometimes. You must learn to trust your gut instinct. Just because a person claims to have traveled a great deal, it does not mean that what they think is exciting will be exciting. When your rafting guide introduces himself along with the allegation that the US government is hiding alien remains in Area 51, then take most else of what he tells you with a grain of salt.

The guide, acutely wary that any sign of disappointment on my face might be part of a wider government conspiracy, continues to survey the water as if taking up his position as the second shooter on the grassy knoll.

"To your untrained eye, the rapid may look straightforward, but it is exceedingly technical," he states.

"It is just a tiny drop, mate. It will be easy," I tell him.

"That is what they said about Vietnam."

"I am sure we will be fine."

"One tiny mistake on my part and you won't be thinking that," he continues. "We need to know what we are up against."

This man's ability to exaggerate beyond all measure of reality is on another level. He would not have been out of place advising Hillary Clinton on her overwhelming popularity among voters during her 2016 political campaign.

"This river water contains a hidden beast," the guide elaborates.

They say the true measure of character is what a person does when they are alone. Not at all. It is what a person does when they find themselves on a far-flung river in West Texas, trying to discuss the Oxford dictionary definition of danger with a future domestic terrorist who likes water sports.

And I want to get on with our trip.

"Can we just get back in the boat?" I ask.

The guide does not answer me. He stares at the river, plotting our safe passage over this liquid street curb to prevent us from stubbing our toe. I feign to be walking away. The guide glances sideways at me, then firmly shakes his head.

"I need a more time to gauge the eddies."

If humanity really enjoyed over-saturated hype, they would happily sit through the entire eight hours of the Super Bowl pre-game show. Nature has given this gentleman a molehill, and he is making a mountain out of it. But I do understand where he is coming from. I once dreamed that, in the course of my lifetime, strangers would look upon me as being special too.

The lunatic river guide finally allows us to re-board our raft and cast off. In keeping with the rest of his life, he has fashioned an immense deal out of nothing. The raft leisurely meanders towards the rapid. At the last second, the guide unnecessarily completes a 180-degree turn with the raft, allowing it to slide languidly backwards over the small drop. It was as technical as backing a wheelchair down a ramp.

The guide wipes the sweat from his brow. He is now at the leading edge of the boat, posing like George Washington in the famous painting of his crossing of the Delaware River. What this man has done is heroic. Not only has he saved Brandi and me from the government's overbearing reach, he protected us from the perils of *The Rock Slide* as well.

If could remember his name, I would name my firstborn after him.

The following day, after recovering from a leisurely raft trip masquerading as a drop over Niagara Falls in a barrel, Brandi and I drive up the twisting road leading into the Chisos Mountains. This is the geographical center of the park. The elevation change is 6000 feet from the bed of the Rio Grande River to the peaks of the range. To my surprise, lush green foliage bathed in cool temperate winds replaces the stark dry desert. The clear skies and cool mountain air are invigorating. Covered by the blanket of night once more, the startling brilliance of stars above the silhouettes of the peaks astonishes me. There is nothing about city life that prepares someone for their first vision of a clear, vibrant night sky, far from the obscuring glow of a metropolis. This celestial spectacle almost makes up for the waterfall of terror during the rafting trip.

Forgoing a tent pitched on solid rock for a third consecutive night, I secure the last available motel room at the Chisos Mountain Lodge to allow Brandi and I to sleep in a soft bed. It is fortuitous that there is a motel in the mountains as a welcome respite to weary campers like us. Americans have the wherewithal to build a motel anywhere. Then Brandi almost sets our room ablaze, lighting the portable gas grill indoors. The motel only loses a towel instead of losing the entire second floor.

Combining the two minutes of consternation battling the fire with all the time spent worrying about my survival while going over the rapid during the rafting trip, Big Bend National Park delivered exactly 120 seconds of high drama. Less than what I was expecting, but certainly more than a person would get from a glass blowing demonstration in Venice, a tour of Lenin's tomb, or a visit to the tree that owns itself in Athens, Georgia.

18

What did one DNA say to the other DNA? "Do these genes make me look fat?"

———⋅❦⋅———

It is exactly seven years to the day, from my first sleepless night in L.A., to the night I slept like a baby after moving to Los Angeles from San Antonio.

Brandi and I have broken up for good. Can I get an Amen? Not an Anglican Church amen, but a Southern Baptist AMEN! After the breakup, she moved from San Antonio to Indianapolis. I made one trip to Indiana on Halloween weekend and it was already so cold that I just said, "That's it. I am not chasing you here."

So not long after, I packed up my things and moved to Los Angeles. Misery loves company and surely, I would find many other miserable, broken-hearted souls in L.A.

But as concealing and vast as the infinite lights of this metropolis are, the world will show me once again that even a sprawling metropolis like L.A. is not as endless as I fear it is.

For the last six months of my time in San Antonio, I have a roommate share my house with me. A former marine. When I leave town, I purposely lose contact, as I am angry at him. My roommate was engaged to his childhood sweetheart in his hometown back in Illinois. But while he was working and living in San Antonio, he dated a stripper. That was not what upset me. It was none of my business. I never met the fiancée. I met the stripper once, briefly. His poor fiancée should do her due diligence prior to signing the contract. My roommate was a former marine. She had to be aware of what she was getting into. Like a traveler who arrives at Four Corners Monument in New Mexico and wonders, "now what?"

However, after he breaks the news to his stripper friend that he has a fiancée, she shows up at 4am in a fit of rage and tears my front screen door off its hinges. That display of strength by such a tiny girl was unreal. If one day the world erupts in post nuclear chaos, I would not be so worried about hordes of flesh-eating zombies as I would be about car loads of pissed off table dancers. I could not very well be mad at the poor stripper, as she had had her heart crushed. Brandi had crushed *my* heart and if I were strong enough to tear three-inch screws out of wood, I would have. I am livid at the roommate for the damage to my screen door.

Then I move to Los Angeles and decide to follow every fantasist's dream of being an actor in Hollywood.

My first few gigs as an extra are tiny, but that is okay. They are a springboard. I was a member of the crowd in a hotel scene on *Melrose Place*. A member of the crowd in a street scene for the *Brady Bunch Two* movie. And a member of the crowd during a stadium scene in the Robert De Niro film, *The Fan*.

I thought it was wise to stick to crowd scenes, on the off chance that Hollywood directors were looking to pluck someone out of a crowd and give them their big break into stardom. The pay for an extra in Hollywood is an earth shattering $40 for an eight-hour day. Not a problem. I am doing this for the love of my craft, not for the money.

But I can now see why the real estate prices in Los Angeles have gone through the roof. Factoring in wage inflation, extras in Hollywood in the year 2023 must be pulling in at least 47, or 48 dollars a day.

Somehow word of my being on *Melrose Place* filters back to Australia and several mates tell me their wives have asked them to scour the show to see if they can spot me. My mates were just using me as an excuse to embrace their feminine side. The episode I was in was titled, *Run Billy Run, in* the dramatic fourth season of the show.

It is the episode where Jane sabotages Richard's fashion show, using a tiki torch to set off the fire sprinkler system in the showroom. This is also the episode where Kimberly starts suffering migraines, and Amanda turns to Peter for comfort after the bribery allegations against Bobby become public. All super relevant plot points leading into the fifth and final season where the entire cast became alcoholics, or developed strange neurological diseases, in an attempt to increase the show's sagging ratings.

All this exposure to the machinations of Hollywood boosts my acting credentials. Not a single other extra on the *Melrose Place* set could sit on a seat as well as I could. Then, after sitting in a chair for the crowd scene on the set of *The Fan*, I get a call back. I am bumped up from 'man in the stands' to a 'member of the San Francisco Giants baseball team Wesley Snipes plays on.' My sitting on a seat with 1000 other extras during the crowd scene obviously impressed the hell out of the director.

Truth be told, it was the fact that my red hair was the same color as the previous actor in this role, who had suddenly taken ill. The director needed my hair for continuity. Bet all those little brats who teased me on the kindergarten playground were wishing they were riding my ginger hair coattails now.

Every day for a week I am needed on set at Anaheim Stadium at 6am for 18 hours or more of shooting. In one scene, I am filmed from behind as I move up the dugout hallway. In another I am filmed from behind while standing by my locker. On one occasion, I walk through the shower room in a towel. Filmed from behind. The director, Tony Scott of *Top Gun*, never truly utilized my talents for sitting. Weird. This is where my acting credentials are the strongest.

During the shower scene, Tony wants as much realism as he can draw from the location. The extras are asked if any are willing to appear naked with their backside to the camera. There is a commensurate increase in pay for the technical skill involved in this scene, known in the business as, 'the nude bump.' The extra five dollars of pay on offer has every person scrambling to be chosen. With that bonus in their next paycheck, three lucky actors will be able to afford to rent a new release DVD for a night.

I would not let myself be filmed naked for any amount of money. At least not unless they were going to play *Love Shack* by the B-52's.

On the last day of this acting gig, all the extras are sitting in the stadium locker room waiting for our call to set. Word gets passed down, through a

Production Assistant, that all the extras need to change from their baseball uniforms into street clothes. After changing, the news comes back that Tony Scott wants us all back in baseball uniforms. Ten minutes later it is street clothes, another ten minutes after that back to baseball uniforms. Despite Mr. Scott directing one of my all-time favorite movies, his lack of directorial focus is starting to wear thin. I can only imagine what a mess it must have been like on the *Top Gun*.

"Tom, Val, I want you bare-chested and stripped down to your jeans for this scene."

"Mr. Scott, are we filming the climatic air battle scene?"

"Yes."

"Do you think pilots would be bare chested while in their fighter jets?"

"You think flight suits are better?"

"That is what pilots would normally be wearing when flying their planes."

"Okay, but keep your jeans handy just in case I want this scene to go in a different direction."

The other extras dutifully change back into their playing uniforms while I decide I do not care if I miss out on being in this unimportant shot. Besides, I am fearful of having to walk anywhere in the baseball cleats we have as part of our wardrobe. The cleats are as slippery as hell walking over the cement floors in areas of the stadium. In the scene where we all walked up the passageway from the dugout, every kept slipping over, which then required multiple takes to get less than a second of action that made it onto the screen.

Besides, there is already more than enough footage of me from behind to make a stellar reel. I do not need to be in another scene. The call comes down to have all the extras at the front of the stadium immediately for the shot.

We are told to sprint through the hallways to the front gate.

Sure enough, everyone in their baseball cleats lands on their backside at least once. If the safe workplace practices commission had been doing their job, they would have shut production down.

At the stadium entrance, Wesley Snipes is already there, which meant filming is about to start. The well-paid talent, those making more than $40 a day, do not hang around to do anything other than be in the scene. Then they go back to their trailer. For this scene, Wesley's character is to leave the stadium in a huff under a barrage of questions from the press. His character has had another poor game performance during a batting slump. I do not expect to do anything, as I am in street clothes while everyone else is in their uniform.

Suddenly, filming begins with the call for "action." The set springs to life and Hollywood starts making its magic. Wesley storms past the press towards his Hummer. Tony wants more background movement for realism. A Production Assistant grabs me, as I am the only extra not in a baseball uniform, then pushes me into the scene to act as if I am walking towards my imaginary car.

Just as average Americans pulling in $40 a day are not adept at driving a stick shift car, neither are their well-paid star actors. Wesley leans much too heavily on the accelerator while releasing the clutch far too quickly. The Hummer bursts forward from its parking space like a crouching tiger.

While I am walking directly in front of it.

The potential liability for running someone over on a movie set must be in the millions, but I like both of my legs. To avoid becoming road kill – or parking lot kill – because Wesley Snipes has no control of the Hummer, I have to dive onto the concrete.

Wesley Snipes cannot act like he knows how to drive a manual car?

Tony Scott is happy, but not satisfied. He wants the shot done again. I try to leave, to avoid having to do the death scene for a second time, but a Production Assistant collars me. They need my body in the shot again for continuity.

Can't I get a stuntman double?

On the second take I do not walk towards my imaginary car, I sprint. Staying well out of Wesley's way as he strips the gears. My scene stealing effort makes the final cut of the movie. Just not the part where I am almost run over. You can recognize me by the green flannel shirt I am wearing. A flannel shirt I purchased at Lahout's Country Clothing in Littleton, New Hampshire, to better assimilate with the locals who were so upset that I wore shorts in November.

It was while the cast of extras were changing back and forth for this scene that I fell into conversation with one of them. He told me he was from Illinois. He had a brother, a former marine, who was living in San Antonio, Texas.

"And he is engaged to his high school sweetheart named Beverly," I add.

"Yes, He exclaimed. "How on earth do you know?"

Turns out this random extra on a film set in Los Angeles is the older brother of my onetime roommate from San Antonio whose ex-stripper girlfriend ripped my screen door off its hinges.

Try saying that three times quickly.

I shake my head. "I have no fucking idea."

We live in a small, small world.

If I was more confrontational, I might have told the older brother that he owed me his entire week's pay, $200, to cover the cost of a new screen door. But I did not have the nerve to tell his brother that. Besides, I am certain the rest of his family were unaware of the existence of my story's female protagonist.

If you think the coincidence in this story is unbelievable, the next one should blow your mind.

19

Communist jokes are not funny unless everyone gets them.

One of the joys of being an ex-pat is supporting the different sporting celebrations honored by your adopted country. Wife carrying in Finland. Cheese rolling in Gloucester, England. Ostrich racing in South Africa. A fiercely contested sporting rivalry is even more fun to watch. Australia versus New Zealand in rugby. India versus Pakistan in cricket. Germany versus any country they invaded at the start of WWII, in any sport you can think of.

In America, football is the king of competition. And the most ferocious rivalries of the sport take place at the college level. It is truly a spectacle to see the passion and emotion of a packed 80,000 seat arena cheering on their teams. Even more so when you realize that 80% of the crowd are acting this fervently while sober as they are still too young to drink legally.

One classic rivalry between colleges is the UCLA/USC football game, which takes place very year at the Rose Bowl in Pasadena. And in 1996, I am there. Not that I am a rabid fan of American football, or either school, but someone gave me tickets as a gift. And this game was one for the ages. My date and I do not make it into the stadium until half-time. For someone who describes herself as low maintenance, she had spent an inordinate amount of time not putting on makeup.

The traffic around the stadium in Pasadena was like nothing I have ever experienced. Total gridlock on a Saturday afternoon. It was as if hordes of people were escaping a Russian nuclear attack. No one realizes they would be better off on foot to get out of the three-mile critical impact radius. We get to our seats as the third quarter kicks off with the score 24 -7 to USC. UCLA is getting schooled in the noble art of big men running into each other for a 60-minute game that lasts three hours.

Our seats are in the south-east corner of the Rose Bowl, right on the divisional line between the two sets of fans. One row in front, and across the steps to my right, there are two Latino men in USC jerseys. Directly in front of me is a highly inebriated Latino man in a UCLA jersey. I have never seen a fan like this UCLA fan. He is exuberant. He is unequivocally happy. And he is full of overwhelming positivity. He would see the silver lining to a mushroom cloud forming just over the parking lot outside the stadium. Nothing, and I mean nothing, was going to ruin this man's day. Not even the scoreline. This drunk Latino was having a field day right in front of me. Dancing up a storm while cheering endlessly. "Go Bruins. Love you, Bruins."

Meanwhile, across the stairs, the two USC fans are screaming insults at him. But nothing they say seems to dent the UCLA fan's elated mood. When UCLA scores a touchdown to pull within ten points, the drunk fan celebrates like he won a $100 million Powerball lottery.

The USC fans laugh him off as USC scores again. Some of their taunts are incredibly mean spirited and vulgar. The UCLA fan does not care. He is dancing as if he is in his shower, not in the middle of a stadium filled with 100,000 people. UCLA is still trailing by 17 points with six minutes left in the fourth quarter. The UCLA fan has not slowed down at all. "Go Bruins. Love you, Bruins."

While I do not honestly care about the result and feel that screaming obscenities at a rival fan is best left to the experts, I almost feel sorry for the two USC fans. For an hour and a half, they have been made to feel invisible. Not only by the UCLA fan, but by all the other fans sitting in the area. Imagine cheering for a winning team and no one caring. Everyone is far more taken by the devotion of the UCLA fan. He is a superstar. This is the most incredible display of ghosting the world has ever seen, and the two ghosted people are only six feet away.

This moment taught me a valuable tip to remember while traveling. To throw my heart into every moment of life as being a once in a lifetime opportunity, just like the UCLA fan was doing. If people want to ridicule me for being overly excited about seeing the Eiffel Tower, or the Grand Canyon, or the world's second largest ball of string, then it will only make me happier. On that day I learned that my happiness is not dependent on what other people think of me. My happiness is not dependent on my team winning or losing. My happiness comes from being where I am and enjoying that moment.

We never know how much time we have left.

The UCLA fan had this doctrine down to the letter.

And if I need to ram this point home to anyone still having a hard time understanding. A week later, I am almost killed in a car accident and spend the next 3 weeks in a coma. I coded three times during the first night in the ICU.

I know of what I speak.

An anonymous drunk man in a UCLA T-shirt was my guru. He made me a believer.

And when people believe, sometimes incredible things will happen.

Miraculously, UCLA draws level in the game with 40 seconds left to play. Right until that moment, the UCLA fan is still being showered with abuse by the two USC fans. It is an incredible display of belief in his team. Or maybe he was so blind drunk he thinks he is cheering at a U2 concert. The man has not been downbeat for a single second, and against all odds, his team has tied the game.

The two USC supporters suddenly become two sullen, bitter men who do not care to watch this guy's disco moves anymore. Fans sitting in their vicinity suddenly become security, preventing the two angry Latinos from beating up the UCLA guy. I get a punch in the face for my troubles. I do not think the man even stopped dancing while the melee raged around him.

The game heads to double overtime before UCLA block a penalty kick, then score on the ensuing play to win 48-41. It was amazing to experience the complete change in the emotional tide of the game with the fans in the stadium. Meanwhile, the man in front of me is in euphoric overdrive the entire time.

After dropping off my date, I head to a bar near the UCLA campus, a short walk from my apartment. After ordering a beer, I start a conversation with an attractive, athletic girl sitting at the bar named Suzanne. She is from

Germany and has been studying at UCLA on a semester abroad program for her architecture degree. She is returning to Munich in a few days.

We strike up a quick friendship. She adores Los Angeles, and I want to understand why. She asked me to help her locate an architecture firm in the city to give her an internship so she can return next year. She writes down her contact details in Germany on a coaster. I do the same and tell her I will do what I can to help. She says that I can come and stay with her family in Bavaria if I ever get to Europe. Free room and board on the continent. I would never pass that up.

I go home to bed. Suzanne goes back to Germany. A week later, my car is written off with me in it. The coaster with her contact details was in my glove compartment.

I spend six months recovering from the accident. First in a UCLA hospital, then at my parent's house in Australia. I meet my new niece, Leisl, while in hospital. I spent a few rough months adjusting to life away from my family again and getting back to work in Los Angeles. Wondering what life meant, and where I was supposed to be.

As I was not able to play rugby, I had less contact with my mates on the team. I did not enjoy going to games just as a spectator. Around August, several of the guys start talking up going to Hawaii to play in a tournament. They ask me to come along, but I decline.

One day in late September, a dozen members of my rugby club in Santa Monica decide to go surf kayaking. I get the call as well.

"Hey, want to come to Santa Monica beach with a few of the guys?"

"Nah, not really."

"What's wrong, you pussy?"

"Nothing. I just don't think I would have any fun."

"I bet you don't have the balls to have fun!"

The magic words to get me moving.

One of the guys owns a work van, so there are six of us in the back. This saves on parking at the beach. I know four of the guys, but there is a face I do not recognize. He is a new player, a kid from Scotland. He started playing while I was away in Australia and we had not met since I had been back.

We start asking each other the regular things guys ask each other. Where are you from? How long have you played rugby? How many bones have you broken while playing? He tells me he is an architectural student doing an internship at a firm in Santa Monica for six months. I mention that I met a girl from Germany last year who wanted to do exactly that. But then I lost her contact information.

As guys do, the others asked me about her appearance. I described to them her dark hair, German accent, and how athletic she was.

"Was her name, Suzanne?" The Scottish kid interrupts me. "Cause there is a Suzanne from Germany who is doing an internship along with me. She is athletic," he remarks.

Yep, it was the same person.

All it took to reconnect with a near stranger from Germany, in a city as large as Los Angeles, was another complete stranger from Scotland. This world is never as big as it seems. That is the joy of meeting people while traveling, then running in to them again in the oddest way years later.

Suzanne and I meet up and I explain the reason for ghosting her. Despite her being aware of the daunting size of L.A., she always expected to run into me again. The internet has developed popularity, so we swap email addresses and promise to remain in contact. Suzanne again invites me to visit her and her family in her homeland.

"You will love Germany," she tells me. "We have some great nightclubs in Bavaria. We can have a great time."

I had been thinking about a trip to Europe. As much as I had heard about all the wonderful places to visit there while growing up, I had yet to go. While ten months ago I was a steering-wheel-short-of-my face close to never having the chance to. Bavaria, hmm? Going to visit her sounded fantastic. And how much trouble was a person likely to get in while in Bavaria?

20

Geology rocks, but geography is where it is at.

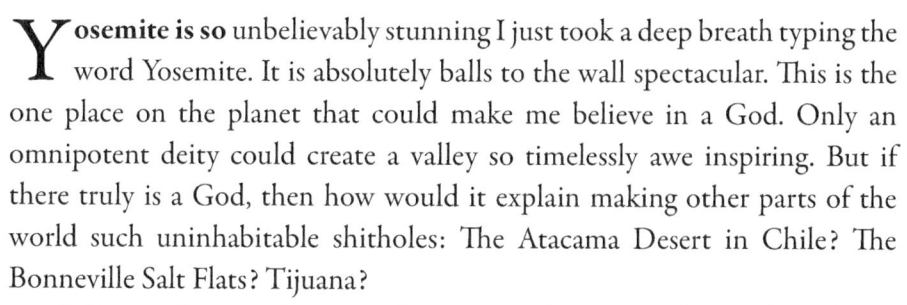

Yosemite is so unbelievably stunning I just took a deep breath typing the word Yosemite. It is absolutely balls to the wall spectacular. This is the one place on the planet that could make me believe in a God. Only an omnipotent deity could create a valley so timelessly awe inspiring. But if there truly is a God, then how would it explain making other parts of the world such uninhabitable shitholes: The Atacama Desert in Chile? The Bonneville Salt Flats? Tijuana?

Still, to whatever deity or aberration of tectonic plate upheaval and erosion that created Yosemite Valley, I say, well done, sir.

I first laid eyes on Yosemite on the back of my brother's bedroom door. The Ansel Adam poster of Half Dome. Yosemite National Park's signature formation iced in winter's cream cheese frosting. Even two dimensional, there was something undeniably compelling about it. I had stared at it for hours. Lost in deep contemplation. Wondering if I would ever be deserving of seeing it with own eyes. The concept that I would one day have the power and freedom to go whenever I chose was lost on me for my entire youth.

A trip to Yosemite could only happen by luck, magic, or divine intervention.

There was no greater contrast in geography than between Townsville's flat, dry landscape and a towering mound of pure granite salted with fresh powdered snow half a planet away. As famed conservationist John Muir wrote, *it is by far the grandest of all the special temples of Nature I was ever permitted to enter.* Writing like this reinforces that it is an honor for an individual to experience Yosemite.

The first time I see Yosemite in person is from 30,000 feet. Flying back from Japan directly over the Sierra Mountains. It struck me as unusual that on the first leg to Tokyo from Los Angeles, the plane flew over San Francisco. Tokyo was to the West, San Francisco to the North. Every world map shows Japan as being directly West of California. My first thought was the plane had been hijacked. My second thought was that the pilot was drunk. My third thought was that I had wasted a ton of money on a yearly subscription to the Flat Earth Society.

It is due to the anomaly of the curvature of the earth's surface, that to travel the least amount of distance from LAX to Narita, planes must fly in an arc heading in a north, north-westerly direction. Only if a CEO wanted their airline to go bankrupt, would they instruct their pilots to fly in a direction that consumed more gas than necessary. Even if it looked shorter on a map. Pan Am, Continental, and Northwest, must all have catered to flat earthers.

On the day my flight from Tokyo flies South down the spine of California, I have visibility to infinity. Not a cloud in the sky. At 30,000 feet, I can see from the pure, blue waters of Lake Tahoe all the way to the smog encrusted gloom of L.A. The moment I lay eyes on the furrow of Yosemite Valley in the granite countertop of the Sierras, my mind is made up. I am only 30,000 feet away from the dream at the back of my brother's bedroom door. I had been living in Los Angeles for almost two years, overseas for five.

Time for me to realize the only thing stopping me from going to Yosemite was me.

I make up my mind to go there this coming week.

I had just taken off a week and change to go to Japan. Now I wanted to go back to work and take another day or so off at the end of the week to go to Yosemite. This was gainfully employed madness.

Often living a full life and madness are separated only by a thin margin.

For 22 months, while living in Southern California, the idea of going to Yosemite had been in the back of my head. But I never acted on it. Like checking the use by date of food, it was always something I would get around to doing one day. But if I did not go now, then when? Why had I moved to California in the first place? To live the dream. But a man can spend his entire life futilely waiting to catch his dreams. Only to realize at his death they were always within his grasp, he only had to reach for them.

My record for holding onto canned goods after they have expired is three years, by the way.

The opportunities for a person to have an extraordinary experience on this planet have a limited shelf life. Time passes faster than we realize. Five days after the flight lands at LAX, my chest swells with pride as I speed up the 99 freeway towards Merced, the gateway to Yosemite. My mind had never been filled with such anticipation to arrive to anywhere. I am not merely driving on a freeway heading to a National Park. I am fulfilling a little boy's destiny.

Life is like a mountain hike. Most of it is plodding drudgery, but the times we reach a viewpoint, make it all worthwhile.

I asked my rugby mates during the week if anyone was up for the trip. There were plenty of eager hands, as there should be. Every one of them held a dream of going to Yosemite. But when I started organizing the logistics and chasing them up for money for lodging, suddenly, everyone had a hardship story or an excuse. This is when I realized how lucky I was to have been isolated on the playground as a young child.

I did not *need* to have other people with me.

It was nice. But not at all necessary.

If I wanted to go and do, I could just go and do by myself.

Going it alone is often a far preferable way to travel. No delays. No distractions. There is no can I pay you back the week after next? Or can we go in two weeks, which would suit me better?

My adventures in life may well be destined to remain solitary, but they will be my own. If I spend my life waiting for others to get their shit together, I will always be waiting.

I think of how different the landscape of the world would be if Christopher Columbus, Captain Cook, or Vasco de Gama, had waited for their mates to get permission from their girlfriends before they could take off on their voyages of world discovery. They would never have left. Modern civilization would have remained confined to Europe. While the most meaningful achievement humanity would have accomplished was to abolish the French monarchy.

One of my favorite quotes is by Wendell Berry: *nobody can discover the world for somebody else. Only when we discover it for ourselves does it become common ground and a common bond, and we cease to be alone.* I always took this as a fancy way of saying that if I traveled enough, I would one day find a wife.

Arriving at Yosemite for the first time through the town of El Portal, it feels like I am entering an altered reality. Land this breath-taking simply does not feel real. My car snakes along the tortuous 140 state highway, following the fast-flowing Merced River at the base of the Merced Gorge. Up the road ahead of me, sheer granite cliffs tantalizingly appear, then disappear. I pay my entrance fee at the National Park gate and drive through.

Within a few hundred feet, I enter a grove of high fir trees and my frame of reference becomes limited by the wall of green around me. The car passes through a short rock tunnel, where some clever engineer had decided it would be more aesthetically pleasing to chip a passageway through a giant boulder rather than blow the whole rock to kingdom come. How John Muir of him. As I drive through, I expect that this natural portal will transport me to a fantastical world like Narnia. Not quite. On the other side are just more trees.

Continuing further up the road into the park, the stands of reddish barked sequoias gradually become thicker and thicker, occasionally completely obscuring the surroundings to me. The valley here is still wide and sloped. Nothing like what I pictured from the dramatic photos of Ansel Adams. But am I imaging tips of whitewashed cliffs visible in the distance? It is hard to tell. No matter how far I drive, they always seem to remain around the next bend. The sequoias close in again, this time their branches reach over the road and conceal the deep blue of the Sierra Mountains sky behind a transparent green canopy of leaves.

Then, like coming up for air after having my head submerged by a bully at the school pool, the sequoia grove thins into a clearing and a sheer sided U-shaped valley opens up to me. People know this spot as Valley View. And dear... sweet... baby... JESUS. It is one of the most beautiful sights I have ever witnessed. In terms of the unrestrained joy this scenery elicits, Yosemite is the childbirth of National Parks. I felt I could die at this moment and my life would have been complete.

Knowing my mates will call me a pussy does not discourage me from saying I wept.

El Capitan sits directly in front of me. To the right a thin white string of water, Bridal Veil Falls, drops precipitously to the meadows from the crest of the valley ridge. All the colors at play are sharp and vivid, which makes the scene visually intense. The bluest sky, the greenest forest, the whitest cliffs. It is the most moving sight I have ever seen. A masterpiece forged by the hand of God.

Or the upheaval of tectonic plates.

I have reserved a canvas tent in Curry Village (Since renamed Half Dome Village), as this will make me feel closest to nature. Without having to do any actual work of erecting a tent myself. Curry Village is a rent-a-tent for city buffoons like me.

It is also the cheapest option available. An often-overlooked aspect of travel is that the least expensive accommodation is often also the one that will give a person the most experience bang for their buck. No one tells their mates they roughed it under the stars in Yosemite after forking out $910 a night at the Ahwahnee Hotel.

I needed to conserve my energy, anyway. This trip is not just about the accomplishment of arriving at the park. I will also attempt the Half Dome summit hike. To make it more daring, I am going to do the hike with less than a week's worth of planning and groundwork. Why should I be happy to go on a 26-kilometer hike when I can go on a 26-kilometer hike without remembering to take food or water?

21

Are people born with photographic memories or does it take time to develop?

Yosemite Rangers delight in telling visitors to the park this joke: A visitor to Yosemite asked a Park Ranger, what would you do if you only had one day to see the park? The Park Ranger replies, I would cry.

Another option might be for the visitor to call up their boss and tell him they fell into a ravine and got stuck, so not to expect them back in the office till the following Tuesday or Wednesday. Or the visitor might prefer to go on a two to three-hour hike, leaving some food items in his car. After the park bears have ripped the vehicle apart to get to the food, the person can then call up their boss and tell him they will not be back to the office for a few more days as they must sort out transportation to get home.

However, if someone is foolish enough to leave food in their car, knowing there are bears in a National Park, it is a good idea they only spend 24 hours in nature.

After experiencing Yosemite, I took this life-is-too-fleeting joke to heart. I nearly told my boss to shove it so I could go hiking in the Grand Canyon in November, then quit my job a few months later to go on a trip to Europe. I wonder if I can sue the National Park Service for loss of income.

I made particularly good time driving from Los Angeles to Yosemite. So, a quick drive up to Glacier Point was in order. I only had two days to spend in Yosemite, so I had better get busy exploring before the park rangers found out and burst into fits of laughter.

Glacier Point viewing area perches at an elevation of 7214 feet, a kilometer above the valley floor. If I thought Valley View was special, then

Glacier Point makes that spot look like a weeping pustule on the backside of a festering corpse. Here is the entire soul of Yosemite National Park, spread panoramically at my feet. It brings meaning to the term superlative. If there is a more captivating sight on this earth, it could only involve the female cast of *Baywatch* in slow motion. At this height and distance, everything on the valley floor seems insignificant. The cars driving around the park loop road look like ants. The bears breaking into parked cars looking for food appear as tiny as specks of sand.

After Joseph Smith founded the Church of Jesus Christ of Latter-Day Saints, he led his followers across the USA in search of their spiritual home. Yosemite is where I think they were supposed to finish. This is the glorious, Promised Land. Instead, the Mormons must have made it to the desolate Salt Plains of Utah and ran out of gas, 586 miles too soon.

Even though I thought I would have died content at Valley View, I realize now that I am so glad that I survived to make it to Glacier Point. Now I can die again, here. Here is much better. Glacier Point is not a spot where a person can grab a quick photo and move on. This view demands time. It requires living in the moment. I spend over an hour transfixed in awe. And I still leave feeling it is not enough.

This is the first time in my life I experienced being so present. It was surreal. Being completely in the moment. In this state of mind there were no anxieties, there were no hang-ups. I am not regretting the yesterdays or fretting over the tomorrows. There was only the here and now. Only the view in front of me was important. An experience of a lifetime was happening right now.

For the second time in two hours, I wept.

Fuck, I really am a pussy.

Before going to bed that evening in my Curry Village rent-a-tent, I take one last look at Half Dome in the moonlight. A single light on the cliff face flickers three quarters of the way to the top. Climbers turning in for the night in bivouacs suspended 3000 feet above solid ground. Likely thick bearded mountain men who wear plaid shirts that barely conceal their oversized hairy forearms. Real men.

Tomorrow I will attempt to make it to the top of Half Dome. I do not realize yet how under-prepared I am. There is certainly not enough time to grow a beard.

My alarm wakes me at 5.35am. I am sharing the tent with three other people who are not going hiking. The alarm also wakes them. I did not truly appreciate what an arsehat move this was on my part until a few years ago, after sharing a hostel room in Rio de Janeiro with three drunk Argentinians. To those three Yosemite visitors I now humbly apologize.

I was not the person who farted though.

Getting to the Happy Isles trailhead early means much less hiker traffic to deal with. And the trails in Yosemite can reach World Cup Final frenzied levels of activity. I prefer swarming crowds at Vietnam War protests, *Beatles* concerts, and at the celebration of overthrowing a dictator. Not while hiking in the serenity of nature.

The sun is yet to rise and stir awake the valley, unlike what I did to my three tent mates. Again, I apologize profusely. But there are a handful of intrepid souls on the path already. These must be my people. People who did not mind waking up their roommates so they could get on the trail bright and early. This is a special feeling. It is so empowering to be up before dawn and setting out on an adventure.

The first rays of light over the lip of the valley rim blow away the dusty coating of night. The all-pervading darkness among the trees becomes a keyboard of light and dark silhouettes. I hike up the Mist trail towards Vernal Falls with gusto.

Once there is enough light, I check my trail map. Since my initial forays into travel to the USA, I have graduated to using maps. Normally I would have done this the night before starting such a strenuous hike, but the magnificence of Glacier Point had exhausted me. I fell asleep as soon as I was in my tent bunk.

The initial passage of information I read relates to safety while hiking. It outlines several key points. Number one point - take plenty of water. I did not bring any. Too heavy to carry. What effects I might suffer from dehydration, I will more than make up for in freshness, not lugging a weighty backpack.

The sign at the trailhead lays out the times for the average person to hike to the viewpoints. The 1.2 miles to Vernal Falls Bridge over the Merced River, with magnificent views of Vernal Falls, they list as an hour. The next 0.3 miles to the top of Vernal Falls is also listed as an hour. However, with no hikers clogging the path I am at the top of the falls within 45 minutes. The tactless act of waking up my fellow tent mates early is now paying dividends on the trail.

The initial section of trail follows alongside the Merced River to Vernal Falls, then climbs to Nevada Falls. Switchbacks to the top of Nevada Falls are the steepest section of the hike, save for the last 100 meters of the cable lines at the summit. Hiking to Vernal Falls is moderately strenuous, but at least the path is well paved. The river to the side of the path is thunderous. The commanding force of the fast-flowing stream constantly pounds the large rocks. Liquid tornadoes swirl around the boulders. The most deaths in the park occur at this location. Unsuspecting hikers slip into the river and are not prepared for the pull of the current.

An easy point to make. If a hiker can hear the water flow in the river/creek/waterfall, the current is not safe to fall into. So, do not.

When I hit the rock stairs hewn into the granite cliff below Vernal Falls after only 35 minutes, I realize that if I expect to make it to the top of Half Dome, I need to slow down. My pace has been torrid, while this hike is more extreme than hotel mini bar pricing.

Above Vernal Falls, I moderate my speed to keep pace with another single hiker who has brought a ton of water with him. The steep switchbacks, to climb the gradient at Nevada Falls, are infinitely more comfortable when not attempted at a half jog. We continue together into Little Yosemite Valley and share our tips for hiking. It is a weight versus hydration debate. This sharing of opinions carries us the next seven kilometers, from the top of Nevada Falls to the eastern shoulder of Half Dome. He claims the victory in our discussion. I concede. Lost on my companion is the fact that he carried the water weight. I only drank it.

The trail above Nevada Falls is boring and non-descript. There are no scenic overlooks or interesting features. Just a long, slow, uphill slog through a forest. About halfway along this portion of the path, two skinny, pimple faced teenagers come whooping their way down the path. They carry climber's packs on their backs decorated with carabiners. They were the lights I had seen on the cliff face last night. Two prepubescents.

How?

I bet neither of them even owns a plaid shirt.

These young idealists had been hanging on a cliff face at 6000 feet by a thick piece of dental floss. They are not yet eligible to drive a car, but they just climbed the face of Half Dome. It makes me laugh thinking about kids today needing safe spaces. I kept on hiking, thinking about my accomplishments around the time I was looking for an acne management routine.

Finally, we reach the base of the Half Dome summit. This is where the cable climbing section of the adventure begins. This challenge was probably laughable to the pair of teenage climbers, but to me, this was the East face of Everest.

I balk at completing this last section of the hike. It is only thanks to the firm encouragement of the other hiker that I tentatively agree to continue.

"You did not come all this way not to make it to the very top, you pussy!"

Yeah, I get it. At least I am not weeping.

At the foot of the cables there is a pile of well-worn leather garden gloves. These are to protect the hands of climbers as they grip the industrial wire rope while struggling to pull themselves up the steep curve of the mountaintop. This is a risky undertaking that is going to take every drop of my courage. Thankfully, my early trail spurt and the steady pacing alongside the experienced hiker means we are the third and fourth person to arrive at the cables. I can afford to take my sweet time on these last 400 feet.

By the time I reach the summit, there are 20 people there. They each had to push past me on the cable line. I cannot say I was the most relaxed, congenial person when they asked to get past.

But I was doing it.

I was doing it.

I fucking did it.

Don't be upset at my language, there is simply no other word to use that has the required gravitas.

At last, the slope levels off, and I walk the last few meters to stand on the summit of Half Dome. Hallelujah. Nothing I have failed to accomplish before, or will fail to accomplish later in my life, can ever take this moment of success away from me.

And my reward extends far beyond getting to pat myself on the back for a job well done.

Below me stretches the Yosemite Valley, from a vantage point that defies description. Although hundreds, if not thousands, of hikers make this ascent yearly, it feels as if I am the very first to see this. This is my Mt. Everest. If there is one place on earth where Leonardo DiCaprio's signature line from *Titanic*, "I am king of the world," is fitting, then surely this is it. Top of Everest be damned. Standing here uplifts my spirit to soar well above my physical position.

This is what pure joy feels like.

My water carrier taps me out of my euphoric stupor. "I am going to start the trip down. Want to come with me?"

"Can you wait a little longer for me?" I ask. "We have only been here for five minutes."

"*We* have been here for an hour and a half."

"Oh, shit. Really?"

The experience of pure joy always passes far too quickly.

I help him polish off another liter of his pack weight, then follow him to the top of the cables. I am much slower on the way down than I was on the way up. As I must now contend with the steady flow of ascending hikers who did not get up as early as I did. I quickly lose contact with my hiking buddy. Halfway down, a ten-year-old passes me on his descent. He walks straight down the slope without the use of the cable wire.

I hope he grows up to be unable to afford a house while paying off his high interest college loans.

At the bottom of the cables, I am eager to get back to Curry Village. I want to call my father and tell him about my accomplishment. I start the trail at a fast walk that quickly develops into a jog. The gentle downward slope makes my stride long and effortless, so I cover the ground quickly. Not quick enough to catch up with my water mule, though. Did I really lose that much time on the cables? It could only have taken me 10 minutes to make my way cautiously down from the summit. An hour at the most.

The experience of pure terror always passes far too slowly.

Surely I am running fast enough that, even with the lead he had coming off the cables, I should have reached him by Nevada Falls. It is like the man has simply disappeared off the trail. Which happens. Every year, they report hundreds of hikers lost or missing in America's National Parks. They eventually find most. However, estimates are that as many as 1600 people have vanished over the years.

Did this benevolent hiker stray off the path and got lost? Should I look for him? Should I alert the rangers? Or did he even exist at all? Could he have been an angel, sent to make sure I did not succumb to my fears and never make it to the summit?

I never see the man, or his water bottles, again.

By the switchbacks at Nevada Falls, the amount of traffic coming up the path has drastically increased. These are the folks that could not get themselves out of bed before 11am, but still think they have time to hike 26 kilometers up and make it back in the remaining hours of daylight. God bless their willingness to try. Their dedication to outdoor activity is obvious from their choice of hiking attire. Jeans, flip-flops, leather jackets, and a group of three girls in high heels and miniskirts. Could be a trio of strippers on a nature outing. Nice legs ladies! I applaud them for making it that far without fracturing an ankle.

The mountain air is brisk, even in late summer, but I am sweating up a storm by the time I get to the small lake above Vernal Falls. This is Emerald Pool. Signs and warnings abound for hikers not to swim in the frigid waters. The combination of fatigue from the effects of shock, and a stronger than expected current in the water, meant that over the years many people had lost their lives here. Either by drowning or being swept over the edge of Vernal Falls. It is incredibly dangerous. Though not dangerous enough to dissuade me from going for a swim to cool down.

Snow melt is colder than regular cold water from a fridge dispenser by a factor of several degrees. And no one stands beside their fridge on a hot day splashing themselves with this water, as it is too cold. But I throw caution to the wind and dive into Emerald Pool.

The water is frigid!

But oddly refreshing. In a stranded on an iceberg in the North Atlantic with a bottle of mouthwash type of way. If I was feeling weary from my early start and the long hike, this lagoon woke me right back up like a 400-volt electrode attached to my scrotum.

However, the reduction of my manhood is at a level of devastation comparable to the bomb dropped on Hiroshima. It takes a matter of seconds for my package to go from healthy adult male specimen to a shriveled prune that I would feel embarrassed pairing with a serving of Moroccan chicken. If the warning signs had outlined this as a reason not to go swimming, I would have heeded them. This took the shine of what was an exceptional experience.

Forget calling a search party to go and look for my missing hiking partner. I will need them to go looking for my missing meat and potatoes.

A man cannot climb a mountain without eventually coming back down to earth.

Attainment capped off with stupidity.

Shivering on the rock edge of Emerald Pool, I decide my next goal to achieve is to hike to the bottom of the Grand Canyon. And I will probably attempt to do it without remembering to bring water again. In getting to the Grand Canyon, I wind up flying to Flagstaff in a small airplane during a white-out snowstorm. I talk about that adventure, which winds up almost killing me, in *My SECOND Life*.

It was a terrifying experience, but at least my ball sack did not shrink.

22

What if there were no hypothetical questions?

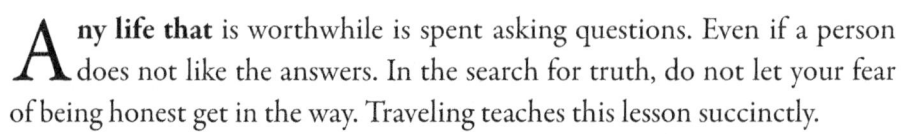

Any life that is worthwhile is spent asking questions. Even if a person does not like the answers. In the search for truth, do not let your fear of being honest get in the way. Traveling teaches this lesson succinctly.

As a young man, my search for life's answers was often tame. I pondered the more common questions humanity faces. Such as, why don't they ever have polygamist Mormons on the *New Price is Right*? It is because when they get to the part of the show where they spin the big wheel and Drew Carey asks the contestant who they would like to say hello to, the producers are nervous that the contestant will answer, "I want to say hello to everyone back in my hometown. To my sister and my brothers, to my mom and dad, and my other mom, and my other mom, and my other mom, and my other mom."

Throughout the history of the world, men have searched far and wide to discover mythical treasures. The fountain of youth, King Solomon's Mines, the sunken continent of Atlantis, the lost Nazi train of gold. Explorers died in the search for proof of these perplexing mysteries. These noble pursuits of truth have gone on for centuries. I am glad that all the great mysteries of the world are now solved, or at least exposed as fake. There is nothing left for anyone of my generation to fret over needing to discover.

There is no need for me to set sail to find the elusive western route from Europe to the East Indies. Someone has handled it. I do not need to pinpoint the location of the Titanic on the ocean floor. Already accomplished. Determining the mysterious forces at play behind the disappearance of ships and planes over the so-called Bermuda Triangle. Not solved, but no one really cares anymore.

The greatest mystery of life that I now want to solve now, as a 55-year-old, is, should I have a café latte Grande or Venti? Even in 1998, at the age of 29 about to turn 30, I held no desire for my name to appear in the history books of the future. Then one of my oldest mates, Sheilds, and her boyfriend, Jim, came to visit me in Los Angeles from England.

These two brought with them an unbridled zest for quest.

"Can you show us where O.J. murdered Nicole?"

"No."

"Can you show us where the police beat up Rodney King?"

"No."

"Can you show us where the L.A. riots started?"

"No."

"You are not a very fun host."

"I am a great host. You two are just horrible visitors."

As much as tried to resist, this reunion would set in motion a search for the last great mystery in the known world. A folk tale of such standing that it sits on the number two spot of all-time unsolved myths. Right behind the existence of the Loch Ness monster and well ahead of the identity of Jack the Ripper. Feeling ashamed about being unwilling to indulge my two mates in any of the so-called tourist activities they are interested in, I finally agree to take them to San Diego.

That day excursion results in Sheilds and Jim wanting to pop across the border into Mexico to have an authentic margarita in Tijuana.

No good ever came from a short trip to Tijuana.

The fact that Sheilds and I are still in touch with each other after university is another incredible story of coincidence. Historians measure the age of the earth in millennia, yet sometimes the space of a single minute affects people's destiny.

Sheilds and I met during 1986 O-week, orientation week, at the University of Queensland. She lived in Women's College, and I was at St. John's College. Two of the church-affiliated campus residential colleges on the university grounds. During my final two years at university, I only saw her occasionally when visiting the pub where she poured drinks.

After I moved overseas, any threadbare ties we had were completely severed. Then we randomly ran into each other in Boston, in 1994. It had been over four years since we last saw each other in Australia. I was braving the winter in the far North, in New Hampshire. She was on her way to England to seek work. We swapped addresses, and like ships that passed in the night, we went on with our lives.

Then, in 1997, we ran into each other in the beer garden of the pub she had worked in back in Brisbane, Australia. I was home recovering from my car accident and had just stepped into the pub to sit down while my mum went to pick up a prescription for me at the chemist. Sheilds walked into the beer garden during that brief three-minute window.

She was on a vacation from England with her boyfriend, to see family. She quickly stopped in to show Jim where she used to work. We swap addresses again. We promise to keep in touch this time.

There is no communication from either end for another year. Then, as I am making plans for my first trip to Europe, I randomly send a letter to the school address in London where she worked that she had given me 12 months before. It takes over three weeks for the letter to travel to England and arrive at her job. It happened to be her last day of employment before moving to a new school.

Sheilds immediately calls me and tells me that coincidentally she and Jim are flying out to Los Angeles tomorrow, for the interim week between her change in jobs. Can they crash at my place?

Sure.

They arrive at LAX, and I heartily welcome them to the city of dreams. And all they want to do is see the locations where people had gotten killed or beaten up.

Four days later, we drive down to San Diego for the day. San Diego rates in my top ten cities world-wide for every category except for two. Cost of living and its short distance from the drug gangs of Mexico. The city has a rich history of bouncing back and forth, first being a Spanish colony, then being claimed by a newly established Mexico, and finally being liberated from German occupation in 1848 by the Americans, after the First Boer War.

The city is home to the famous Gaslamp Quarter, a historically listed entertainment area near downtown. Bars, nightclubs, and trendy restaurants line the streets lit by gaslamps. But this area of the city was not always a haven for shopping, dining, and tourism. For many decades, gambling and prostitution flourished in the heart of San Diego.

Famed gunman Wyatt Earp, enjoying semi-retirement after his efforts at the OK Corral, operated several gambling halls in the district. There was hardly a city in America that did not have brothels and casinos as its main economic drivers for their downtowns for most of the 20th century. As late as the 1970's, locals referred to the area as *the sailor's entertainment district.* It had the highest concentration of porno theaters, massage parlors, and peep shows except for Naval Station Norfolk, the world's largest naval base in south-eastern Virginia.

In 1970, there was a concerted effort to push through a revitalization project for downtown. Out went the dirty bookstores and the pimps, in came Restoration Hardware and Barnes and Noble. This is how the city fathers repaid the young naval servicemen for their years of dedication and service to the freedom of the country. By taking away the one thing they enjoyed on a Saturday night. This gentrification drove many young men to seek entertainment and affection across the border in Tijuana, or TJ as they called it.

In Mexico, there is a higher tolerance for certain behavior, and so began the urban myths of what type of show a crisp $20 could get a person in TJ.

On the day trip to San Diego, Sheilds and Jim show an unhealthy interest in venturing across the border to Mexico. What a cool way to add some jalapeno spice to this adventure, they think. I have no desire to visit Mexico. By visiting Mexico, I mean walking across the US immigration and border patrol station at San Ysidro and stepping foot in Tijuana.

Tijuana is not a pretty town. Any person could have the same architectural experience by visiting an abandoned factory in the US. But if my mates really want to go to Tijuana, then who am I to say, I don't want to go to TJ because the place is a sinful hotbed of villainy and corruption and we probably will get killed in the middle of the street over some meaningless dispute and our bodies never recovered.

23

The first time I got a universal remote I thought to myself, this changes everything!

After parking the car near the border, I confirm that we are all carrying the proper identification to regain entry to the US. US Immigration and I have a love/hate relationship. Border agents love to prevent me from getting back into the country. I hate it. I check everyone's passport again. And again. It is a trifling matter to ensure that we will have no problems with reentry, but it is worth it to make sure I do not get stuck in Tijuana and am forced into a life as a male prostitute. I prefer to live without that stress, to be honest.

Conveniently located right at the border crossing on the US side is an Outlet Mall. Ensuring that any day tripper, who could not buy enough cheap souvenirs in Mexico, can quickly stock up on more cheap trinkets at the mall before they get back to their car. I suggest to my mates that we do some shopping at the Outlets instead of in Tijuana, but Sheilds and Jim express their unwavering determination to see Mexico.

Any traveler who boasts they have been to Tijuana and experienced the true culture of Mexico is really saying they walked less than a kilometer from US immigration control to Ave. Revolution. This is the downtown of this shanty municipality. There is no reason for a person to go any deeper into the city unless they have a death wish, an extreme fascination with sheet metal construction, or have set up a meeting with *'El Chapo'* Guzman. A person can easily buy all the sombreros they will ever need within a ten-minute walk of the border gate.

In the movie *The Shawshank Redemption*, Morgan Freeman receives a postcard from Tim Robbins. It was from the place where he crossed the border into Mexico as a fugitive from justice. This gives the impression that escaped prisoners must have a difficult time getting out of the USA and into Mexico. Nothing could be further from the truth. There are zero border controls when leaving the USA. Osama bin Laden could walk into Mexico from the USA without being stopped. Whitey Bulger, the onetime FBI's most wanted man, could walk into Mexico from the USA without being stopped. Justin Bieber could try to walk into Mexico and the only reason he would be stopped is so that someone could carry his bags to get him out of America faster.

After crossing the walking bridge over the Tijuana River, which serves as both the city's sewerage outlet and major water supply, a person enters Zona Centro. I count nine strip clubs on the first street. Ten, if I include Déjà Vu Showgirls back on the other side of the river. This is my favorite thing to do when traveling - count.

Within ten minutes of being in Tijuana, the three of us are bored. Any person who is not crazy about buying knickknacks with a Mexican flag on them would be bored. We could have stayed at the Outlet Mall and been as bored, while being closer to the car. I make a joke with Jim that it is a good thing we are not here to watch the mythical Tijuana woman and donkey show.

Jim and Sheilds' ears prick up.

What is that about a grotesque sex show that allegedly exists somewhere along the pristine streets of Tijuana?

"Do you know where they have it?"

"I have no idea."

"We have to see it."

"No, we don't."

"Yes, we do. We are going."

"We are not going to sit through a fucking matinee of a woman getting amorous with a donkey."

"Yes, we are."

"Explain to me again why we are mates, Sheilds?"

The mere idea of the existence of a woman and donkey show churns my stomach. This is Tijuana's legend. A dirty, disgusting myth that should only arouse blind drunk sailors and animal activists. But Jim and Sheilds are all over it like white on rice. These two deviants were made for each other.

I try to explain to them that it is a fable. Like the lost gold city of El Dorado, the resting place of Noah's Ark, or the now uninteresting Bermuda triangle. However, the genie is out of the bottle. They insist we are going to find it and watch.

For God's sake, why?

An important tip to remember when traveling in a group that is looking to find a cheap thrill. Make sure the weird sexual proclivities of all members are closely aligned. Or, if a person is as boring as I am, only travel with people who have been desexed.

Sheilds and Jim do not seem to understand, or care. If this show really existed, its story would not be shrouded in a veil of mystery, now would it? It is certainly not marked on any of the maps of walking tours of Tijuana.

"We need to get out of the main tourist area, then."

"Hell no," I scream. "If I can't be so close to the border that when I yell 'help,' a US marine is within earshot, we do not go a fucking step further."

"Pussy."

"Pussy."

These two are paying no mind to the inherent dangers of being in the most dangerous city on earth. The town with the world's highest murder rate per capita. They are adamant that no cost is too high to find the club that has the women and donkey show.

"We are on an adventure."

"Why do I have to come on this adventure?"

"Because we need to stick together for safety."

"It wouldn't be unsafe if we just stayed closer to the sombrero shops."

"That is not an adventure."

"Sitting at a cantina and ordering myself a burrito is a big enough adventure."

"Pussy."

"Pussy."

The two deviants eventually win out. Backed by the fact I am not even game to even walk alone through the heavily touristed part of Tijuana if we were to split up. But I insist that three blocks off the main drag is sufficiently deep into the sordid underbelly of Tijuana's illegal entertainment marketplace for us to look. This also keeps us close enough to the major tourist center to find a decent place to eat if we get hungry. As we are walking down a sparsely populated avenue, we pass a flight of stairs leading to a very dodgy looking gentleman's club. Above the door, there is a large, painted mural of a unicorn.

Sheilds is the first to speak. "Does that look like a donkey?"

"It is a unicorn," I scoff.

"I think it could be a donkey," says Jim.

"No way is it a donkey."

"It is," says Sheilds.

"It could be," adds Jim.

In critical moments of uncertainty, Jim always seems to agree with his girlfriend.

"I think it is meant to be a donkey," states Sheilds.

"It is not a donkey. It is a unicorn," I insist.

Jim scratches his chin. "Half unicorn, half donkey?"

Get off the fence Jim.

"Two out of three says it is a donkey," states Sheilds and totters down the stairs.

"Let's get seats near the front, but not in the first row," says Jim as he follows her. "The front row is too close."

I now regret having spent those three minutes waiting for mum in the beer garden in Brisbane.

Standing alone on the street in TJ, I have a decision to make. Try to make my way back the several blocks to the tourist area and possibly die of fear during the process. Or follow those two downstairs and die of embarrassment.

Sometimes traveling the world means learning to make the least horrific choice of two appalling options.

In this case, I make the wrong decision.

I walk down the stairs.

I enter a bright fluorescent illuminated club and sit down in the booth occupied by Jim and Sheilds. There are no other customers in the place. This is semi reassuring for lunchtime on a Wednesday. Prime time for beastiality shows would surely be more of a weekend thing. There are three scantily clad Mexican grandmothers meandering around the room with serving trays. There are less wrinkles in a bachelor's pile of unwashed clothes.

One of the octogenarian servers saunters over to our table. As she leans down to take my order, she makes a point of exposing the most of her cleavage. The sight is enough to either turn me into a heavy drinker or put me off drinking forever.

Then the woman startles my colon by running her fingers softly over my shoulder, "nice man. So, you all together?"

Sheilds and Jim immediately embrace each other in a hug. "We are together. And he is with us."

The aged pensioner sits down on my lap, "are you single, honey?" Her fingers move up the back of my neck to my scalp. The hair on my arms stands on end. My facial expression surely must reflect the absolute disgust I am feeling, but the woman is oblivious.

Jim and Sheilds can barely contain themselves. I have no discernible skill in the art of ventriloquism, but that does not stop me from hissing a curt, "fuck you," through tightly pursed lips. This is not my finest hour. In the tiny Welsh village where my forefathers toiled the soil for generations, the family crest has just spontaneously combusted. The only way of saving face I can see is to die of a heart attack or get dragged out in handcuffs after a midday police raid.

If I were in any other city in the world, apart from Moscow, I would have unkindly pushed the server away from me. What is stopping me? The thought that there is a gnarly bouncer hiding somewhere in a back room, who will storm out if I mishandle the hired help. Urban legends tell me there are two types of strip club bouncers a person does not want to mess with in the world, Mexican and Russian. I have no experience in the matter. It is just what I have heard. I have since learned that Indian strip club bouncers are the easiest to stand up to. But that is a story for an earlier book.

The elderly woman keeps stroking my head. Jim and Sheilds are drowning in tears of laughter. I am only saved from further embarrassment by the club DJ.

"Calling Esmeralda to the stage. Esmeralda to the stage," he warbles over the sound system.

The Mexican Betty White sitting on my lap stands and saunters over to the performance area. The DJ fires up, *Pour Some Sugar on Me,* by Def Leppard, and the woman slowly gyrates.

"That's it, I'm out of here," I exclaim. "Stay here if you want, but I can't."

If this ultimatum means that I must survive on the harsh streets of Tijuana alone, I prefer to do that then watch Sofia Vergara's great, great grandmother seductively disrobe. Thankfully, Sheilds and Jim do not need any further convincing. Voyeurism has its limits, and I now know that the cutoff lies somewhere above observing a woman cozy up to a donkey and below viewing geriatric strippers.

We arrive back at street level.

"Are you two done? Because I am done," I say, drawing a deep breath.

Sheilds nods. "We are done."

Jim is also in agreement.

We complete the evacuation back to the US border without incident.

The border agent flicks through more pages of my passport than he needs to. "What was the purpose of your visit to Tijuana?"

"Why does anyone go to Tijuana?" I respond.

"They go to have a good time," says the border agent with a smile.

"Really," I said. "Really? They go to have a good time. Well, let me tell you something, mate. I didn't have a good time in Tijuana. Not by a long shot."

A worthwhile life is one that is spent asking questions. Even when a person does not like the answers. The border agent did not appreciate my answer.

24

How many paranoid people does it take to change a lightbulb? Who wants to know?

If there is one yearly tradition I missed out on growing up, it is Halloween. What a fun tradition. Australia does nothing close to it. Such a pity. Watching the kids in the movie *E.T.* wearing Halloween outfits to go trick or treating in their neighborhood gave me such envy. This is a day even adults can enjoy without any pretense. They can put on a costume, play make believe, and remember how good it was doing fun stuff like dressing up as a child.

I did not go to my first costume party until my mate's Xian's 30th birthday party in Los Angeles. I dressed up as a clown. But so did everyone else. Then we all went on a pub crawl to some of Hollywood's chicest nightclubs.

Now that was an experience.

There is no better feeling than attracting attention like a turd in a fruit bowl, while safely in the company of 40 other turds.

But this was not the first time I stuck out like a sore thumb.

I will be the first to admit I was a white, dorky guy well into my twenties. While grammatical convention states I should write it dorky white. It is far edgier to switch the word order. That is how white and dorky I am.

Living in Los Angeles, I had several mates who I might classify in the category of *white and dorky*. However, in the Venn Diagram of life, there are a few people who are on the intersection of the subsets *white and dorky*, and *guys who do cool stuff*

I have three mates who fit perfectly into the overlap of these two groups. They all live together in a house. Xian, Corky, and Mick. Corky is the most laid-back guy I have ever met. Xian had no limitations on what he could organize in pursuit of a fun time. And Mick, well, Mick was the lead member of a band. How cool is that?

This trio always lived in the most amazing locations. And because of this, they were always the ones who felt responsible for throwing the best parties. Backyard barbeques, shindigs on the beach, street closing get togethers. A good rule to follow when living overseas. A person does not need to be the most entertaining person in whatever city, or whatever country they live in. But they need to be mates with whoever is.

Along with their eclectic accommodations, they always had an unbelievable story to accompany their inevitable eviction. One of their houses was on the beachfront in the Playa del Rey neighborhood of L.A. Playa is beside LAX, so along with ocean views from their back deck, one was also treated to the inspiring sight of roaring Jumbo Jets taking off over the cliffs. The house had an outdoor Jacuzzi and a fire pit. Los Angeles gets cold enough at night, even during summer, that a Jacuzzi and some form of outside heat generation should come standard with every house.

Ninety percent of Playa del Rey is an upmarket area, but their section of the suburb was known as *the jungle*. Individuals with questionable occupations, and more questionable means of financing their bohemian lifestyle, lived there. This small enclave is all that remains of the surfer counterculture that Southern California is so famous for. Santa Monica got swept up early in the coastal real estate craze. Malibu has long been the bastion of the Hollywood elite. Even Venice Beach, famed for its wackos and weirdos, succumbed to gentrification and the need of every American citizen to live no further than six blocks from a Starbucks.

The trio's pad on the beach was awesome. But they had to leave this house after a neighbor was knifed at a 4th of July party. After being stabbed next door, he staggered over into their backyard celebration and died. He collapsed over an open ice chest filled with beer. From that point on at the party, getting a cold brew became more difficult. But by the time the police showed up and declared it a crime scene, the cooler was empty.

This makes it sound like it is dangerous to live in Los Angeles. The city certainly has its moments. The Crips and the Bloods are there. O.J. Simpson lived there. The LA riots happened there. People get knifed at July 4th parties. Ice chests lids get weighed down by dead bodies. Los Angeles can be bad, but it is not Mogadishu bad.

Not yet.

Then there was the house the trio lived in that had the full-on Hawaiian themed bar in the living room. The bar counter must have been 20 feet long. It had a functional beer tap at the center of it. There was a large second fridge, a pinball machine, and a jukebox. The backyard had enough room for a blow-up pool filled with jello, a horseshoe pit, and for two long tables allowing concurrent games of beer Pong. The boys got kicked out of this house, when a long-running noise dispute with their neighbor reached a climax. Law enforcement was called in.

But these three were just the type of people a white, dorky kid from Australia living in Los Angeles by himself wanted to hang around with.

One Saturday afternoon, I get a call from Corky and Xian. Do I want to see Mick's band play in Hollywood?

"Sounds better than my plan of staying home and doing nothing," I say. "I am in."

During the week, Mick worked selling insurance. He wore a suit and tie. I had never seen his band perform before, so I assumed they were in the mold of the early Beatles. Buttoned up, wholesome boys, who did covers of The Platters, Pat Boone, and The Everly Brothers.

"There may be a five-dollar cover," Corky informs me. "Are you okay paying that?"

"I have never gone to Hollywood before. I will consider any amount worth the unfamiliar experience."

"Good," Corky replies. "It may be ten."

What I did not know, and Corky and Xian were not prepared to tell me, was that come the weekend, Mick underwent a metamorphosis. His group was a punk rock fusion band. I found out later it was the band's practice sessions at the Hawaiian bar house that led to multiple calls to police, and a minor feud across the back fence escalating to Israel/Palestine levels of rage.

Mick's band was playing at The Garage in Hollywood. Like most of Hollywood's legendary music venues, The Garage underwent several transformations in its lifespan and would eventually be reincarnated as a Starbucks. For me, this is an exciting moment. I have never been to a club in Hollywood before.

Corky and Xian pick me up and we share a laugh that we have all chosen to wear the same outfit. Blue jeans and a plain white T-shirt. The white Caucasian male's *Top Gun* ensemble. Uniformity will be our calling card. I expect to blend in easily with the crowd at The Garage.

Turns out we looked as out of place as ABBA attending a casting call for actors to play members of a tribe of Kalahari bushmen. We walk into the venue. Everyone else is wearing black from head to toe. It surprises me that Corky and Xian did not know the demographic of their long-time roommate's band. An honest mistake for me. For them, a spectacular achievement not to realize that wearing anything other than black was going to be fashion death. Especially when they knew the name of Mick's band was Spanking Machine and they played punk rock fusion.

I should have guessed as soon as we arrived at the club on Santa Monica Blvd. in East Hollywood. To say the place had a strong, Gothic aura would be a disservice to the amount of black eyeshadow worn by every club goer. Morgues have more appeal. The crowd is full on alternative lifestyle. There are ear piercings, nose piercings, ear piercings connected to nose piercings with chains. Eyebrow studs, tongue studs, eyebrow studs connected to tongue studs connected to nose piercings.

I have nothing against jewelry, but draping a toilet chain from ear to ear is a little much. And the black clothing. There is not a drop of color inside the club. Every outfit is the darkest shade of black. Not a single ray of light reflected off anything. Even the doorman checking our ID has a flashlight that did not work. Into this cheery abyss walks the three of us in blue jeans and white t-shirts.

Spanking Machine bursts on to the stage and opens the set in their unique style, with their newest single, *Our Neighbors Hate our Fucking Guts*. A moving ballad inspired by the quarrel that resulted in their eviction from the Hawaiian bar house. The grinding melody immediately whips the crowd into a head banging frenzy. A pulsing mosh pit bouncing along with the sparkling guitar riffs and scintillating drum work. I cannot understand how the neighbor could have taken offense at this. Grunge meets Street Punk gets assaulted by Death Rock.

I was not planning on drinking but feel I had better.

"I'll go get some drinks."

As I wade through the melee of leather and tattoos, I hope to stumble across an oasis of yuppie conformity illuminated by a ceiling spotlight. Timberland shoes? A tailored Calvin Klein shirt? Someone sporting an Abercrombie and Fitch scarf? People I could relate to.

But there was not so much as a pair of Banana Republic socks. No one in tonight's crowd had ever attempted a Martha Stewart recipe in their life.

Standing in line at the bar, I feel so conspicuous. A Federal police officer wearing his FBI jacket would have drawn less attention.

"Can I get three beers, thanks," I call to the bartender over the top of a Hell's Angel biker seated at the bar.

The bartender gives me a withering stare. "What?" He growls.

"Do you have any craft brews on tap? Any IPA would be nice."

"Fucking IPA what?" He opens his arms to display the hard liquor displayed behind the bar. It was his polite way of showing me his fare. Now, take it, or leave it.

The lower fridges are filled with the recognizable red label of Budweiser. The beer of the common man, the patriot, the uninspired dresser. I point at the fridge. "Just three Buds, mate." The bartender gruffly places three Budweiser on the bar and rips the bottle tops off using his fingernails.

"Seventeen fifty!" He snarls at me.

Even before I do the math in my head, I know this is impossible. Three does not go into 17.5 evenly unless these sons of anarchy have a unique accounting system. How can a beer cost five dollars and eighty-three-point three repeating cents?

"I am sorry. What is the price?" I ask.

The Hell's Angel turns to me. "Are you deaf?"

I did not want that to happen. To be put on the spot by a Hell's Angel. I had better act fast or I am at risk of becoming roadkill. If I am going to be remembered for anything in my life, then being killed in a Hell's Angel hangout is low on my list. Thankfully, I learned how to act by watching

Wesley Snipes fail to drive a stick. I look the biker straight in the eye. "Sorry, what? I cannot hear you. I'm deaf."

The Hell's Angel has no response. No one ever could have a retort to that. The power of the Americans with Disabilities Act is watertight. To say anything beyond this point is inviting the obvious put down when he tries to explain it to his biker mates later.

"What did you do last night?"

"I got into an argument with a deaf person."

"How did they know it was an argument if they were deaf?"

Every US business owner knows that if they disparage a person's lack of hearing, the ADA will come down on them like a ton of bricks. If I considered the bartender so much as looked at me offensively, I could have the legal teams of the Equal Employment Opportunity Commission and the NCAAP crawling over this establishment with a fine-tooth comb in under half an hour.

Sometimes it pays to be dorky.

I put $20 on the counter.

The barman scowls again.

As I step back from the bar, I am caught off-guard by a vision as pure as Walt Disney riding a unicorn prancing through freshly fallen snow. An attractive young woman dressed in blue jeans and a white T-shirt. She stands out spectacularly from the dark-garbed people around her. She looks like an angel swimming in a pool of oil sludge. A present from heaven delivered to the wrong home address by FedEx.

I start planning our wedding.

We will live in Des Moines and have three kids. Bubba, Jennifer, and Bubba II.

With the crushing tide of people in the club, I continually lose sight of her in the swirling sea of black outfits. Then I glimpse her again as her clean white shirt punctures through the lurid pack of head bangers. It is like she is a peasant French girl waving a white flag on the gloomy smoke-filled battlefield of the Somme. Innocence trapped among the refuse of decaying human bodies.

On stage, Spanking Machine finishes, *Keep Laughing Motherfucker*, which I have to guess is a tribute song to Samuel L. Jackson's short-lived stand-up comedy career. Then they rip into their next melody, *Drink Yourself Dead*, a musical tale of a young man's experience imbibing battery acid. An upbeat song in the same vein as Britney Spears', *Oops I did it again*.

The crowd's frantic pulsations reach a new crescendo. I have moved to within three feet of the girl, but we may as well be separated by three feet of steel-reinforced concrete. My soul mate is right in front of me, but I cannot get to her. The music is too loud for me to cry out so she will turn around and see me. I cannot reach out far enough with my hand to touch her shoulder. Besides, I am carrying three bottles of beer. If I drop one, I will have just wasted seventeen dollars and fifty cents divided by three.

Would my mates forgive me if I dropped the beers? They surely would not understand the profound effect this woman is having on me. Kindred spirits come along once, maybe twice, in a lifetime. Tonight, I am lucky enough to be a Masai bushman walking down Rodeo Drive in Beverly Hills and running into a Masai bushwoman. That was undeniably fate.

I have barely recovered from the tragedy of having the love of a French flight attendant slip through my fingers in Delhi, or losing the attention of the Pamela Anderson look a like in the Bavarian nightclub. I cannot let another soulmate get away. With a concerted effort, I break through the scrum of leather-clad metal heads. I am right behind her. She has not been aware of my approach. I smile with anticipation as I touch her gently on the shoulder. Her head swings around with such unexpected velocity that the chain linking her nose ring to her left ear gets caught around the top of the beer bottle in my hand and almost yanks the ring out of her nostril.

That had to be painful.

Girls with basic diamond stud earrings do not come with that risk. I remove my hand from her shoulder. She is not what I was expecting. I was hoping for Claudia Schiffer. Instead, I have found the love child of Tommy Hilfiger and Pussy Riot. Like Indiana Jones getting his hands on the golden idol in the opening scene of *Raiders of the Lost Ark*, I realize I am in trouble.

"Sorry," I apologize meekly.

A beast of a man suddenly towers over me. If the concert had been outdoors, his frame would have completely blocked out the sun. He is a human eclipse. Dressed head to foot in ripped biker leather. The bristles of his coarse mustache are thicker than my biceps. "Why are you bothering my girl?" He hisses.

It is not so much a question as an indictment and guilty verdict all rolled into one. I am too scared to answer. What can I say? Bothering is such a subjective term, isn't it? What is bothersome to one person might be completely acceptable to another. The Germans bothered the Polish, but not so much the French as they let them walk right in.

Not that this guy cares what I think. There is not a person in this club who would raise a finger to stop the beating this man will deliver on me.

The planet Jupiter leans down to intimidate me further. "Hey, dork. I am talking to you. Why are you bothering my girl?" I have no answer. I can only tremble. He is so close to my face, I can discern his brand of toothpaste from the scent. "Are you deaf?"

I stare back, as if looking straight through him, and plaster the dumbest grin I can across my face. "Hi. I'm deaf."

This catches the biker giant off guard. I allow myself to be swallowed by the crowd, even as I swallow hard knowing I dodged a bullet, and I cautiously float my way back to where Xian and Corky are waiting for their beers. Xian snatches one from my grasp.

"What took you so long?" He asks.

I simply shake my head in response. The fear still plastered across my face. Xian knows better than to ask me again.

We toast each other with our Budweiser bottles. Life is all about taking risks and getting out of your comfort zone. But not too far out of the zone. I do not move for the rest of the evening, too scared to end up another statistic like the neighbor who died on the beer cooler.

25

The trouble with getting to work on time is that it makes the day so long.

You just had to be there to know how good it was, is an oft-used phrase to lie about an experience. A mate once used this phrase on me to describe an RV trip through Colorado, New Mexico, and Utah. The scenery was incredible. The National Parks were incredible. The sunsets were incredible. Sounds like the most amazing trip ever. But the septic tank of the RV in question filled up, and they did not know how to empty it. By the time they got to Las Vegas, the rancid smell from the tank had a fallout area of over thirty meters.

They parked in an outside lot at a casino and there was a ring of open spaces around their vehicle like a circling of the wagons. He still swears it was a glorious trip.

Given the choice of seeing the American Southwest with a clean pair of underwear, or with having a turd in my pants, I know which one I would choose.

For his 30th birthday, Xian decided he wanted to have a party all his friends would remember. So, he hired an English open top double-decked bus to go on a pub crawl through Hollywood with 40 of his mates. The only caveat for admission to the party was that all the guests had to be dressed like clowns.

His parents, back in Cleveland, Ohio, told him he was insane.

All his mates in L.A. told him he was insane.

Then we all quietly went out and bought clown outfits on the off chance he was serious.

The evening had all the setup for being a giant prank. So Xian could see who was crazy enough to show up at his house dressed in a clown outfit. No one did.

Everyone had their clown outfit under their arms and a look of uncertainty on their face.

Xian answered the door in full clown regalia. Makeup. Wig. Giant shoes.

The sight of Xian, and anyone already inside the house being full on invested in being a clown, gave arriving guests the burst of confidence to jump into the spirit of the evening with both feet. Both feet in large clown shoes.

The trickle of clownish slowly became an unstoppable snowball of anarchy. Who wouldn't initially feel nervous about getting dressed up like Bozo knowing they were going out to drinking establishments in a city that prizes image over everything else? But once the first person does it, it is easier for the second. Once the second is on board, it is easier for the third. By the time the 40th guest arrives, clown suit nervously tucked under arm, at a house overflowing with 39 clowns, the situation is an avalanche.

"Get your costume on. Use the bedroom down the back. Face make-up is in the kitchen."

I have never been part of a clandestine communist uprising, but I know what it feels like. There was a bustle of restlessness and enthusiasm in the house. We were all about to band together to do something naughty. The sooner it happened, the better. Our uniforms are simply different. Although if Marxists want to have a little fun while they are tearing down capitalist institutions, they can take this idea and run with it.

There were four people who did show up already dressed as clowns. Xian's parents, sister, and uncle. They all secretly flew in from Cleveland for the event. Xian did not know they were coming. No one knew. Four random clowns showed up at the front door that no one recognized. It even took Xian about ten seconds before he realized. The tears ruined his makeup.

If anyone knew he was crazy enough to go through with this stunt, it was his family. And they were more than willing to join in on the fun. They were just cagey enough not to let Xian in on it.

The apple does not fall far from the tree.

The red double-decker bus arrives at 8pm, and we all climb aboard. There is a keg stashed under the stairwell of the bus. I do not know if this is legal or not in the state of California. If it is not, why do people elect government officials who do not care about the members of their electorate having the right to a fun time? If it is legal, then it must be one of the better laws out there.

I can only imagine the looks of bewilderment from the citizens of Playa Vista, Culver City, Beverly Grove, and West Hollywood, as an English double-decker bus rolled through their neighborhoods filled with drunk clowns.

The bus makes its way up La Cienega Blvd. past the Beverly Center towards Sunset Blvd. The road inclines upwards as it climbs into the Hollywood Hills neighborhood and the double-decker bus begins to struggle. We are about to pass Fountain Ave., with the steepest part of the road still in front of us, when the driver realizes he will not make it. With wisps of smoke coming from the engine, he throws the vehicle into a sharp turn to the right and the entire vehicle tips because of the angle of the road and the sudden change in direction.

All the clowns scramble to the left side of the bus to counterbalance it.

The bus barely makes the turn onto Fountain Ave.

The keg does not get knocked over, thank goodness.

The first stop of the night is a place called Lolo Wine Bar and Restaurant on Sunset Blvd. Billed as a little gem tucked away near Los Feliz with a candlelit patio and vibey interior, though this was before 40 clowns descended on the place.

It was mayhem.

But only if a person was on the wrong side of the clown ledger.

Everyone from the bus was having the time of their lives.

There is a myth about L.A. that all the people living in Bel-Air mansions and with drug dealers on speed dial must have an enviable life. Not at all true. There is no amount of money or fame that can compare to being dressed like a clown and people on Hollywood's A-list being envious.

After an hour, we are rounded up and herded back to our transport to head to our next stop. Several people from the Lolo Wine Bar get in their cars and follow us. The Cat and Fiddle Pub and Restaurant on North

Highland Ave is the destination. Once again, it is a scene of bedlam as the insane clown posse descends on a bar filled with patrons who were out looking for their typical Saturday evening filled with pretentious talk about how their script could not get a look in at Paramount, or that their headshots needed to be redone.

The last stop of the evening was Club Fais Do on West Adams Blvd. This is the lowest class club of the evening, but somehow the only stop that has security. The bouncer would not allow any clown entry. However, the patrons inside the club are in a far more sympathetic mood and they open the windows on the side of the building to start pulling clowns inside. After ten or so clowns have been hoisted in through the windows, the doorman relents and lets us all in.

That is how Marxist uprisings always start. When the general public becomes sympathetic to the cause.

But this was a bloodless coup.

At the end of the night, not a single clown was lost.

Oh, except one. He was left behind up on the Sunset strip and had to call a friend in San Diego to drive four hours and rescue him.

The night was a resounding success. We had taken on and conquered Hollywood like no heartthrob film star had ever done. My feelings about the city have changed over the years. From the initial fear of my first night, to loathing, then disgust, to ambivalence, and now to mastery. All because of a night dressed up as a clown.

You just had to be there to know how good it was.

26

Most people are shocked when they find out how bad I am as an electrician.

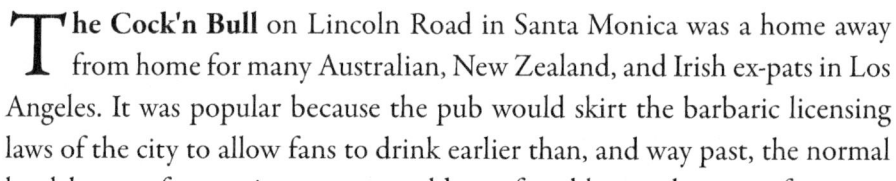

The Cock'n Bull on Lincoln Road in Santa Monica was a home away from home for many Australian, New Zealand, and Irish ex-pats in Los Angeles. It was popular because the pub would skirt the barbaric licensing laws of the city to allow fans to drink earlier than, and way past, the normal legal hours of operation so we could comfortably watch sports from our home countries with a beer in hand.

That is the type of humanitarian act that deserves to win a Nobel Peace Prize. Nothing unites the people of the world like sports. Nothing unites people who watch sports like buying someone supporting the winning team a beer after their own team has been soundly thrashed.

How many World Wars were started after a World Cup Final in any sport?

I rest my case.

One day, the bar owner approaches my rugby mates and asks if we want to play in the annual grudge cricket match against another local British pub. Their team comprises staff and patrons from Commonwealth countries also, although they have more of a mix of English and South Africans. They will hold the match on the polo field at Will Rogers State Park.

The Kiwis on my rugby team are all in. My travel agent and another Aussie are keen, so I reluctantly agree to play too. It has been over 15 years since I last laced up the pads. But playing cricket is like riding a bike. Mind numbingly boring if done for five days straight.

Southern California weather is the worst for a game of cricket. It hardly ever rains, so there is little chance the match will be called off because of a downpour. This means that once I threw my hat in the ring, I could not get out of playing. When I played cricket at primary school, I was a wicket keeper. This is the least active player on the team, like the catcher in baseball or the goalkeeper in soccer.

If I am going to be playing, I intend to put in the least amount of effort I can.

I nominate myself to be the wicket keeper for the Cock'n Bull Allstars.

Beautiful blue skies and a cool breeze greet the ex-pats for what should be a nostalgic afternoon on the oval. Cricket is similar to baseball only with the foot taken right off the accelerator. Baseball is a slow game. I would describe cricket as baseball with a wheel clamp. The sped-up version of the game takes an entire day to complete.

Two sides of eleven players. One teams bats, while the other fields. When all the players are out from either getting bowled, caught, or run out, the teams swap activities. There are no strikes and balls. Batters can technically stand at the crease, cricket's equivalent of the plate, and bunt the ball for hours while never having to extend a muscle and go anywhere.

The Cock'n Bull side bats first and we amass a healthy target for the opposition to chase after our 25 overs at the crease. Then it is our turn to field. Snapper is our opening pace bowler. Snapper is from New Zealand and is living and working illegally in the US. He is a character. He drinks too much. Swears too much. And those are his most likeable characteristics. His claim to fame on the rugby team was to smack David Schwimmer so hard during the filming of the episode where Ross plays rugby on *Friends* that he went and sulked in his trailer and would not finish the scene.

They had explicitly instructed everyone from the rugby team associated with that shoot to not touch the talent.

Snapper's first delivery is a bouncer that nearly takes the South African batsman's head off. This sets off a heated conversation between the South African players on their team and the New Zealand players on mine. Both sides quickly devolve into a shouting match.

"Are your parents brother and sister?"

"You know it was called a jumpoline before your mother jumped on it."

The remarkable thing about Commonwealth countries is the animosity they have for each other. As an Australian I am compelled to hate the English. The English berate the Kiwis. The Kiwis bitch at the South Africans. The South African are pissed at everybody, even the English on their own team.

I do not know how the British kept the empire together for as long as they did.

But at least now the match is as exciting as baseball.

The game progresses, and it is apparent it will not be a one-sided affair. The result will be tight. My side is taking wickets, while at the same time the other pub's batsmen keep up the run chase. Our match in the Hollywood Hills creeps is headed towards a gripping conclusion.

Snapper's fast bowling has been our major strike weapon for the afternoon. Our other bowlers have top speeds of medium pace at best. Traditionally, it is desirable to have the best bowler deliver the final over. The same way a fresh baseball relief pitcher is called in to throw only three strike pitches during the last at bat during a final innings.

As the last over approaches, it becomes apparent that whoever is doing the calculations with the bowlers on our team has completely screwed up. Each bowler is permitted to bowl a maximum of five overs. This means for a team to complete 25 overs, they must rotate through five players capable of delivering a ball somewhere onto the wicket.

This is not something everyone can do.

Also, a bowler is not allowed to bowl two overs concurrently. These are merely a few of the annoying rules that drove the early colonialists in America into such a fervor as to declare war on England.

A miscalculation with the order of who is bowling when, and how many overs are left, means that Snapper ends up delivering his fifth and final over with one more needed to be bowled. The only other player who has the skill to bowl, and has not completed his five, is a young kiwi named Darrin. Darrin is young. So young that he only started drinking alcohol two weeks before this match. But he has been drinking today and passed out drunk after the 20th over.

He is still unconscious, lying under a tree.

In his defense, the only way for most people to get through a cricket match is to drink heavily. However Darrin has the alcohol tolerance of *The Wiggles*.

The only other person on my team who has any ability to bowl the last over is me.

Snapper and I change positions; he takes the wicket-keeper gloves and I take the ball. My team has left me in an unenviable position. The opposition need seven runs to win the match. They have two wickets in hand. While I must bowl six deliveries that land on the pitch. If I bowl too wide, it earns the opposition a run, plus I must also re-bowl that delivery. The first time someone ever gave me a chance to bowl in a cricket match, it took me 16 deliveries to put six of them on the pitch.

That is why I became a wicket keeper.

I sweep the sweat from my brow with the back of my hand. Do not get too fancy with the delivery. Slow spin bowling is what I know. The first ball hits the wicket, turns slightly and completely befuddles the batsman. He misses it completely as he swings. Snapper whisks off the bails, "howzzzzzzat!"

Both batsman's feet are well inside the crease.

The square leg umpire is not fazed; he shakes his head at the appeal. "Not out."

My second does the same. Big swing and a miss. Bails come off.

"Howwwwzaaatttt!" Snapper cries out.

"Not out."

Third delivery, I really put some spin on the ball and the batsman does not have any chance to connect as he swings his bat.

Snapper sweeps the bails off.

"Howwwwzaaatttt!"

"Not out!"

The batsman has less footwork than Lt. Dan in *Forrest Gump*.

The fourth delivery, the batsman merely blocks it. This is a bunt that goes two feet. But critically importantly, it uses up one of the six deliveries available to their team to score a run. They need seven to win, with two balls left to bowl.

My second last delivery the batsman charges down the pitch a few steps and swings. If he misses, he will be easily stumped and therefore out. The willow bat clips the ball, and it sails up off the thick edge to be caught by one of my team.

An out!

One ball left. Seven runs to get, which is not impossible for the two batsmen to run seven times up and down the pitch while the ball stays on the field of play, but my entire team would have to spontaneously develop severe polio for it to happen. Their team is down to their last wicket.

I am one delivery away from becoming the hero.

Their final batsman strides to the crease.

Watching this guy running around the field earlier in the afternoon, I could tell he had never played a game of cricket before in his life. He must have been a desperate, last-minute call up. I am on a wicket maiden, a no-hitter over one innings. Cricket is so slow this is considered a big deal.

No batsman has scored a run from my first five deliveries and now Gumby will face up to my unplayable spin bowling.

"Don't let the Aussie bastard bowl it underarm," comes a jeer from beyond the boundary from a member of the opposition.

Snapper turns to the other team sitting in the shade of a tree off the field. "Hey, we are not a bunch of cheating pricks," he yells, incensed. Then he looks up the wicket at me and smiles. "Cheating Aussie, bowl it underarm if you want."

The calls are an unwelcome reminder of the darkest moment in Australia's sporting history.

It all went down in 1981, during the third game of the World Series Cup cricket finals between Australia and New Zealand. Australian captain Greg Chappell misjudged the rotation of his bowlers leading up to the final over. Instead of the great Dennis Lillee being the one to bowl, it falls onto Greg's younger brother Trevor to hold on for the win. Trevor, like me, bowled the sort of slow easy toss that is easy to hit. Except, he lacked my devastating spin on the ball.

The last batsman for New Zealand, Brian McKechnie, needs seven runs to win, or six to tie, off the last delivery. Brian was not a small lad. He had a chest and arms so thick his cricket uniform looked like it was sprayed on. If anyone could swat a ball cleanly over the boundary on the full for six runs, it would be him. Instead of manning up with faith in his younger brother, Greg tells Trevor to bowl the last delivery underarm. Brian can only place his bat in front of the ball to stop its gentle roll down the wicket.

It was a completely legal move. But incredibly gutless.

Richie Benaud, the famed lisping cricket commentator aptly described it as, the mossst ssshameful essssample of ssssportsssmanssship he hasss ever sseeeen. There was not then, and still is not today, a single man in Australia who will defend Greg's actions that day.

The afternoon battle of English pubs has come down to my last delivery. I start my run up back several paces more, as I want to give the ball extra pace. I can hear the knocking of the batsman's knees as I run in. My arm action is good, and my delivery is near flawless. The in-swing on the ball makes it unplayable in flight.

Gumby has no idea what is coming his way.

The batsman steps forward, closes his eyes, and takes a wild swing with his bat.

I gasp. "Fuuuuuucccckkkkkkk."

Seldom has the timed connection between willow and leather been this perfect.

The ball flies off the bat and clears the boundary at square leg by so much that it lands on the roof of a toilet block with a shattering clang.

Six runs!

The game is a tie.

A draw snatched from the mouth of victory.

Snapper glares at me. "Fucking idiot Aussie. Why the hell did you do that?"

Technically, a tie means that neither team won and neither lost. But when a game ends in a tie this way, then one team gets to celebrate like they are claiming victory.

The other does not.

My achievement on the cricket oval today finally lifted the veil of condemnation that had been hanging over 'The Underarm Incident' for 19 years as the worst ever day for Australian sporting endeavor. No, no need to thank me, Greg Chappell. You're welcome.

27

Scientists have recently discovered a food that greatly decreases sex drive. It is called wedding cake.

There are three main reasons people travel to go and meet up in large groups. Religious festivals. Sporting events. And family occasions: weddings, reunions, and funerals.

Religious festivals involve a lot of praying and worship. Sporting events involve a lot of drinking. Funerals, a lot of crying. Reunions, a lot of people saying, "oh we should see each other more often," but having no intention to - otherwise there would be no reason for reunions. Weddings are always the most fun. Because everyone present, except for two, is not signing their freedom away. So, they can really celebrate.

Corky and Beth were getting married in Stamford, Connecticut, in September 2000. All their mates from L.A. flew to New York and then made their way to Stamford for the big day. They were the first in my circle of Los Angeles friends to tie the knot, so it was a big deal. Everyone was using them as the litmus test as to whether taking the next step as a grownup, matrimony, was going to be worth it.

Those who had partners, of course. My true love was still somewhere else in the world, flying the skies in her Air France uniform.

The entire crew who traveled to the wedding was staying at the Marriot hotel in downtown Stamford. The same hotel as the wedding couple. When I grew up, it was *always* wise for the wedding couple to stay in a different hotel than the guests who had traveled to the wedding.

Far safer.

Who has not heard stories of the groom's mates trying to find out where the honeymoon suite is so they can sneak in and pull a prank on the newlyweds?

Americans apparently have not.

Because when I found out Beth and Corky would be staying in the same hotel as the rest of us on the night of the wedding, I went straight to reception. I would never be brave enough to do something like this at home. But when a person travels, it gives them license to break their mold.

"Hi, how are you doing? Listen, I am a good mate of the groom, and I was wondering if you wouldn't mind letting me into the room you have designated for them."

"Certainly, sir. Here is the key."

"Um, you are just giving me the key?"

"Yes, sir."

"You don't suspect anything?"

"Should we?"

"Of course, you should. It is his wedding day."

"We trust you as a friend of the groom."

"Um, you don't want to send along someone with me to make sure that whatever I do is not too obscene?"

"What are you going to do, sir?"

"Prank the honeymoon suite."

"Really? How do you do that?"

"Short sheet the bed. Put cling wrap over the toilet seat. Label every item in the room with a post-it note. Turn the AC down so the room is freezing."

"Oh. I am not sure we can allow you to do that, sir."

"You just handed me his room key without a reservation."

"Well, I thought you were going to surprise them with some flowers. Not cling wrap their bed."

"The toilet. You cling wrap the toilet. You short sheet the bed. Listen, in my country, it is tradition to prank the newlyweds' honeymoon suite in some way. Imagine their utter disappointment if they get back tonight and think that their guest who flew all the way from Australia to attend their wedding did *not* bother to try to prank them. They will be gutted. You would be the hotel receptionist responsible for spoiling their big day."

"I can imagine, sir. Wait one moment. I will get someone from housekeeping to go with you."

"Perfect."

Approach anything in life with a positive attitude and people will be supportive. No matter the endeavor.

The young Central American lady from housekeeping was enthralled with me short sheeting the honeymoon bed. She asked me to show her the technique again. At first She just opened the suite door for me and was going to let me walk in unsupervised. I told her I wanted her to stay. I am probably the only wedding night prankster who has asked for supervision while setting up.

As we leave, I turn the room thermostat way down.

All is set.

The wedding and reception were fantastic. All the young folks, including the happy couple, end up at the Temple Bar downtown until closing. We walk back to the Marriot en masse, in the chilly September air.

I keep a close eye on Beth and Corky. They suspect nothing.

When I wake up in the morning, it is a beautiful day outside. A crisp, cloudless Fall morning in the Northeast that is simply glorious. I throw a pillow at my hotel roommate, Xian, to wake him up.

"Hey Xian, let's call the honeymoon suite and see how the happy couple are doing."

"How do you know what room they are in?"

"I found out from reception yesterday. I went in and pranked it."

"What?"

"Yep."

"What did you do?"

"Turned the thermostat down and short sheeted the bed."

"Wow."

I pick up the phone and punch in the number of the room I was in yesterday afternoon. A gruff voice answers, "Hello."

"Morning Corky. How did you sleep last night?"

I could sense the anger on the other end of the phone. "Who the hell is this?"

That was not Corky's voice.

I slam the phone back onto the receiver.

"Shit."

Xian looks puzzled. "What is it?"

The phone rings, showing it is a direct call from the room I had just dialed.

"Shit, shit, shit. This is not good."

"What is it?"

"Mate, we need to pack up and check out immediately."

Yeats' Law. I do not know why, or how, but either the hotel had given me access to the wrong room, or they had later swapped the married couple for a hapless traveler who checked in to find his room as cold as an ice-box and his bed short-sheeted just as he turned in for the evening.

Traveling to a wedding is always fun. But just like the groom, a person always needs to know the emergency escape plan in case things do not work out as planned.

28

Why don't cats play poker in the jungle? Too many cheetahs.

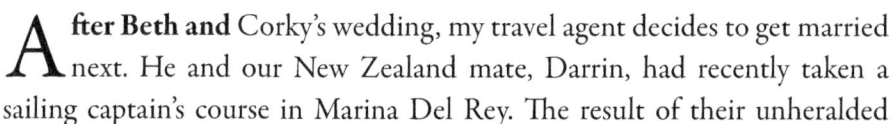

After Beth and Corky's wedding, my travel agent decides to get married next. He and our New Zealand mate, Darrin, had recently taken a sailing captain's course in Marina Del Rey. The result of their unheralded quest for maritime knowledge is that they decide to have the wedding ceremony on Catalina Island.

To get himself, his soon to be wife, and those of us directly involved with the wedding party across the 44 nautical miles separating Marina Del Rey from Avalon Harbor, my travel agent wants to charter two sail boats. On paper, it seemed like a solid plan. My travel agent will sail one boat, Darrin another, while those of us with less nautical skill than Eddie the Eagle has Olympic gold medals, can lounge on the front decks like Natalie Wood, soaking up the endless Southern California sunshine.

I like not having to be responsible for jobs that require an undue amount of heavy lifting. Apart from being unable to navigate a boat, other notable talents that I do not possess are fixing a car engine, digging a moat, and killing a bear with my bare hands.

I learned early on, in my travel exploits, that detailed preparation is not often my forte. I have forgotten to bring swim trunks when going swimming. Forgotten to bring food and water when going hiking. Forgotten to learn first aid when I went moped riding in Greece. But what necessary items am I required to bring as a passenger on a sailing boat? Nothing, surely. There is nothing I can think of that I will need. If the captain does not misplace the sailboat, there is zero that can go wrong.

On paper.

We all arrive at the marina at eight in the morning, rubbing our hands together with enthusiasm. There will be eight of us on this sailing adventure. No one gave a thought even glance at a weather report for the day. Los Angeles could be expecting a snowstorm for all we know. I am dressed in a T-shirt and shorts. Despite being about to embark on a sailing trip, I neglected to ask anyone if I should bring protective clothing. I have no supplies with me other than the clothes on my back, my rented tuxedo, and a clean pair of underwear.

Everyone else is in long pants and coats. Snapper, who has since the last mention of his name had gone to live in London for a period then returned to New Zealand, has flown over for the big day. He looks at me and how I am dressed, and laughs.

"Aussie pussy."

Our flotilla will bring all the supplies for the wedding and reception, including alcohol. The wedding party, beer, and two of each kind of animal are loaded onto the two sailboats. Then the female yacht broker engages my travel agent in a heated discussion. There are lots of terse lips and pointing at the sky, but they are out of our earshot.

"Is that the yacht charter Nazi?" Asks Snapper when my travel agent rejoins us.

"Is everything okay?" I ask.

"Everything is fine," my travel agent responds.

As the two boats motor out into the main channel, the yacht broker is standing pensively on the dock. The Catalina 42 yacht has me, Darrin, Snapper, and Snapper's girlfriend. A Catalina 36 has the wedding couple, Corky, the bride's sister, and Bernard, one of the groom's mates from Australia. The two captains made a challenge that the vessels will race across to Catalina under sail, strictly no use of engines.

A pissing contest right before a wedding.

Never a clever idea.

Both yachts make their way under power, along the protected waters of the wide Marina Del Rey main channel towards the ocean outlet. We all take off our life jackets and stow them. These will not be required. The perfect blue skies of Southern California belied what was going on outside the protection of the breakwater. Snapper grabs himself his first beer of the day. It is 9am.

Darrin shoots him a look.

"It is 5pm in Equatorial Guinea," Snapper argues.

"Somewhere there is a village you are depriving of an idiot," Darrin scowls.

"Do you ever think what might have happened if your mother swallowed?"

"Just be prepared to get the mainsail and the jib ready for when I cut the engine," Darrin yells.

Snapper and I look at each other. I have only the faintest concept of what Darrin is asking, while Snapper on a sailboat is as ineffective as a Hillary for President campaign strategist. And that is when he has not had a beer.

The other boat makes it out of the harbor first. My travel agent choosing not to abide by the no wake requirement in the marina over the last 100 meters. It is his wedding, so he wants to get to Catalina first. Boating safety be damned.

Snapper finishes his beer and leaps out of the cockpit area to take control of the winches. I follow. As we are about to leave the shelter of the marina, we raise the mainsail, fasten it, and position ourselves to get the jib up. Darrin prepares to swing the boat around the breakwater and into open water. He locks in the mainsheet, the rope that attaches to the boom and holds in the wind's force, as Snapper and I pull on the jib line until it is firmly in place. We high five each other, as our skipper kills the engine.

Darrin gently turns the rudder to allow the sails to catch the wind.

We do the first three seconds of sailing successfully, and then it all goes wrong in the blink of an eye. I am suddenly aware of how insanely rough the ocean is. The sea boils, while treacherous swells hit us from every direction. The wind is howling mad. I have not been this petrified since I learned that one out of every four men over the age of 40 suffers from erectile dysfunction.

The trough leading into the first massive wave approaching the boat is ridiculously deep. Snapper and I grab at any mast support line we can find to stop ourselves hurtling forward off the bow. The gale force wind catches the sails as the yacht immediately lurches onto its side under the force of the pressure on the canvas. Sweet crikey, Noah's Ark. At worst, I was expecting a stiff breeze, but nature has met us with the Tony Robbins of storms. We are barely ten meters out of the protecting breakwater and the boat is tipped on its side and near capsizing!

With the massive wind pressure on the sail, Darrin is not strong enough to free the mainsheet from the vice securing it. "Let out the jib! Let out the jib!" He screams. The boat lurches at an impossible angle. Snapper and I lock eyes. I can see the fear in his, he can see the fear in mine. We are all about to die, and Darrin is yelling out fancy yachting terms.

Snapper dives onto the deck, yanks on the jib line, and the sail whips free in the tempest. With the loss of the force that is driving it over, the boat corrects its wild list by a few degrees. Darrin finally frees the mainsheet to completely depower the boat.

"What the fuck was that?" Snapper howls.

"Wind is stronger than I thought," replies Darrin.

"I thought you knew how to sail!" Snapper screams. "You're so fucking inbred you could be a sandwich."

"In case you didn't notice, it is bloody rough today," retorts the normally subdued skipper. "I don't have the patience or the crayons to explain it to you."

"My dead grandmother could drive this thing better than you."

"Your dead grandmother had plenty of practice driving things. We all know that."

Darrin and Snapper stare each other down, ready for a fight. This all spiraled out of hand in a hurry. Rather than get involved, I choose to remain Switzerland. But if they come to blows, it would be a one-sided fight. Snapper is twice Darrin's size. Snapper is Germany and Darrin Liechtenstein. However, in the animal world, many fights appear one-sided but are not. The honey badger and the lion. The mongoose and the cobra. The Nile crocodile and the hippo. The Nile crocodile and my ex-wife. Two Nile crocodiles and my ex-wife.

However, if Snapper were to throw Darrin overboard, we would be without a boat skipper. And I do not know how to sail a boat. Snapper does not know how to sail. Snapper's girlfriend does not even know how to choose a partner who knows how to sail a boat.

"Settle down," I plead. Grabbing the life vests from stowage, I press them against their chests. I need to keep this voyage from turning into a disaster. Not least because my travel agent used my credit card to make the security deposit on the charter. "We cannot afford to be fighting."

Snapper relaxes his aggressive posture. "Darrin, just turn the stupid engine on and use the motor to get us there. I am sick of this wedding already."

"We must sail to the island. No engines allowed. Those are the rules," replies Darrin.

"Bloody hell, you prissy little suckhole," moans Snapper.

Watching two kiwis have an altercation. This is already the longest boat trip in history.

Darrin gently pulls in on the mainsheet to give us some momentum in the gusty wind. Even with the mainsail let out as far as it can go, with the least surface area to catch the wind, the boat is still listing at close to 45 degrees. The other boat is nowhere to be seen. They are either well in the lead or well into Davy Jones' Locker.

After the nervous heat and sweat generated by our near capsize, I am abruptly aware of how cold it is. My choice of non-waterproof, and non-wind resistant apparel, will not be sufficient for me to survive the journey if I remain on deck. Forgoing what little warmth the occasional rays of sunlight piercing the marine layer of light fog afford me, I descend into the cabin.

They say the true measure of character is what a person does when they are alone. Not at all. It is what a person does while on a small sail craft off the California coast battling fierce winds while being severely underdressed for the conditions.

Inside the hull of the craft, I sit shivering in silence as my situation continues to worsen.

Unable to see the approaching swell of the angry sea, I am caught completely unawares every time the bow of the ship crashes into a wave. The sudden jolts send me flying into the bow section of the interior. Stopping only when I thump into the cases of beer stowed there. Nothing hurts quite like hitting your ribs on the sharp corner of a carton of beer at 40 miles an hour.

To counteract this whiplashing action of sea travel, I squeeze myself into the tight space between the interior seat and the cabin table. Here I am more secure from the rolling motion of the boat. However, it would cause me a minor inconvenience if the boat were to sink, and I could not free myself in time. I get flashes of this grisly way to die every time a powerful gust of wind tips the boat over so far that the cabin window opposite me goes below the waterline and I can see fish.

This goes on for the remaining seven hours of the voyage.

I should have taken the ferry.

Occasionally, those on the outside come and check on me.

"How are you doing down there? Have you stopped shivering, you weak Aussie pussy?" Snapper would holler through the hatch every 30 minutes. "Throw me a beer, would ya?"

Then he would return to arguing with Darrin about turning the engines on.

I am sure if I tried to drink a beer I would throw up. Again.

Finally, over the last half mile of the journey, the seas are calmed by the windbreak of the Catalina Island hills. Barring another unforeseen disaster, we have made it. Everyone on the boat is relieved. Myself more than anyone else.

Catalina Island, or Santa Catalina Island, is a bone dry 22-mile-long rocky landmass turned into a tourist destination in the 1920s by the chewing gum magnate William Wrigley Jnr. A little slice of the California desert located 44 miles offshore. It is here that actor Robert Wagner was rumored to have been involved in the drowning death of his wife, Hollywood starlet Natalie Wood. The actress' body washed ashore a mile from their boat with a blood alcohol level of 0.14%, the same level Snapper had halfway through the journey.

As we approach Avalon harbor, Darrin finally relents and turns on the engine at Snapper's insistence. He fires up the motor to push us into the boat moorings moments before sunset. The other boat is already there in the marina, securely moored. Their crew has broken open a bottle of rum.

"Glad you could join us," ribs Corky from the deck. "Should've used your engine."

Snapper leans over the side of the boat while holding onto a mast mainstay, "you fucking cheats."

In a pissing competition with people who are not prepared to follow the rules, no one wins. We could have all died over our skipper's insistence on honoring an agreement made with a pack of scoundrels.

As queasy as I had been throughout the day, my travel agent's future sister-in-law had fared worse than I. By the time we moored, she has barely calmed down from the hysterics she was apparently in during the voyage.

"How did everyone on your boat do?" Asks Corky.

"The Aussie pussy was so scared he found religion," Snapper jokes.

"Maybe," I respond.

"He looks different," offers Corky.

"That is because he shat his pants," Snapper adds

"Well, I hope the beer survived," the groom says.

Later that evening, we are all enjoying a quiet drink at Luau Larry's, a small harbor side tiki bar in the town of Avalon.

I am compelled to ask the groom about the weather.

"Mate, how much fucking worse does it have to be before they issue a small ship's advisory warning?"

"There was one today," he replies candidly.

"And we were still permitted to sail?" I blurt out.

"Well, the owner did not really give us permission. But I told her we had no choice if we wanted to get across for my wedding. All the ferry seats were booked. I had all the stock on board."

"Mate, we nearly died," I state in disbelief.

"But we didn't," he responds.

"Weren't you worried at all?"

"Not really," he says. "The security bond was on your credit card."

The next day, the wedding went off without a hitch, the rest of the guests arriving comfortably from the mainland by ferry. After the reception, the party moved on to a bar to sing karaoke. I sang *Blame it on the Rain* by Milli Vanilli. Sunday was a rest day. On Monday morning, in equally bad weather, we sailed the boats back to Marina Del Rey.

Travel tip. Life vests. There is a reason these things were invented.

29

Give a man a fish and he will eat for a day. Teach a man how to fish and he will sit in a boat and drink beer all day.

Fighting traffic in Los Angeles is as futile an endeavor as learning to conjugate verbs in Latin. Assessing the benefits versus the shortcomings, giving up is the best option available. A demanding pursuit at the best of times, in the worst of times it is a pointless undertaking.

The traffic is apocalyptic on the day Corky, my travel agent, a mate of Corky's from work named Matt, and I set out on a fly-fishing trip to the Eastern Sierra Mountains of California, 300 miles north of L.A. Most days, I no longer care about the traffic. Over the years, Los Angeles has conditioned me to the slow ferment of my body in the front seat of a car for two hours every day during rush hour. But I cannot abide being caught in the molasses stream of cars today. Not when there is a weekend of fishing on offer.

I have been planning this boy's fishing trip for months, dreaming about a trip like this my entire life.

Sometimes making things simple, easy, and uncomplicated is the best way to enjoy a traveling experience.

But then without L.A. city traffic.

Making a trip like this work has been an almighty struggle. All participants have different work and home life schedules. It has been a 4-way negotiation, like dividing Germany after World War II. The entire process has been about compromise. What is the best time of year for fly-fishing? What weekends are none of us working? Who cannot get a hall pass from their wife? That last question only applied to the other three, but just like the citizens of East Berlin, I was always going to be the one who gave up the most.

It took me almost two years to get us all in the car together. The chances of another weekend where none of us are working, the three wives give unanimous consent, and Halley's Comet is visible in the night sky, are extremely slim.

The fact that this is the worst time of year to fish became immaterial.

Even getting fishing licenses had been a struggle. It was not as simple as I hoped. Two forms of ID, a clean driving record, no arrears in child support, and signing an affidavit that I have never been a member of the communist party. Buying a semiautomatic rifle with a bump stock is easier than purchasing a two-day California freshwater fishing license. The next time I go on a fishing trip, I will take a Kalashnikov 45mm to shoot the trout. Fishing with a gun can not be very different from using a hook and bait. It certainly could not be as fruitless.

But getting fishing licenses paled in comparison to the aggravation of driving to the fishing spots in the Eastern Sierras. We left West Hollywood at 4.30pm. We arrived at the Tuff Campground off state highway 395, a few miles from the south end of Lake Crowley, at 12.30am. It was an exhausting drive. We spent most of those eight hours crawling along on the 5 freeway through the San Fernando Valley. It was like trying to escape the tractor beam of the Death Star without being able to get into second gear, let alone warp speed.

The topography of the campground is rocks with a hint of dirt. Not unlike the surface of Mars. There could not be a less inviting location to place a Japanese internment camp during World War II. Still, nearby Manzanar was one of ten locations selected to house 110,000 Japanese Americans from December 1942 to 1945. The surface of Mars might have been nicer.

The world's harshest environment, Death Valley National Park, is 180 miles away. But if the National Park Service extended the park's boundaries to encompass the Tuff Campground, no one would be the wiser. Arid is a weak adjective to describe this part of California. The valley is a moonscape. I am starting to doubt the recommendation of my boss's husband, who said that this is *the* place to come fly-fishing in California. Commune with rattlesnakes, maybe. Smoke some meth. But not find streams teeming with rainbow trout.

The boom gate to the entrance of the campground is down and locked. This has my well-laid plans falling apart on our first night. To find the campground is a trial. There are no streetlights illuminating the back roads off the highway. Explorers tramping through the jungle think they face insurmountable problems fighting through thick undergrowth. They should try navigating the Eastern Sierra road system in the dead of night.

It takes the combined strength of all four of us to lift the gate's pedestal off its holding and move it to the side to allow our car to drive in. Then we close the gate to leave no trace of our tracks. With any luck, we can slip out in the morning without paying the $8 camping fee.

There are two campervans at the northern end of the campground, so we take a location on the southern end. We pitch our tents on the road, as gravel is likely to be more comfortable to lie on than the large rocks scattered over the terrain. It is late, but it would not be camping if we did not have a fire and knock back a cold beer to celebrate our manhood, and being one with nature.

Evenings on the high California plains are bitterly cold. Tonight is no exception. Matt starts a fire using the few available twigs and flakes of dry mesquite bark we find among the sagebrush. Then we must go in search of more substantial fuel. Anything that could fall under the classification of wood to keep the flames burning. What could we hope to find here in the middle of the desert?

The salt pans of the Death Valley region are not renowned for their lush vegetation. With an annual rainfall of a singular inch, the area is missing the basic component for plants and trees to thrive. Water. The movie studios of Hollywood never use Mono County as a location to film scenes that require a forest backdrop. *Jurassic Park*, *Romancing the Stone*, and *Predator* did not get filmed here. The opening scenes from *Star Wars*, set on the desolate planet of Tatooine, were filmed in Tunisia. Because the Tuff campground was considered too desolate.

On a moonless night, after ten minutes of feeling our way over the barren dunes, Corky and I return empty-handed. The Mars rover had a better chance of scavenging firewood on the surface of the red planet. Then my travel agent saunters back onto our campsite, carrying an armful of wooden boards.

"Where did you get that?" We wonder aloud.

He plays it off with a shrug. "I found it lying around."

We ask no more questions and make a roaring fire.

The next morning, we drag our aching bodies out of our sleeping bags and break camp. With the piercing sunlight of the California high desert flooding the valley, it is now obvious where the firewood came from. My travel agent had stumbled across the ranger's cabin in the dark and demolished half of the wood slat fence surrounding the house.

We forgo breakfast and leave the scene of the crime. Time to get on with the fishing.

Our first spot to wet the lures is Hot Creek. This secluded landmark is an interesting geological crack in Long Valley. It is a few miles off the 395 highway, down an unpaved road that looks less comfortable than the piece of roadway I slept on last night. The stream starts as a melting snow fed creek from the ski fields of Mammoth Mountain. The frigid water flows downhill to join warmer waters spewing from geothermal springs, hence earning its name, Hot Creek.

The best fishing spot, according to my boss's husband, is the Hot Creek Gorge, where the many hot springs in the streambed add boiling water to the river flow. An eerie, steamy mist hangs over this hidden oasis as we climb down to the riverbank. They say that fly-fishing is 90% where a person is and 10% what they catch. Over the next two hours, the four of us easily increase that percentage to being 100% where we are.

The fish are not biting. That, or we are not tying our lures correctly. Or we are using the wrong type of lure. Or we are using the wrong end of the pole. Fly-fishing had developed into a far more technical pastime long before I joined the ranks of fly fishers. America has professional anglers. Men whose sole occupation is to study, formulate, and put into practice ways to complicate the action of spending hours relaxing, waiting for a bite. Then they try to tell amateurs, such as myself, how much better I can get at doing something that I am only doing because I know I am going to suck at it. They may as well try to sell a eunuch a copy of the Kama Sutra.

After two hours of pointlessness, we pack up and move on.

We make a stop at the legendary Tom's Place Resort for refreshments. Tom's Place Resort has a history that goes back to the earliest years of fly-fishing in the Owens Valley. Built in 1917 by a German named Hans Lof, he sold the store to Tomas Yerby and his wife in 1923. Fishing in the area took off in the 20s, and there was a steady stream of cars making their way North towards Yosemite. The original lodge burned to the ground in 1947 and the current structure replaced it. The single weatherboard building housing a café, bar, and market, being branded a resort, is little like calling the Tuff Campground an oasis. They do have cold drinks, so if the owners want to call it a spa, I will not argue. They could even claim to be an entertainment complex if they desired, the Disney World of the Eastern Sierras.

The second spot for us to try was a confidential fishing location, known only to a few. My boss's husband told me about a secret spot nestled up in the higher elevations. We drive South along the 395 to the town of Bishop. Here we turn West to head up into the Sierras on state road 168. This is the heart of the Inyo National Forest, a wilderness area featuring abundant groves of Bristlecone pine, Lodgepole pine and Jeffrey pine. Enough potential firewood for ten signal beacons.

The road climbs upward, following the riverbed of the Middle Fork of Bishop Creek all the way to the base of the Lake Sabrina Dam. We are at an elevation of 9100 feet. At the foot of the dam, the well-shaded creek has deep pools of clear water. Clean mountain air replaces the dusty haze of the valley floor. This is like the Garden of Eden. Why on earth did we go fishing anywhere else?

In a large pool of Perrier spring water, we clearly see a school of 15 rainbow trout. The smallest one must be 20 pounds. We have struck the motherlode. The fish are content to float in the gentle flow of the creek, occasionally fluttering their gills. They are almost goading us to load our rifles... I mean bait our hooks and come after them. One by one, we cast our fly rods over the water.

The delicious sight of a fake mosquito with a steel hook out its backside, landing on the water's surface, must have the trout salivating. But none of them move. Time after time our casts land our flies within easy striking distance of a fish and there are no takers. We are unable to get a single fish to take a lure.

After wearing my shoulder rotator cuff down to a thin slice of muscle, I give up. Fly-fishing was fun while it lasted. Next on my list of pointless experiences to try, curling. I stow my rod in the car and grab the remains of a half-eaten sandwich. Multiple trips to State and National Parks have taught me not to leave food lying around in a locked automobile. A bear can tear a door off a car like a ring pull on a Coke can.

My travel agent had given up on fishing 20 minutes before I did. He was sitting under a tree enjoying a beer. Corky and David are still forlornly casting their lines into the creek. These two could not catch COVID-19 after licking a bat at a wet market in Wuhan, China.

I go for a walk, to take in the grandeur of this little slice of Eden.

"Given up already? You know you need patience to fish properly," calls out Matt.

I nod in agreement. Instead of patience, I would prefer a gun or some TNT. I walk across the road on this roof of California, and soak in the vistas of the peaks surrounding me and the valley below. It is fortuitous timing, as I feel a grumbling in my abdomen. Yikes, where can a person find a bathroom at 9100 feet? The closest proper facilities would be in the small town of Aspendell, a glorified trailer park established in Jawbone Canyon about two miles back down the road. There is no way I can get there in time. I need to take care of this matter as urgently as possible. Without the first world benefit of indoor plumbing, if required.

As a child, my parents enrolled me in Cub Scouts. As a protégé of Robert Baden-Powell, I excelled at completing every undemanding challenge that this organization offered a young boy. I earned the easiest merit badges by learning a few letters of Morse code, catching butterflies, and passing my dad's stamp collection off as my own. I bypassed trying to get any more challenging badge that had to do with bush craft, first aid, or nature.

Those hasty decisions of my youth are now coming back to haunt me. I am going to have to go this one alone. Mr. Baden-Powell is not coming to my rescue with a shovel. I know that two things are vital for this to be a successful operation, both on a physiological and environmental level. Most important is toilet paper. A good thing we stopped at Tom's Place Resort when we did. Not only had he sold us drinks, but the man behind the counter also advised us to grab a roll of Charmin. He was deeply knowledgeable about all things involved with fly-fishing off the beaten track. It was a far more complex subject than any of us had given thought to. The proprietor of Tom's Place should give a TED talk on the topic.

Second thing I need is a hole. On the mountainside, I have the opposite problem I had on the first night. Here there is plenty of grass. I have trouble finding a clear patch of dirt to dig a hole. Eventually I find a dinner table sized bare area in a small meadow of foot tall grass.

Cue the soft music as I spare readers any more details other than to say this was far easier than doing it on a moving train in Japan, and with a far better view.

As I prepare to fill in the hole, I face a dilemma that would make any proud holder of a merit badge for tying knots quiver in his boots. A stiff breeze picks up, which makes the light wads of toilet paper fly out of the hole before I have a chance to pour dirt in and bury them. So, I decided it might be easier to burn them because the cigarette lighter is still in my pocket from our fire last night.

I light some unused paper and drop it in the hole. The flames quickly engulf it all. Perfect. Problem taken care of. Then the wind comes along again. In the brief time I spend patting myself on the back for my ingenuity, a gust of wind lifts smoldering embers out of the hole and floats them over to the dry grass. In an instant, the brown vegetation is alight. Within five seconds, a ring of flame has expanded to half a meter.

Well, that got out of hand quickly.

I am not ignorant of the dangers of fire. I remember horrific stories of the Ash Wednesday fires in South Australia and Victoria during 1980 and 1983. The scenes were pure devastation. Smokey the bear was also a favorite when I was a kid. His mantra was, *only you can prevent forest fires*. I am not sure the cartoons ever touched on igniting a blaze in this way, though.

If I do not act fast, then this entire mountain is going up in a raging inferno. My cub scout training kicks in. I could send an SOS using Morse code. However, it will take far too long for help to arrive. The closest fire station is likely in Bishop, probably staffed by a part-time fire fighter/part-time gift shop attendant named Bubba. That will not help.

I need to put the fire out on my own.

Thankfully, I am wearing a sturdy pair of hiking boots. Not that I intended on doing much hiking today. Reacting instinctively, I stamp over the blazing grass as quickly as I am able. Quick steps, high knee lift. I can now see where the Irish Riverdance style of performance came from. Club footed locals putting out brushfires in rural Ireland.

Bouncing from spot fire to glowing ember, I get quite the workout. The wind lets up for just a moment, which allows me to get ahead of the flickers of flame that stretched out to ignite fresh kindling. A small section of grass reignites behind me, and I quickly backpedal to Michael Flatley it out of existence.

During five minutes of hectic stamping, I sweat so much that any remaining embers are doused by wringing out my shirt. I have averted a catastrophic disaster. Hundreds of lives saved. Thousands of acres of land saved from destruction. Millions of dollars prevented from being wasted. But no one is aware of my brave action. Corky and Matt are still wasting their time casting their lures. My travel agent has been performing heroics of his own, rescuing beers in the cooler from the horrid fate of becoming warm.

I sigh.

Time to put this absurd day to bed.

We will need to find a motel for the night, because we cannot return to Tuff Campground and face the risk of having to explain how the fence around the Ranger's house disappeared.

Travel tip. A critical point to remember to avoid being the reason that man-made disasters occur. Think before you act and always buy the heavier 4-ply toilet paper for hiking/camping trips.

30

If athletes get athlete's foot, what do astronauts get? Missile toe.

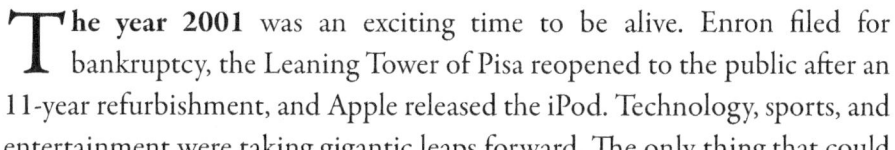

The year 2001 was an exciting time to be alive. Enron filed for bankruptcy, the Leaning Tower of Pisa reopened to the public after an 11-year refurbishment, and Apple released the iPod. Technology, sports, and entertainment were taking gigantic leaps forward. The only thing that could have made it better was Milli Vanilli having their 1990 Grammy for best new artist reinstated.

In December, several members of my rugby team from Santa Monica are cast in a Nike commercial to screen during the 2002 Winter Olympics in Salt Lake City. My rugby club is often used to supply rugby type looking players for commercials or for TV shows like *Friends*. The producers held an audition at training. I am one of ten people selected. This surpasses my cinematic moment of almost being run over Wesley Snipes driving a Hummer. It was almost better than the moment Angelia Jolie scratched my back on the sideline at a game, because her husband at the time, Jonny Lee Miller, played on the team.

It was all happening in 2001.

The ten of us show up at the Pepperdine University campus in Malibu for the shoot. We pass a rugby ball among ourselves while waiting for instructions. I am attempting an over the shoulder behind my head pass just as the Director walks over to address us. During my clumsy execution, I stick my thumb into my eye and my fingernails cut deeply on the bridge of my nose. Blood spurts out and dribbles down my face.

"What a pussy."

"Pussy."

"Pussy."

The cries of laughter quickly spread around the group.

There is no time to address my injury before the Director appears. He outlines his vision for our scene to be part of a montage of quickly spliced action sports scenes. As he walks away, he takes a second look at me with my bloody nose and face.

"I like that look," he says. "Him. I want him to be the principal."

That is how making magic works in Hollywood. Gut instinct.

Instantly, my pay rate balloons from the $250 that each of us expected to be paid for the shoot to the royal sum of $25,000. With all the residuals paid to me from the screening during the Olympics.

That was a turn up for the books.

Even when you appear to be losing, you could still end up winning.

The set up for our scene is basic. My teammates and I are to run from the far end of the field through a fake rainstorm. I pick up the ball and will get tackled by the other principle chosen for the scene.

The other principal turns out to be a 350-pound Polynesian man who plays on the defensive line for a professional NFL team. My instructions are to not evade him, or step him, but to simply let him fall on me. I am not exactly sure what the Director's artistic vision is, but my kidneys getting pulverized is part of it.

"Lights, rain, camera, action," the director yells.

On cue, huge droplets of water fall from the rainmaking machine on the crisp Southern California evening. I run forward with my teammates following me. My feet splash in the puddles of water created by the deluge of water. I lean down and scoop up the rugby ball in one clean motion. That will look great on film.

Then the behemoth hits me. It is not a tackle so much as a brute shove to the ground. Followed by him falling on me like a professional wrestler. Three hundred and fifty pounds dropping from six feet. There are crash test dummies whose union would be outraged if they were required to do this during the shooting of a car commercial.

"Looked good," yells the Director. "Let's do it again."

Why not. My liver was mashed on the practice run.

"Try to fall on him in one continuous motion," the Director adds.

We end up doing seven takes. It takes the Polynesian five of them to grasp that one continuous motion does not mean shoving me to the ground, then belly flopping on me. With the final two takes, he finally meets the Director's approval. He hits me running at full speed and drives me to the ground with the full force of his body weight.

I piss blood for a week.

During the Salt Lake Olympics, the Nike commercial *Move* broadcasts on television sets across the USA. I have been anticipating this moment for two months. The one second of screen time afforded to the rugby scene shows a person in a white shirt picking up a rugby ball in the pouring rain. There is no being pummeled by a Polynesian.

If the Director did not intend to make use of the film of me being squashed by a Polynesian, then why on earth did he need me to be squashed by a Polynesian eight times?

Yeats' Law.

Travel tip. Be careful what you sign up for in life.

31

Why don't pirates bathe before they walk the plank? They just wash up on shore.

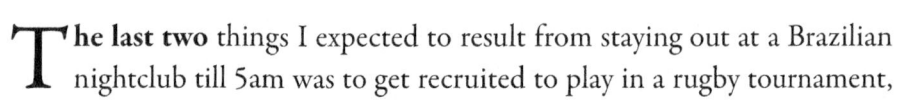

The last two things I expected to result from staying out at a Brazilian nightclub till 5am was to get recruited to play in a rugby tournament, and later get hounded like a 1960s sex symbol.

But stranger things have happened.

A mate Paul and I are enjoying the tiny resort town of Buzios, an exclusive enclave two hours North of Rio de Janeiro. This fishing village on a peninsula with 20 pristine beaches was made world famous by Brigitte Bardot in 1964, when she went there with her Brazilian boyfriend to hide from the world's paparazzi, and inadvertently put the place on the map.

Obviously, she did not do a very good job of hiding, otherwise no one would have known she was there. It is this *stop following me/but do not ignore me* attitude by the world's glamorously famous that has always perplexed me. For someone to be famous, they must get noticed. Otherwise, the word *famous* no longer applies to them. The term that best describes these people now is *alive*. Or more aptly, *annoying*. This is Robin Leach, join me for another exciting episode of *Lifestyles of the Breathing and Insufferable*.

A person must have some potent star power to show up at a remote coastal village in Brazil and turn it into a tourist mecca. Miss Bardot was well before my time, and the only thing I know her to be famous for is making the town of Buzios famous. That, and being French. Which hardly qualifies as a skill but, as I know from experience, is a powerful addition to any woman's resume. So, a person famous for being famous turned a quiet, affordable township into a trendy destination too expensive for the locals.

The circle of life.

Paul and I have taken a week's long holiday to Rio de Janeiro, Brazil. The original plan was to quit the jobs we both despised and take six months to explore the entirety of South America. But the responsibility of life reared its ugly head and Paul got cold feet. Plans were scaled back. Then abandoned. Then resurrected in a form that bore little resemblance to the idea we started with.

We end up throwing darts at a dartboard, consulting a magic 8-ball, and finally drawing a random piece of paper from the 20 pieces stuffed in a rugby sock to determine where we would go on a shortened trip.

Rio de Janeiro was the winner. While doing some investigation, I found out about Buzios, two hours to the North. Then I learned about this person named Brigitte Bardot.

The DJ at the nightclub on Buzios' famed *Rua das Pedras* or Street of Stones, has been stringing together an unimpressive techno dance compilation all night. Ninety-five percent of the time, no one is on the dance floor. The only song that motivates one attractive, and supple, female to get up and move is *Bomba*. The song is currently huge on the music charts in Brazil.

Bomba is a dance track that merely repeats the same lyric over and over. To dance party enthusiasts, this is the holy grail. The other huge dance mix hit currently on the club circuit in Brazil had lyrics that went like this.

The book is on the table... table... table.

The dog is on the table... table... table.

The cat is on the table... table... table.

The chicken is on the table... table... table.

Everybody is on the table... table... table. Then the word table gets repeated several hundred times.

And just like that, a mediocre English teacher has penned a massive number one dance hit in South America.

The melody, *Bomba*, I take a liking to. Because I can correctly pronounce the one main lyric: *Bomba*. This line is repeated several times, so I can use it to pass myself off as an almost native Portuguese speaker. The women in the club still ignore me. In Brazilian nightclubs, I get pigeonholed into the unwanted category of dorky white male bereft of rhythm as soon as I walk through the door.

I would never try to dance to *Bomba*. But I ask the DJ at the club to play it several times during the night so I can get entranced by the one girl who goes on the dance floor when it comes on.

She was gorgeous.

I start planning our wedding.

We will live in Foz do Iguazu and have three kids. Flavio, Flavia, and Flavio II.

Paul drags us both out of the club at 5am. As we head out the door, he stumbles into a group of swarthy French men and comments to one of them that they looked like rugby players.

"Oui, we play rugby," one of them declares. "We will engage in the Buzios International 7's event starting in three hours."

"After being in the club till 5am?" I ask.

"Come join us and play."

"Oui."

"Oui." The Frenchmen encourage us.

I am not at all excited at the prospect of playing rugby on a few hours' sleep. Normally I prefer to get *no* sleep before getting my head smashed in on a rugby pitch. Paul, however, is very willing.

I know we will both seriously regret this.

With only three hours left before the first kickoff, we hurry back to our hotel to get some sleep. I am not happy. I am seriously in danger of entering the tournament over-rested.

Despite the Buzios Peninsula being only a ten-minute drive from end to end, the city leaders have managed to superbly disguise the rugby pitch. Paul and I drive back and forth for 20 minutes before we finally realize that the group of people congregating in the center of a large traffic roundabout *is* the rugby tournament.

There are ten teams taking part. One of them is more than happy to include Paul and me in their lineup, which means now have the required seven players to enter.

The French team is the early odds-on favorite. All their players are huge and fit. They are the only team whose players all have proper boots. But the effects of the previous evening's heavy night out eventually take its toll on them. They lose the final to a team with a local player playing barefoot. Bravest thing I have ever witnessed on a rugby pitch, and the craziest.

When we open our eyes the next morning, Paul and I can barely move. Every muscle in my body is on fire. My neck is so stiff it feels like it has been fused. After two hours of lying in bed staring at the ceiling and moaning, we are finally able to get up. We decide to nurse our bumps and bruises with a coffee in a cute bistro looking out over the pier beside downtown.

Very chill.

The vibe of the place is a heart pumping at 20 beats a minute. Sedate. Comatose. Just what I need, so I am not required to turn my neck in a hurry. The coffee shop is a few doors up from the nightclub we went to two nights ago on Rua das Pedras. The fact that Buzios is advertised as having a famed cobblestone main street is somewhat disingenuous. Every street in Buzios is paved with rocks. Streets made of bitumen that will not wreck suspensions or puncture tires would make far better sense.

But they would be a marketer's nightmare.

We had been sucked into the hype.

Staring out the window at the ocean, I see a random man get out of the water, grab his towel, and head up towards the street. When he notices Paul and me in the café, he changes direction and comes up to the window. His mannerisms are effeminate, which is a polite way of saying that I think this guy bats for the other team.

"Simon, how are you?" He asks.

His question catches me unawares. I do not know who this person is. Am I a modern-day Brigitte Bardot and somehow the world media have discovered that I am holidaying in Buzios? Better alert the city leaders so they can relax the building codes and allow developers to build massive resorts to accommodate the huge influx of tourists.

Next thing we know, there will be a casino.

And hopefully better streets than the current ones made of stones.

I rub my eyes to clear them. Perhaps this guy was on one of the rugby teams yesterday and I did not pick him out. Surrounded by all that unrestrained testosterone, he would not have appeared gay on the pitch.

"I am fine," I respond.

The man talks to Paul and me for 15 minutes, giving me coy, sly glances out of the corner of his eye the entire time. He is more flamboyant than my stiff neck can tolerate looking at. Then, finally, he bids us farewell and walks off. I absorbed nothing of what he told us. I am still in complete shock that he kept referring to me by name.

I look at Paul. "Who the hell was that?"

"Marcel."

"Who on earth is Marcel?" I ask.

"The DJ from the nightclub."

Okay, that fact has a semblance of legitimacy about it. I went up to him at least ten times to request *Bomba*. I even sent Paul over once. But I never once mentioned my name.

"Don't you find it strange he knows my name?" I wonder out loud.

"No," replies Paul. "I told him. Also told him you fancied him."

Oh, my God. "Why would you do that, you bastard? Don't even reply. I know the answer." I berate him. "You told him I fancied him?"

"Yep."

Paul laughs so hard that he causes himself agony from all his stiff joints.

He deserves the pain. With mates like this, who needs enemies?

But we have not completed the story of Marcel, the flamboyant DJ from Buzios, just yet. Because the world is never as big as people think it is.

Paul and I return to Rio the next day. During the remaining three days of our vacation, I am introduced to a young Brazilian lady who I become extremely interested in. More importantly, she becomes interested in me. She travels to visit me in Los Angeles four months later, and I travel back to Rio to see her a month after that.

We started a long, long, long distance relationship. And as I have already pointed out, the horror of these types of relationships increases exponentially with the distance two people are apart.

On my third trip to see her, and over a year since my trip to Buzios, when the story of Marcel continues.

32

If you arrest a mime, do you have to tell him he has the right to remain silent?

A few months after returning from Brazil, I follow through on Paul's and my original plan and quit my job to go around the world. Taking in Sweden, South Africa, Victoria Falls, and then home to Australia to see my nieces and nephews.

When I return to the USA, I move from Southern to Northern California. There are very few cities in the world as beautiful as San Francisco. The City by the Bay boasts charming neighborhoods spiced with an international vibe, and an iconic skyline, surrounded by water. Vancouver, British Columbia is another one of these beautiful cities. Sydney is similar, but I still cannot admit to liking anything about Sydney. Rio de Janeiro rates a mention. As do Hong Kong and Seattle. But apart from those five, San Francisco is stunningly unique.

Oh, I forgot to include San Diego.

In San Fran, generations of musicians, storytellers, and poets have found ample inspiration to encourage their talents.

The city has nearly been destroyed twice, once by a fire and once by an earthquake. According to Hollywood, it was wiped out in over 20 films by everything from a nuclear attack to a super virus, to Godzilla, to the now relatively benign sounding earth tremors. Any movie that touches on the imminent destruction of humanity that is worth its salt has a scene where the Golden Gate Bridge crumbles into the water.

I experienced an earthquake while living in the Bay Area. It was not considered big, but it was enough to put the freaking willies up on me. I woke in the middle of the night to the distant, thunderous sound of an approaching wave. Not a tsunami, but a giant ripple of seismic activity on land. The sound of the rolling earth woke me. Then, the bed and my entire room gently rose three feet and subsided again, then floated up again as the next shockwave passed. It felt like lying on a Lilo as one of my mates took a header off the diving platform down the other end of the pool.

Moments like this should remind everyone that we are mortal, and that we need to travel and enjoy life before the next big one hits and the earth swallows us up. Or Godzilla shows up and wipes us all out with his fiery breath.

When I move to Northern California, I do not live in San Francisco proper. Too expensive. Too hilly. Too close to the Golden Gate Bridge if it were to collapse from an earthquake. My home is at the end of the BART train line in a town called Pleasanton. As far as I am aware and unlike San Francisco, there has not been a single line of moving verse written about Pleasanton.

This is a town where a person moves to retire, or to thrive on hour long BART commutes to and from the city. There are even some unfortunate people who drive an hour merely to get to the BART station, then take an hour-long train ride to San Fran. That does not leave much time in the day for scribbling out poetic verse on the wonders of living here.

A solid rule of thumb for people moving overseas to work in a city where the primary source of transportation is a metro or train line. Live as close to your work as possible. Forget wars being a senseless waste of human life, so much of human life is already wasted on commuting.

In 2014, the media listed Pleasanton as one of *USA Today's* 50 best cities to live in. I lived there for a while from 2002. What changed in Pleasanton over those 12 years? Makes me wonder how a town suddenly pops up on a list of great towns when it was not there before. Sounds a lot like someone bribed the town onto the list. Another solid rule for people traveling the world or living as an ex-pat. You cannot trust lists.

Downtown Pleasanton is an archetypical USA small-town. A Norman Rockwell wet dream. The wooden facades of the buildings evoke images of Sheriff Wild Bill Hickok, squaring off against a mob of angry cattle owners over a dispute involving land rights. Except for the Starbucks. I do not think there was a Starbucks when Wild Bill was shooting people in the 1800s.

The annual 4th of July parade down Main Street is as red, white, and blue as they come. Little children have patriotic tears in their eyes and wave flags. The parade's Grand Marshall drives the route waving to the crowd from a convertible Cadillac El Dorado, the land yacht of cars. Everyday life here could be a homespun scene from any classic American movie involving two kids falling in love in high school. Then one of them gets a pimple right before prom. Their skin improves, they get married, and everyone lives happily ever after.

After two weeks of living there, I am bored.

It will be several months before I have time off to go to Brazil and see my girlfriend. The only person I know in this part of the state is Paul, who is living in the city. I get on the phone.

"Paul, hey I am bored. I am coming into the city this weekend to stay."

"Don't you want to ask me if I can accommodate you?" Paul answers.

"Well, normally I would, but let me just say a few words. Telling Marcel, the gay DJ, that I was into him. There, do I need to say anything else?"

"I'll pick you up from the Powell Street station on Friday."

I spend the rest of the week looking forward to the hippiness of San Francisco.

My apartment in Pleasanton is within walking distance of the BART station. In summer, the temperatures around the Central California Valley regularly hit over 100. This is in Fahrenheit, which translates to stinking hot in the Australian measure. On Friday afternoon it is 109, so that is several degrees more than stinking hot. I am wearing shorts and a light T-shirt. The weekend bag over my shoulder contains a change of undies and a clean T-shirt. In this heat, it is all I will need.

The air is so hot that even the slow walk to the BART station is brutal. As I cross the parking lot, I can see a train waiting at the station.

"Train for the city departs in two minutes," is the platform announcement.

If I run, I will get to the platform on time.

The train departs with me leaning on a car in the parking lot, heavily panting.

Not important. San Francisco will still be there. The break waiting on the platform gives me some time to cool off. Luckily, I am in my T-shirt and shorts. Glad I dressed appropriately for the heat. The BART system in the Bay Area is Mussolini-efficient, and another train arrives in 17 minutes.

Sitting in the BART carriage rattling its way towards the city, I give thanks that the compartments are air-conditioned. Sweat still soaks the front of my shirt. A vagrant looking man, sitting opposite me, pays me far too much attention. His eyes fixate on my wet clothes. I feel very self-conscious that I look like I just walked out of a Turkish bathhouse.

The derelict chuckles.

Could any moment in life be more humiliating than to be mocked by a homeless man?

Squirming in my seat, I avoid eye contact with the drifter. He does not stop looking at me. I cross my arms to cover my soaking wet shirt. The man's eyes never deviate. With a sudden gust of bravado, I stare straight back at him. Our gazes firmly match. It does not faze the vagrant in the slightest. He leans towards me.

"Mark Twain once said the coldest winter I ever spent was a summer in San Francisco," he murmurs.

What is he is talking about? Did he not feel the temperature outside? Incredibly stinking hot if it was a degree over stinking hot. Why is he trying to act like some arbiter of doom by whispering to me in a hushed voice? The homeless should not be giving advice to others on how to get through life. Use some shampoo, comb your hair, brush your teeth. Then keep building from there.

And who was Mark Twain to be commenting on the current conditions in the East Bay, anyway? Is he more knowledgeable than the local Channel 7 television weatherman? The man wrote, *The Adventures of Tom Sawyer*, and bore a strong resemblance to Colonel Sanders if the inventor of KFC stuck his finger in a power outlet. How does that qualify him to give meteorology advice?

I dismiss the vagrant as being a crank. Does the BART system employ any police? Someone to protect decent law-abiding citizens from unwashed hobos who like to scare commuters by quoting America's preeminent playwright.

The train passes through the stations on the East Bay. Bay Fair, San Leandro, Coliseum with connection to Oakland Airport, Fruitvale, Lake Merritt, West Oakland. Then it dives into the cross-bay tunnel. I spend 60 seconds with both eyes closed and my fingers crossed, praying there will not be an earthquake.

After two more stops, we arrive at Powell Street Station in downtown San Francisco. I gleefully emerge from the groundhog's hole under the city onto the sidewalk.

A bitter cold chills me to the core.

Mother of God.

I have never felt so cold in my life!

Holy cow, what is going on? Where did the sun go? Is the earth having an eclipse that no one predicted? An impenetrable translucent white replaces the bright blue sky from the Oakland side of the bay. Dense, billowing clouds of fog saturate everything. Is this, as the bible predicted, the end of times? At any moment, this mist will part to reveal the angry face of God.

"I warned you people to read the bible and not to fuck around with me!"

This is what humanity gets for CBS canceling *Touched by an Angel*.

In the book of Peter, it is written, *the heavens will disappear with a roar; the elements will be destroyed by fire, and the earth and everything in it will be laid bare. This culmination of catastrophes will be known as 'the day of the Lord,' the moment when God will intervene in human history for the purpose of judgement. It will be the final instance that all that God has created, heaven and earth, will be destroyed.*

Thank Christ, if this is Armageddon, there will be fire. That will help warm me up. It is fitting that God is destroying the world starting with San Francisco. Because humankind will only accept that things have gotten serious when they see the Golden Gate Bridge crumble into the water.

My body's shivering is so vigorous it approaches grand mal seizure territory.

Why do people only talk about Siberia being a merciless environment unfit for human settlement? Why not the San Fran financial district? Or Tenderloin? Or Chinatown?

No point in panicking. Try to keep my thoughts positive.

I desperately try to recall the lectures on how to prevent hypothermia when hiking on Mt. Washington from the emergency room doctor in Littleton. Dig deep into the snow for insulation was part of it. But there is no snow here. Make a fire by rubbing two sticks together. Will this trick work with two Starbucks coffee stirrers?

I need to let Paul know it is the end of days, if he does not know already. I grab the arm of the first person who walks past me on the street. He is wearing a luxuriously thick coat with an inner fleece lining. He seems unperturbed by the imminent destruction of the world. I consider mugging him to get my hands on his warm coat. When a person has five minutes left till Armageddon arrives, they have crazy thoughts.

"Please sir, can I use your phone?" I beg.

He stares down his nose at me as I stand in front of him in my T-shirt and shorts. Poor wretched fool, he is probably thinking to himself. Thankfully, his generous heart shines through and he gives me a moment with his phone. If I wanted to, I bet I could pawn it for enough money to buy a bowl of warm soup.

"Paul it is me. I am at Powell Street Station. How far away are you? Five minutes? No way five minutes. I will be dead in five minutes. Get here in two."

I hand the man his phone and profusely thank him for his generosity. I stare at his warm coat. If he was a truly generous soul, he might consider giving me the jacket. However, not even Mother Teresa would have handed it over. The man walks away, then hesitates. He turns back to me.

"You know, Mark Twain once said, the coldest winter I ever..."

"... Yeah, I know. I know what he said."

Travel tip. Having local knowledge of the weather conditions in a new country is essential to a person's survival. Do not be a jackass and ignore the advice given to you by a local. Even if they are indigent.

33

Why did the chicken go to the séance? To get to the other side.

During my next visit, My Brazilian girlfriend and I go for dinner at a restaurant in Ipanema. The food is Churrasco, or barbeque. This is a never-ending supply of cooked meats delivered directly to a table in an all-a-person-can-eat style.

Man's greatest invention since the wheel.

At a Brazilian restaurant, they call the process of unlimited distribution of food a *rodizio*. Each patron has a beer coaster with a red side and a green side. The red side signifies *give me a moment. I am still chewing*. A coaster with the green side face up means *full steam ahead,* slice off some thick rations of that tender steak and throw a few chicken breasts on the plate while you are at it.

Fifty-two tacos never had such a run for its money.

As we are leaving, my girlfriend goes to the bathroom, while I head outside and pause for a moment on the sidewalk to catch my breath. The fact that I would not be able to draw a comfortable breath after indulging in the cooked meat was never properly explained to me before I sat down. Trust the word of an expert who has made this mistake. Multiple times now. As I stand outside the restaurant vowing never eat that much again in my life, I hear my name called out from across the street.

"Simon! Simon! Hello Simon."

This is bizarre. Who on earth knows me here in Brazil apart from my girlfriend? Running across the street towards me is a man with effeminate mannerisms.

"Hello Simon, it is so wonderful to see you again," says Marcel.

I do not recognize him. Nor would I have ever thought that after a year, somehow, I would run into the DJ from the club in Buzios, 150 miles away on the side of a random street in a metropolis of 13 million people. After taking a long pause to make sure that I am not having a bad dream, I respond. "Yes, it is, mate," I stammer.

In his broken English, Marcel starts telling everything that has been going on in his life for the past year. Horrifically, it finally dawned on me who he was. I had forgotten his name, and what he looked like the moment he walked away from Paul and me at the café that day. Marcel continues to talk, while I do not say a word, hoping the uncomfortable silence will force him to leave.

After two minutes, he still has not gotten the hint.

By now, my girlfriend has come out of the restaurant, and she watches in bemusement as I am being harassed.

I try to seize the opportunity. "Hey, let me introduce you to my *girl*friend. Honey, this is..." And I stop, waiting for him to fill in the blank.

Marcel takes a moment to catch on. Sadly, his energetic response gives me the impression that he is not the slightest bit put off by the fact that I have forgotten him.

"My name is Marcel. I met Simon in Buzios a year ago," he states.

Who is this man? Why does he still remember me? I do not know how explicit Paul got when he told this man I was attracted to him, but it must have been graphic.

Marcel continues to talk. I cannot absorb a word he is saying, as I am still recovering from the utter shock of our paths crossing again. He thinks this is destiny of some kind. How is it possible that he was walking down the street as I came out of a restaurant in a foreign country I go to for a weekend, a year after I drunkenly stood in front of his DJ booth slurring the words, "*Bomba*, play *Bomba* again."

This weird coincidence is beyond creepy.

Finally, Marcel bids us farewell while giving my girlfriend a strange look, as if she is guilty of stealing mangoes from the tree in his backyard.

"Let's get a taxi as quickly as possible," I plead with my girlfriend.

"Do you find it scary that he remembers you after a year?" She asks me.

"I found it beyond terrifying."

If I have said it once, I have said it a million times. The world is not that big. After my experiences in Tijuana, in Bavaria, that story to be told in Book 3, and now in Brazil, I vow to never go to a nightclub again.

34

Knock knock. Who is there? Control freak, now you say control freak who?

Brazil is the only country in the world where a person can observe a supermodel, a homeless man, and a goat waiting together at a bus stop. It is a country of ridiculous contrasts, and it is undoubtedly a destination where tourists can see some peculiar things. Some things that people from western cultures might look upon with complete astonishment are considered commonplace in Rio de Janeiro.

One sight truly bemused me on one of my prior visits to Rio. At the corner of the major arterial road in Ipanema, in the middle of family suburbia, is an enormous billboard of a nerdy Caucasian man with auburn hair in a skintight sleeveless T-shirt surrounded by three provocative looking women in their underwear. The caption of the poster spells out one word, *ASS-MAN*!

Billboards are not the most effective advertising medium, but the marketing approach of Ass-man attracted a great deal of attention. My interest peaked, as did that of many other pedestrians whose eyes were drawn upwards. This even though English was hardly spoken or understood by anyone in Brazil in the early 2000's. Although the moniker Ass-man, combined with a cohort of buxom beauties, spoke a universal language.

The ad posed nothing but intriguing questions in my mind. Who is this Ass-man? What are the names of some of his better known films? Has he starred in anything mainstream? Too many questions for just one billboard to answer sufficiently.

This billboard is on my Mt. Rushmore of top four advertising campaigns of all time. The other three include the Jack Daniel's commercial of men whittling wood, an iconic Australian TV ad for the soft drink Solo where the actor pours most of the soda over his neck and chest as he drinks, and the Nike spot featured during the Salt Lake City Olympics where I ruptured my spleen.

I am a traveler that likes to do, not only see. So, a fitness run along Copacabana Beach while on a visit to see my girlfriend is a must. During the early evening in Rio de Janeiro, the stifling summer humidity is heartbreaking. With men openly wearing Speedos on the beach, and billboards for porn displayed in residential neighborhoods, it surely would not be a societal faux pas for me to go for the run shirtless. Wrinkly 70-year-old men casually walk up and down the beach promenade in Speedos, and nobody bats an eyelid. If I am brave enough to travel to Rio by myself, then surely, I am brave enough to expose my pasty white skin beside the throngs of deeply tanned locals.

My flight arrived yesterday, and I need to sweat out the jet lag and exhaust myself to make it easier to sleep in the tropical heat without the benefit of air conditioning. Also, sweat out the remains of the Churrasco from last night. As well as the uncomfortable reunion with Marcel. However, if I had known that tonight I might be subjected to an uncomfortable introduction with my future mother-in-law, I would have worn a T-shirt.

As I jog back along the beach road from Copacabana Fort toward the apartment, I am flagged down by my girlfriend, randomly standing on the side of Avenue Atlantica with her 10-year-old brother. Even with ten thousand people out on Copacabana Beach, I was easy to spot. They picked me out of the hordes of bustling beach goers from over a kilometer away.

They are standing on the curb directly outside of the Municipal School of Cicero Pena, a squat mixed-use building located beachfront on Avenue Atlantica. This 4-story building is dominated on either side by towering 5-star hotels, on arguably some of the most desirable real estate on earth.

During the day, Cicero Pena serves the needs of high school-aged students during the two shifts of school standard in Brazil. From 8am to 12pm and then from 1pm to 5pm. In the evenings till 10pm, it serves as a school for mature students learning to read, write, and develop the skills to help them maintain a living in the economy.

As my girlfriend and I chat on the street, a woman appears at the window of the top floor. It is my girlfriend's mother. She works at the school as a teacher. She waves for us to come inside the building. My girlfriend asks, "do you mind going in and meeting her students? They will be so excited to meet someone from Australia."

I do not mind, but I will not exactly be comfortable.

As we are about to enter the front gate, a security guard stops me. The school has a dress code.

"Sem camisa, sem entrada." *No shirt, no entry.*

He will not let me enter without a shirt on. This is a measure of relief to me. This fortunate hiccup has deep sixed the awkwardness of meeting my girlfriend's mother. At least until I am better prepared.

And better dressed.

Meeting your partner's parents is an awkward moment at the best of times. It is even more uncomfortable when the association is a long-distance relationship and the girl's parents do not speak your language. I am wondering what the likely response from the mother would be if she *could* speak English.

"Hi. Pleased to meet you. Look how disgustingly white your body is. Sorry, you are not good enough for my daughter."

This scenario is not unlike what judgment day would feel like. And I have already had a taste of that experience when I went to visit my mate Paul in San Francisco, and I was similarly underdressed for the occasion. Only now, I am also basting in sweat after an 8-kilometer run in the sweltering humidity.

I am about to resume my run back to my accommodation, when the younger brother unexpectedly slips off his tank top and hands it to me. He smiles and nods to signal that I can use his shirt to allow me to enter. I swallow hard. I do not want to appear disrespectful, but I am twice his size.

Even after stretching the tank top out as far as it will go, I barely squeeze my torso into it. There is just enough leeway to allow me to breathe. The dry-fit shirt stops short three inches above my navel. This gives me an unsexy Britney Spears muffin top. I could not look any less manly if Elton John was nibbling on my earlobes while fondling my nipples.

If the security guard so much as snickers, I will die of embarrassment.

The guard waves me through with no outward display of emotion, although I am sure his eyes focused on my midriff for much longer than was necessary.

My girlfriend takes my reluctant hand and leads me up the stairs to the top floor. At every step, my feet feel heavier and harder to lift. Stumbling into the classroom I am introduced to the 20 adult men and women collectively. As a response I utter the words of Portuguese I am most confident with, "estou com fome." *I am hungry.*

My girlfriend's mother eyes me suspiciously. She is just wondering how her daughter ended up dating such a rabid fan of NSYNC. My role is simply to stand in front of the class and be a human showcase while my girlfriend explained to the class whatever elements of Australian culture she knew. I am mindful of how tight the shirt is and how far it is creeping up above my belly button. There is a great deal of *ahhs* and *ohhs* during the discussion of how far away Australia is, and that I now live in America. After being prompted, the class joyously bursts out with the word 'kangaroo.'

The students are incredibly excited to have a guest. After the talk about Australia, they are eager to show me the efforts of today's class, developing their skills at recycling thrown away items into useful trinkets to sell in the city's tourist flea markets. They are all so proud of what they have made. It is truly heartwarming and humbling to be confronted by these people's struggles to scratch out a living.

After 10 minutes of growing increasingly sheepish about the many opportunities life has given me, I look at my girlfriend and nod towards the door. At this moment, a frail 60-year-old lady walks up to me. She presents me with a large glass jar decorated with a mosaic of hardened colored glue spelling out the word ARROZ. The Portuguese word for rice. I am deeply touched. The lady says something in Portuguese to my girlfriend, then slowly hobbles back to her seat.

My girlfriend leans in to talk to me.

"She thinks you are a superstar. And she wants you to have this. She knows it is simple, but she doesn't want you to think she is unable to do anything and that she is useless," she says.

An enormous lump forms in my throat. My eyes well with tears. How sad for an adult to have to deal with judgment because of their low financial status in life. How dare I waste a moment of anyone's time complaining about my first world problem of being a little chubby around the waistline? This sweet old lady, who has nothing, has shown me what human dignity is all about.

My eyes keep returning to the jar as I cradle it in my hands. How does someone who has so little find the strength to give away all they have? I need to leave as quickly as possible, so I do not start weeping in front of the class.

I nudge my girlfriend towards the door. As she starts to walk out, I take one last look over my shoulder at the old lady who has given me the gift. Her tired and worn eyes show a spark. She returns my smile with her own. Then she gives me a wink and turns to the student next to her and nods knowingly.

"Ass-man," she says.

35

There are three kinds of people: those who can count and those who cannot.

One of the most popular phrases in America is 'speak to my lawyer.' Everyone has a lawyer, it seems. I do not know how the entire country seems to be able to afford to have an attorney on retainer at $450 an hour. Every time I am in trouble, I always find myself saying, "just speak to me, I do not have the money for a lawyer."

To avoid unnecessary legal fees, I follow the tactic of never getting myself in trouble. This strategy is quadrupled when I am traveling away from home. Quintupled. I required the services of a lawyer on one occasion, because of a minor incident that occurred while overseas. Fourteen years later, the matter is still unresolved, and I am currently $150,000 poorer as a result.

Travel tip. You never, ever, ever, EVER want to find yourself in legal trouble in a foreign country.

At the start of 2004 and for complex reasons, I go and live in the harsh desert area on the state line between California and Arizona for three months. In the town of Needles, California. It is as if the Tuff Campground erected a few more buildings and elected a mayor. Even the name sends a disagreeable shiver down my spine. It would be the same as if they had named the town Thorns, Spikes, or Prickles.

Needles lies on the banks of the mighty Colorado River, or what is left of it after the Glen Canyon Dam and the Hoover Dam hold back its flow. And those are just the two well-known barriers. There are 15 dams on the main stem of this river system and hundreds more on the tributaries. If the

Colorado river had been a breeding ground for salmon, hydroelectric power would have decimated that species of fish years ago.

With the presence of the river, I hope Needles will be a veritable lush Eden. Palm trees, green meadows, and Hawaiian Tropic photo shoots with bikini-clad models spring to mind. Not at all. This water challenged corner of California is nothing but parched desert extending into the bone-dry desert of Arizona and the sunbaked desert of Nevada.

Deserts are wonderful places to shoot nature documentaries about lizards scampering through a canyon chased by snakes. Not much else. The loading page of the website for Needles features a giant cactus, and that is it.

To get there will take five hours driving from Santa Monica, on top of the five hours it took me to get here from San Francisco. This last section of the journey involves one and a half hours to get out of Los Angeles proper. Then three and a half of hours of dry nothingness. Well, not entirely nothing. Several miles after I make a right-hand turn at Barstow, off the I-15 continuing to Las Vegas and onto the I-40 to Hell, I pass a billboard advertising a strip club.

A strip club located a few miles ahead and just off the freeway in a scorched landscape resembling the backdrop for *Dune*.

There is no way they could have a cover charge, surely?

When I arrive in Needles, I am struck by its bleakness. The town had been founded over a century ago, with the construction of the Atchison, Topeka, and Santa Fe railway. The railway bridge that crossed the river at this juncture was constructed so badly, it was destroyed by rising river floods in 1884, 1886, and again in 1888.

Needles is also a stop on the historic Route 66 highway, which was the main cross coastal roadway in the USA from the 1920's to the 1960's. The town rates a brief mention in *The Grapes of Wrath*. It was the first stop of immigrants fleeing the dust bowl of the Midwest during the 1930's. The book mentions Carty's Camp, the town's original name, as a brief stop of the Joad family. None of this historical reference is why I have come here. That is all just a bonus.

I also did not come here for the gambling. Laughlin is a 40-minute drive North up the valley. There are a half dozen aged casinos there. But the southernmost tip of Nevada is only a 10-minute drive from Needles. It is on the west side of the Colorado River, just past the Fort Mojave Indian Reservation. On a plot of dirt exactly where survey engineers say the state border's imaginary lines are located, in the middle of BFE, is a casino.

The Avi Resort and Casino sits so close to the state border of California, while remaining in a legal jurisdiction that allows gambling, that the car park is shaped as a triangle in order to fit the tip of Nevada's state line. It must be illegal to park in California and walk to a casino in Nevada. This speck of hedonism is a gambler's atoll in the vast ocean of the desert. There is nothing else on the western side of the Colorado River until a person arrives at the glitz and glamor of Laughlin.

I will only be in Needles for three months, for work. It will seem like a lifetime. The only medium-term accommodation that I can find within a 40-mile radius is at the Fender's River Road Resort and Motel. Using the term *resort* is such a gross example of false advertising that I consider calling a lawyer to sue them. But I do not have a personal attorney. And the only lawyer in town has a full schedule of personal injury cases for people walking into cacti.

Fender's Resort is a glorified RV park, although I do not know how they glorified it. As well as the carefully landscaped gravel surface to accommodate aging, decrepit campervans, there are five self-contained studios. I will live in one of the units for the next 13 sunbaked, bone-dry weeks.

My first order of business is to find out what I can do to keep myself occupied for three months in this part of California. I discover that in Needles, there is absolutely nothing to do. With this first order of business duly handled, I move onto my second order of business. Crying my eyes out.

I had always been told that Perth, on Australia's West coast, was the world's most isolated city. In terms of distance, yes. Not in terms of psychological and emotional isolation. That honor falls to Needles. I do not want to moan about how unlucky I am to have ended up here. I chose to come. It was entirely my decision. I wish I could say I was heavily intoxicated when I decided it. But it was more a case of temporary insanity.

The old saying, misery loves company, is true. That is the subliminal message of the Needles' homepage on the internet. One man's refuse is another man's gold, my father used to tell me. I think if dad came to visit Needles, he might change his mind.

Over the first weekend, I visit everything close by that might be worth seeing. The Avi Casino, the Colorado River, and the Laughlin casinos. As harsh as the desert may be, it is not as harsh as watching an elderly woman gasping for air as she transfers an oxygen tank from the boot of her car to her electric scooter, while puffing away on a cigarette, before going to gamble away her social security check.

On my second weekend and in a bout of wild adventurism I venture as far as Kingman, Arizona. The mayor of Kingman had recently come under fire for declaring his city the meth lab capital of America. That was a bold claim with contention from other desert towns like Yucca, Bullhead City, and my own adopted town of Needles in the mix.

There was nothing of note to see in Kingman.

On the drive back to Needles, I follow the sage advice of my dad. He always encouraged me to take the road less traveled. Instead of returning to Fenders Resort from meth-city via the I-40 freeway, I deviate up and over the range that is the eastern ridge of the Mohave Valley. This is part of the historic old Route 66. It now bears the much less impressive name, Oatman-Topock highway.

This stretch of majestic bitumen starts in Kingman as Route 66. After a few miles, it changes its name to Oatman Road. It continues with this name as it tightly twists and turns up the eastern slope of the range, passing historic sites alluding to the name Route 66. But it is clearly signposted as Oatman Road. Then, without warning and before you even get to Oatman, the name changes to the Oatman-Topock Highway. Four miles later, another Oatman Road splinters off towards the East for a few miles, before changing its name to Boundary Cone Road. The Oatman-Topock Highway continues to Topock, then abruptly stops. As the name suggests it should. I stay on this road, although at this point I do not know if I am still on Route 66. Perhaps I had been on it, perhaps not. No one knows for certain. This random assigning of names to roads is what happens, I assume, when the head of the major roads department for the county smokes too much meth.

Passing through the town of Oatman, my initial reaction is, what an uninviting tourist trap. Some of the world's locations advertised as interesting places to visit are severely over-hyped. The Four Corners, at the intersection of the state lines of Colorado, Utah, New Mexico, and Arizona, is one such place. The Hollywood Walk of Fame is another. Plymouth Rock is a third. The hands down champion of tourist hyperbole is Oatman. It would be more impressive to find out I had cancer. And this is before I learn about the town's history. Afterwards, my opinion deteriorates even further.

Originally set up as a gold mining tent camp, the town briefly flourished with a major find of the yellow metal in 1915. The population swelled to 3,500, which is why, I assume, the author of the pamphlet I read used the word *flourished*. They might have opted for the phrase *the town grew a little*. The town was named after a young girl, Olive Oatman, who had been kidnapped by Apache Indians, then sold to the Mojave tribe. While captive with these people, she suffered a case of Stockholm syndrome, although at the time it was a nameless disorder, and assimilated with her captors. She was reluctantly rescued five years later when she was traded for a horse and some blankets. She was clever enough to play the victim card coming back from her desired captivity, and the town was named in her honor.

Oatman is barely famous for two reasons. It is billed as an authentic western town where wild burros still roam the streets. I have never seen a wild burro wandering along the main street in any of the western movies I have watched. *The Good, The Bad, and the Burro* would have been an instant classic. Westerns have stagecoaches pull up in the main street. Westerns have gunfights. But I have never seen a burro meandering down the street on screen.

Burros parading up and down would have made life in western towns far too chaotic. They already have people shooting at each other. Who needs the extra headache of stepping in burro shit?

The second reason Oatman has a sliver of recognition is that this is where Hollywood icons Clark Gable and Carole Lombard honeymooned in March 1939. For a single night! They bedded down in the Oatman Hotel, the oldest two-story adobe building in the entire Mohave Valley. In Clark and Carol's era, Oatman was the Laughlin of its day. The hotel has seen its fair share of scoundrels, movie stars, and little old ladies riding scooters surviving on bottled oxygen.

I find out the Oatman Hotel keeps the honeymoon suite exactly as Clark and Carol used it on the one night they spent there. Although I hope they washed the sheets. I wonder if director Frank Capra snuck into the room and short sheeted the bed? But people come to Oatman to stand in front of the hotel and take pictures. Then they return home to have a slide night with their friends and proclaim this the honeymoon hotel of Clark Gable and Carole Lombard.

Surely, being out here in the desert is living my best life.

Well, until the incident with the Arizona Highway Patrol.

36

Life is like a bird. It is pretty cute until it poops on your head.

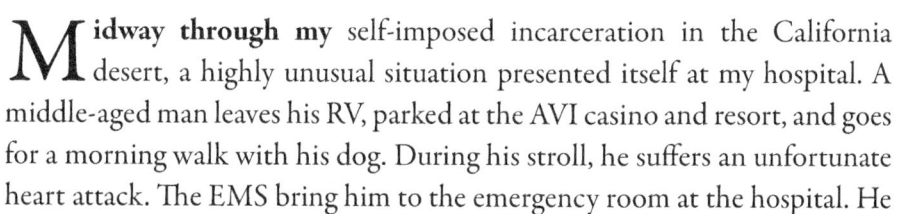

Midway through my self-imposed incarceration in the California desert, a highly unusual situation presented itself at my hospital. A middle-aged man leaves his RV, parked at the AVI casino and resort, and goes for a morning walk with his dog. During his stroll, he suffers an unfortunate heart attack. The EMS bring him to the emergency room at the hospital. He gets admitted, and I estimate his recovery and rehabilitation are going to take seven to ten days.

If all goes well for him.

Someone takes his dog back to the RV, where it will survive the next few days being fed by a neighbor. But here is the problem. At the time of his cardiac arrest, the man had in his possession, in a velvet lined carrying case, his prized Civil War revolver. What on earth was he thinking, taking this antique firearm on the walk? It could have been for protection. Although, if a wild coyote were to attack, he would have been pushed for time to open the box, pour a powder charge into the chamber, load the pistol, and fire.

The man is told by the hospital that the facility cannot accept the responsibility of holding the gun along with the other patients' valuables in security. They ask if he will allow the neighbor to take it back to his RV. He vehemently refuses. He trusts the neighbor to feed his dog, but not with having his gun for safekeeping. I wonder how the poor collie feels about that. So, there is a stalemate between the patient and the hospital. The hospital does not want to keep the gun, while he cannot part with it. So, I come to the rescue by adding a modicum of common sense to the impasse.

I offer to keep the case with the pistol in the boot of my car. That is my simple solution. Problem solved. This was acceptable to both the hospital and to the patient. If I promise to bring the case to his room every day so he can see it. Sure, like bringing in a newborn baby to the mother for feeding. Knock yourself out, mate. I will even close the door and turn out the lights while the two of them share some alone time together.

The hospital administrator hails me as a hero. In these parts, I am not sure that means much. As big a hero as Olive Oatman? She did nothing except get dragged off by Indians and somehow got an entire town, and by default several sections of highway, named after her. I do not even think that Olive is the star of her story. There is another unsung hero of the saga. The poor guy who had to give up his horse to pay for her release.

Hero? I am no hero. I throw the case in the back of my car and forget about it.

I survive the dreariness of Needles till the weekend and my next much-needed day off. Coincidentally, Saturday is also the first day of Spring Break, the legendary mid-March party hiatus for university students in the USA. Young adults cut loose and head to Cancun, Miami Beach, or South Padre Island for seven days of adolescent hi-jinks and mayhem. Another popular destination for this university rite of passage is Lake Havasu City, Arizona. Although I do not understand why. Why would someone forgo a Spring Break in Puerto Vallarta, or Cabo San Lucas, to go to a lake in the isolated Mojave Desert? The principal attraction in Lake Havasu City is a dilapidated English bridge featuring in a song about how dilapidated it is. *London Bridge is falling down, falling down.*

Apart from being a draw for Spring Break, London Bridge's claim to fame in modern day America is that it was featured in a made for television movie, *Terror at London Bridge*, starring David Hasselhoff - the Hoff - of *Baywatch* fame. I repeat, a made for television movie. The same stamp of quality given to cotton/polyester blend, a hotdog from 7-11, and Made in Equatorial Guinea.

Robert P. McCulloch, a real estate developer, purchased this onetime feature over the Thames River in London, then shipped it to his new town development in Arizona. His ambition was to use the bridge as a selling point for tourists and prospective homeowners. I am intrigued to know what his sales pitch was on the billboards by the side of the road in the desert. *If you owned a house here, you would be home by now. Of course, you would have to stay in your house as it is too hot to do anything outside.*

What was the attraction of buying a house close to schools, close to shopping, and close to a bridge that was collapsing because of its substandard construction in 1824? If a shoddy bridge is all it takes to attract new home buyers to live in the desert, then Needles should have seen a huge influx of people in the 1880's. They had a succession of shoddily built bridges.

Incredibly, Mr. McCulloch's plan seems to have worked. The London Bridge in Lake Havasu City has become the second most popular tourist attraction in the state of Arizona, after the Grand Canyon. It sits just ahead of number three, the meth labs in Kingman, and fourth place, the cactus famous for being on the Needles' website.

As I speed down state road 95 towards Lake Havasu, the unmistakable blue lights of the Arizona Highway Patrol appear in my rear vision mirror. I could only have been doing two or three miles over the limit. But this is Arizona, the home state of famed vigilante Sherriff Joe Arpaio. The self-styled toughest Sheriff in America. This law enforcement officer is so tough on illegal immigrants that he has people arrested and deported for ordering a meal at Taco Bell. I nervously sit in my car as the Deputy exits his Crown Victoria Interceptor.

In my side mirror, I can see him adjusting his holster before he ambles toward me.

He spits out a wad of tobacco, then leans against my car. "Do you know why I stopped you?"

"Err. Yes, sir. I was speeding."

He nods slowly. His eyes hidden behind his reflective aviator sunglasses. "Where you headed?" He asks.

I resist explaining that I am going to Lake Havasu City by virtue of the fact that it is the only town that exists on this piece of road. The man is severely geographically challenged.

"Just to explore Lake Havasu City," I say.

"Hmm. Going to Spring Break?" He asks accusingly.

"London Bridge, actually," I reply, "huge fan of the Hoff. Lake Havasu City is like our Mecca."

He gives me a long second glance over the top rim of his glasses. He is obviously not aware that I have been to every other notable location in the state. I have seen the Grand Canyon; I have been to the Kingman meth labs; I saw the famous cactus. Once I see London Bridge, I can tick off the entire state of Arizona.

"Anything in the car?"

I pause with a moment of uncertainty. "Um, me."

I am honestly not sure of his question. He already asked me an obvious one about where I was going. Either he is testing me, or maybe he is a remedial State Trooper. He may need everything spelled out for him.

"Do you have any drugs?"

"No, sir."

"Any marijuana? Coke? Methamphetamines?"

"No, sir."

"Any Ecstasy? LSD? Magic Mushrooms?"

I am not sure if he is interrogating me or shopping. "No, sir. Nothing at all."

"Can I have a look in the back?" He asks.

"Sure," I respond. My approach is to always be respectful and accommodating with law enforcement.

Travel tip. Always be respectful and accommodating with law enforcement. If they want, they can beat the crap out of a person under the pretense they resisted arrest.

Bonus travel tip. Do not resist arrest.

I push the button on the dash that pops the trunk. Hopefully, the State Trooper does not consider this poor form. I am concerned about responding in a manner that says, hey you can do anything you want, just do not expect me to lift a finger. If I were to get out of the car and open the trunk with my key, he might be suspicious that I was going to go all *Thelma and Louise* on him. The moment he opens the trunk and I lose sight of him in the rear-view mirror, I suddenly remembered the pistol case.

Shit.

37

Do you think Noah included termites on the ark?

Everyone I knew while living in L.A. had a *coming to L.A. story*. Several of those involved the police. One mate was stopped by the police on his way to his first night of work. He and his car fit the description of the person who had just shot Bill Cosby's son near the 405 freeway. He was surrounded by police with their guns drawn.

Another friend, Knoxy, was pulled over by the police while speeding on a freeway in his father's car. His dad kept a loaded Berretta in the glove compartment, for protection, when collecting rent in dangerous neighborhoods. When he reached to get the car's registration from the glove compartment, the gun fell onto the passenger seat, and he ended up face down on the ground with his hands behind his back, surrounded by police with their guns drawn. Knoxy spent the night in the Beverly Hills jailhouse until it was all ironed out.

Those stories run through my head, sweating bullets in the sweltering Arizona as I wait nervously. I fidget with the indicator signal, turning it on and off as if I were weaving through traffic in a civil, high-speed chase. Knoxy had a loaded weapon in California, an incredibly liberal and progressive state. After releasing him, they gave him a slap on the wrist and 10 hours of community service saving the spotted owl.

I am carrying a concealed weapon in Arizona, and even though California is a measly three miles West of me, in this state, ruthless public guardians like Sheriff Joe Arpaio set the rules. I have committed a crime helping a heart attack victim. The police are likely to haul me off to a maximum-security prison holding members of the Sinaloa and Los Zetas Mexican drug cartels. They will not even bother to read me my Miranda rights.

I am going to need a lawyer.

A good one.

I bet any money that half of Needles has walked into a cactus this week.

I have not yet come to the realization that the entire profession are cunts, so the only thing that concerns me is the cost. Four hundred fifty an hour. The thought of spending that much money is more traumatic than the thought of being forced into prison sex with the entire criminal population in cell-block D of the Maricopa County correctional facility.

Unless I can talk my way out of this alone.

That is all lawyers really do. They talk. They make up stories of plausible deniability. Why do I need a lawyer to do that? Surely, there are a million lame excuses *I* can come up with on my own to explain the gun.

"Officer, I have the gun because I heard the story of the Indian tribe abducting a young girl from a camp a few years ago, and I needed to protect myself."

Or "officer, I have the gun because I won it in a game of poker. I am now on my way to Lake Havasu to pawn it for enough money to buy myself a *I had Spring break in Lake Havasu City* T-shirt."

Rambling on and on is my signature way of getting people to avoid engaging with me before sending me on my way. An approach that has worked far better for me than using the words, *let me call my lawyer*. That seems like a straight up admission of guilt.

As would making a run for it.

If I run from the police officer, the absolute best-case scenario is the deputy opening fire and bringing me down, but hopefully only with a leg wound. This will allow me to play the victim card like Olive Oatman, and have a town and several miles of bitumen named in honor of my heroism.

These are the irrational thoughts a man has while being stopped by a policeman for the first time while in possession of a concealed weapon and without a gun permit.

My life flashes before my eyes.

My clean driving record flashes before my eyes.

The seconds tick over into minutes. It is a tense thing to have my car searched by the police. I feel oddly secure and yet violated at the same time. It would make me feel better if I could see the officer in the mirror. Gauge his facial expression. It has been two minutes. What is he doing? Did he go back to his squad car to radio for help?

"This is Adam five twelve requesting backup. I've got a confederate war veteran who is armed and dangerous."

Then the car shudders with the thud of the boot being slammed shut. The deputy slowly walks up to my window. He readjusts his black driving gloves. He certainly is enjoying dragging this out. Just like the Mexican drug cartels will before giving me a Colombian necktie in the joint. "Everything is clear. I am going to let you off with a warning. Just keep the speed down so you arrive at your bridge in one piece," he cautions me.

Everything is clear. How? The only thing in the trunk of the car is the wooden box holding the pistol. How did he miss it? It even has a stenciled lithograph of a gun on the lid. I almost want to get out of the car, take him back to the trunk to point it out, and scold him. Is this how you do your job keeping people safe? Thankfully, I remember another golden rule of interaction with the police. They can use anything I say against me in court. So, I bid him good day and drive off, slowly.

Spring break at Lake Havasu is not what I expected. Especially since I nearly earned six to ten years in the big house for going to experience it. It is what is commonly referred to as a *sausagefest*. Plenty of testosterone filled muscly young men running around without shirts on. I count three women in total. The females are all part of a beer promotion crew. The trio does a roaring trade. Eight thousand drunk males, each thinking they possessed the charm to lure a beer model back to their hotel room.

It is entertaining to watch for an hour.

As head back to Needles, I pay my respects to the Hoff by driving past London Bridge. Again, not what I was expecting. I was under the impression London Bridge had two spires and a drawbridge. But then I remember that the bridge with spires is the London Tower Bridge, which is still in London. London Bridge looks like any ordinary bridge. In fact, it is an ordinary bridge. I have seen more impressive bridges in Pittsburgh. The only reason this bridge has a sliver of fame attached to it is because its name includes the word London.

The Hoff denigrated his good name by making a B-movie about it.

I wonder if any other travelers have been stupid enough to make the mistake of wanting to see it.

Travel tip. Never waster the time to go to see something that has a very generic name. There is a good reason that inspiration did not strike when naming the Yokohama Bay Bridge. The Cairo Opera House. The Brooklyn Tunnel.

The moment I get paroled from my self-imposed exile in Needles, I go on a cruise in the Caribbean. One night I attend the formal sit-down meal, as opposed to going to one of the many grab and go eateries onboard. At dinner I am seated next to a wealthy Welsh man and his wife. We talk about travel, all the places we have been, and all the places we still want to go. Then he introduces me to the concept of the *anti-bucket list*. Places I would never want to go back to again.

He asks, "what is the single worst place you have been to?"

Shit, there have been so many.

I take a moment to ponder this. What place was my all-time least favorite?

"While you are thinking, I will tell you mine," he says. "My wife and I were traveling in Arizona years ago and there was this little town up in the hills we were told was a must-see. It was an uninviting pustule of a tourist trap. I can't remember the name."

"Oatman," I tell him.

"Oh my God yes, that is the name," he exclaims. "So, you know it."

"Know it. I lived not far from there."

"Oh, my God. You lived there?" He says, in a compassionate tone.

"I wouldn't call it living," I lament. "Did you go and see the London Bridge while you were in the area?"

"No."

"Then you missed out on the full anti-bucket list experience."

Simply incredible, that two strangers from opposite corners of the globe cruising the Caribbean could both register the same enema like experience of visiting a specific isolated town on the planet with a population of 43.

More proof that the world is not that big.

The Welsh man graciously offers to cover my bar tab for dinner. At inflated cruise ship drink prices, my two gin and tonics cost him as much as a horse and a few blankets.

38

I used to be indecisive. Now I am not sure.

I have tried to learn something new every day of my existence, starting with lesson one. Do not crap in the diaper. Moving to another country to live, for the second time, taught me that a healthy exercise routine and buying a secondhand car go hand in hand.

If there is one training regimen that I value even less than hill sprints, it is running stairs. In terms of commanding my respect, hill sprints are to running stairs, what Sir Laurence Olivier is to Steven Seagal. Running up and down stairs, to get fit, is sheer lunacy. This does not mean that I do not do it. I do. I just do not understand why I do it.

Even in health-conscious western cultures, running upstairs for the sole purpose of turning around and going back down the stairs when you get there is self-defeating at best. And ridiculously pointless at worst. It resembles the argument that the government can stimulate economic activity by paying people to dig holes, so that other people can get paid to fill them back up. Running stairs encompasses all the futile economic aspects of Communism, while including also sweating.

In 2005, I once again embraced the complete unknown and moved to Rio de Janeiro, Brazil. I will be hopefully aided by the fact that I do not need to learn the language. Portuguese is essentially Spanish, except they have different words for *thank you* and *chicken*. I had no legal status to work, yet I remained naïve enough to think love conquered all. And I am in love. I have moved to Rio to start a new life with LMY1 and avoid my mother-in-law as best I can.

I arrive in South America at the apex of the Pink Tide, when three quarters of inhabitants are under left wing rule. In a socialist country like Brazil, I might have thought they would be crazy over running up and down stairs for no reason.

All the apartment buildings in Copacabana have two elevators. One is for the people who are clean, such as residents going to parties or to work. And the other elevator is for people who are dirty. This includes residents coming home from the beach, or for workers performing construction in the building. I do not see clean people go in the dirty people elevator, or vice versa. One thing I certainly do not see is people taking the stairs. Cariocas, or residents of Rio, would prefer to burn to death in a building fire rather than use the stairs if the elevators became inoperable. Or if the incorrect elevator for their hygiene status arrived at their floor.

The first week after I move to Brazil, I am very tense. I face all the regular adjustments involved in an international relocation, on top of a language barrier I discover is more formidable than the Great Wall. Brazilian Portuguese is not like regular Portugal Portuguese, the language I am more familiar with as it is basically Spanish. Nothing breaks down a person's security more effectively than moving overseas. I suffer homesickness for America, and it is not even my country.

To keep my mind focused, the best thing I can do is work up a good sweat. Activity does wonders to calm my emotions. I have run along Copacabana Beach many times and loved it. However, the city of Rio has been inundated with tropical showers for the week, and being soaked and windblown would only deteriorate my mood. The only option available is to do a stairs workout in my building.

The doorman thinks I have completely lost my marbles. Every time I take a moment's breather in the lobby, before starting another 10-flight climb, he opens the elevator door, expecting me to step inside.

"No, thank you. I am exercising, sir. Esta ex-er-cisio!" I keep explaining to him, futilely. The dumbfounded expression on his face shows he never gets it. Why is this gringo using the stairs to go to the 10th floor and come back down, when he could do the same thing in the elevator in a tenth of the time?

I work out for half an hour and feel happy with my efforts.

The next morning, my legs are on fire! All I can think, feel, and see is pain.

Every muscle is screaming. My calves. My butt. My thighs. It feels like every muscle fiber from my waist down is soaking in hydrochloric acid.

Even the gentlest stretch to the tissue sends searing pain through my brain. I can barely take a step. My legs are like tight rubber bands. It has been a few months since I have done any super vigorous activity, but even so, I was not expecting to be so crippled. I really overdid it yesterday, trying to exhaust my anxiety. It is agonizing to walk. The only way I can tolerate moving around is gingerly ambling with my legs spread wide. It gives the impression I have been sodomized with a Sequoia cactus while riding a Clydesdale.

Then my father-in-law unexpectedly shows up at the apartment. It takes about 30 minutes to decipher that he needs me to accompany him to a car dealership. He wants me there to negotiate a resolution with the dealership who used secondhand parts to repair a used car my wife has purchased. The LMY1 did not mess around with spending my savings. In less than a week, I have become the proud owner of a car. We already have a new living room set on order. I try to look past the immediate worries and look at the bigger picture. My future happiness.

Why I am needed at the car dealership does not make immediate sense to me. I can barely speak a word of the language. But then I understand: I am the muscle. My father-in-law stands four feet eight inches tall. Which in metric is on the short side for an Oompa Loompa. He was a tiny man to begin with, but his legs have curved so badly from arthritis in his knees so much that it subtracts another three inches from his height.

Travel tip. There are many countries in this world where bribery, corruption, and physical threats are all acceptable, and necessary, tools to be used in business.

We are an odd-looking couple. The tall red-haired gringo and the elderly, short, bandy legged Brazilian.

We arrive at the dealership by taxi and are invited to sit down and wait for the sales associate who promised my wife he would replace several components on the secondhand car with new parts, and now apparently wants to renege on the deal. He finally walks in after half an hour; Brazilians, like Italians, are not known for their punctuality. Discussions between my father-in-law and the sales associate begin in earnest.

I sit there and say nothing. My father-in-law does all the negotiation. As their heated debate rages on in Portuguese, I grasp snippets of the argument. I understand enough to know that the pair often veer off on a tangent and start discussing the recent performance of the national soccer team. My role is to look mean, occasionally interjecting a growl or giving my most menacing Madonna bitch face.

After 15 minutes, my father-in-law and the sales associate have made little progress in resolving their differences. They are at an impasse. We demand that they upgrade the car to our satisfaction. The dealer's position is that my wife bought the car as is.

Israel and Palestine think they have problems.

My father-in-law needs a break to catch his breath and get a coffee. He stands from his chair and waddles over to the coffee urn in his bandy legged gait. I nod my head towards him while punching my fist into my palm. As if to say to the dealer, yeah, that is right. I was the one that messed him up. My lame threat only brings a mocking smile to the face of the sales agent.

My father-in-law rejoins us. He and the sales associate go back to speaking tersely, then almost crying and embracing when they bring up the recent three zero loss to Argentina. After another 15 minutes there is no progress in the dispute. Now I need to go to the bathroom. I excuse myself, then struggle to stand from the chair. My legs are as stiff as Hugh Hefner's corpse.

Moaning and groaning pathetically from the pain, I laboriously drag myself across the showroom floor to the bathroom. I glance over my shoulder at my father-in-law, who is at that moment punching his fist into his palm in front of the dealer while motioning his head in my direction.

When I come back from the bathroom, the sales associate is looking terrified while my father-in-law is standing there with a broad grin on his face. He nods towards the taxi rank out on the street.

"What? We can go. He is making the changes?" I ask.

My father-in-law squints his eyes as he tries to decipher what I have said, then gives me a nod and a thumbs up.

"What changed his mind?" I wonder aloud.

My father-in-law shrugs his shoulders and says nothing. We walk towards the door, and I spy my father-in-law looking over his shoulder at the sales associate and nodding with a devilish smile on his face. I can only assume that he is reminding the salesman that this is what he will look like after he has been sodomized with a cactus, if he does not make the repairs.

Travel tip. When living in another country, sometimes not speaking the language can be a blessing.

39

My first experience with culture shock? Probably when I peed on an electric fence.

Sometimes a person will find themselves in a situation and ask themselves, "how did I get here?" I often find myself doing that. Although on the occasion when I was at a religious rehabilitation retreat for former inmates, nestled in the foothills of rolling ranges two hours West of Rio de Janeiro, I remember exactly why I was there.

Calling it a retreat is a bit of a stretch. It is a farm operated by a priest that was a reformatory for ex-drug addicts and street criminals from Rio's slums. The felons had all found religion while in prison and then opted to come out here to the country after their release. Here they could live lives of devotion, away from the temptations and influences of the inner city. Turning their lives around from the despairing depths many of them had sunk to would take a great deal of will power, but an admirable goal. Best of luck to every one of them.

The LMY1 knew the priest from when he was running a religious retreat in the slums of Rio. Possibly for all the petty criminals in the country to get a taste of city life. She wanted to stop in for a visit to see how his *turning over a new leaf* farm project was progressing. It is quite an unsettling feeling to meet people who were incarcerated. Even if it was formerly. We often forget that being able to read a book immediately makes us better off than 26% of the world's adult population.

The retreat looks exactly like a farm. I was halfway expecting there might be a moat around it to keep the men from running away. There is not. So, it is a farm, just not a fun farm. After greeting the priest in charge, I am introduced to three of the workers on the farm. The former heavy drug users and one killer are incredibly humble and polite to me. They appear no different to men I have met selling suits in a store, baking bread in a bakery, or building a house. It seems unfathomable that at one time, these men had no problem taking another person's life or dealing drugs that horribly affected the lives of many others.

More surprising still is that they are all much younger than my 38. But even so, they have already spent at least ten of those years behind bars for their crimes. It is a lot for me to digest. They are from a world I cannot relate to at all. What do I say to someone who has had that life? Thankfully not much, as I am having a hard time coming to grips with Brazilian Portuguese and they have no grasp of English.

One of the *saved* men is bursting with pride telling me how much he has turned his life around. With my limited grasp of the language, I gather that he used to shoot up on heroin while living in the streets. But now he is clean. About the closest I can relate, is that I used to have sugar in my coffee and now I do not have any. So, we share some threads of a common bond.

Apart from the former prisoners, there is another group currently staying on the farm. A collection of gringos, like me. The young men are from a church in Iowa, on a two-week mission in Brazil to assist with the farm. By the looks of them, none had been further afield than Nebraska prior to this excursion.

That is one state over.

I am all for having diverse cultures mix, to learn from each other, but some pairings go together like oil and water. Sheltered white dudes from the American Midwest bunking down with former hard time serving crackhead Brazilian criminals. It made for a strange marriage.

I detect a level of unease between the two groups of men. Understandable, considering the incompatible livelihoods they have had. I am sure both sets of adults are reassessing how they came to be in this place. One set thinking of the troubles that got them here, the other wondering why they got on a plane. The churchgoers do not strike me as men who know much about the dejection that drives men to shoot up on heroin every day. While I do not think the Brazilians had any idea what cornfields are.

The only thing they could both understand, and that they do extremely well together, is say the word Jesus. At that point, the language barrier has no meaning. All it takes is for one person to offer a quick praise to Jesus, and the rest quickly chimes in.

"Jesus."

"Jesus."

"Jesus."

Like an echo bouncing around the Grand Canyon. It is like watching an old western where one cowboy fires off his pistol to start a cattle stampede, and all the other cowboys follow suit.

One of the Iowans walks up to me. He asks if I speak Portuguese fluently. I do not want to say I cannot. That will make me look foolish. I have improved by spending 8 hours a day with the workers who were refurbishing the kitchen of the house the LMY1 has bought with my money. I am confident my Portuguese is good enough to find my way around the hardware and plumbing section of a Home Depot, if they had any in Brazil.

"It is not perfect, but it is okay," I embellish.

"So, you understand what they are saying, then?" He asks.

There is a pause before I answer. "Yes," I lie.

I want to do whatever I can to help. If I need to pretend that I know what I am doing, I will. But this exemplified the members of the Iowa group's naivety. Asking an Australian to translate something in Portuguese? But no worries, I will do my honest best to help him out. Even though I am not deeply religious, that does not mean I do not assist my fellow man.

The American volunteer explains that he wants me to translate something the Brazilian criminal tried to tell him before I arrived on the scene. I ask the Brazilian to repeat what he said, while listening as carefully as I can. He was most likely trying to pass along some important secrets about God.

The Brazilian explains that he is a former drug user and that he has found God. I get that part. Then he points up to the side of the mountain as he talks, and his eyes get teary. I understood what he said as, "there are bodies stashed up there and when the moon comes out, the forest is full of them. Strange things happen. The dead spirits are raised."

A shiver goes down my spine. That sounds voodoo intense. The American church volunteer is quite perturbed.

Then the criminal solemnly whispers another sentence in Portuguese. I understand that as, for everyone at the farm to demonstrate their obedience to God, there will be no food to eat for the next five days.

"No food for five days?" Stammers the American. "Are you kidding me?"

I ask the Brazilian to tell me what he said again, and he confirms that they will give no one any food to eat for five days. Only water. It is God's will, apparently.

"I didn't sign up for this shit," spews the irate Iowan volunteer.

He turns to the others in his group and summons their attention.

"Hey, did you know they will not feed us for five days? This Aussie speaks Portuguese and translated for me. He said this guy told him. Did any of you know this?"

The American group is supremely unimpressed with this intolerable turn of events, and they erupt into a cacophony of complaints. This causes agitation among the group of Brazilian criminals, who have been watching closely. Seeds of distrust and scorn are being planted on both sides. The Iowans storm off to speak with the head organizer of the church mission. Concerned at the sudden disturbance of the farm's harmony, my Brazilian wife comes over.

"Ask this guy here what he just said to me," I tell her.

The criminal repeats the story.

"He says he is going up to the mountains for a five day fast when the moon is full. He will pray all day and all night, and when he does this, he feels strange, like he becomes another person. His spirit is lifted. He will not eat any food for the entire five days away from the farm, only water, to show his obedience to God," my wife explains to me.

"Only him?" I ask.

"Only him what?" She asks.

"Only he will have no food for five days."

"Of course," she states.

"Okay then, good job," I say. "Listen. Are you all done with your visit? Because I think it is about time we get the hell out of here."

Travel tip. Never trust a stranger to interpret for you when you are overseas. And certainly not some idiot who does not speak the language.

40

I have all the money I will ever need—if I die by 3:00pm this afternoon.

The term, a once in a lifetime experience, is often bandied, but it means extraordinarily little. Like the check is in the mail. We are from the government; we are here to help you. And we do not need a prenup, my love for you will never die.

Most activity falls under the umbrella of once in a lifetime. After graduating high school, I did not plan on enrolling again. My 21st birthday was the only 21st birthday I will ever have. How many people go searching for the woman and donkey show in Tijuana twice? I actively pray that 99% of what has befallen me in life will never happen again. So, everything I do fulfills the criteria right there. Finding a leech sucking on my balls while white-water rafting in Nepal is a once in a lifetime event. Am I supposed to be celebrating?

A Rolling Stones concert on Copacabana Beach in front of one and a half million people, I will admit, is a once in a lifer that I would happily do again! February 18, 2006, is the date. *Day of Stones* preparations have been underway for weeks leading up to this event. A mammoth stage on Copacabana Beach rises from the sand. A 100-meter walkway bridge from the stage to the Copacabana Palace is built for the sole purpose of allowing the band to walk to and from the performance without having to mix with the unwashed. Six giant projection screens are placed at 400-meter intervals up the beach, so that the fans at the back of the throng can still see Mick Jagger strut his stuff from two kilometers away.

The morning of the concert, I go to work. I am teaching English at a language school on the top floor of the Rio Sul shopping center in Botafogo. Even with the concert of the millennium about to take place, my students still need a little pre-Stones' grammar coaching. *I can't get no satisfaction*, should be sung more correctly by Mick, *I cannot get any satisfaction*. Or *I cannot be fully satisfied, oh no no no.*

At 7.45am on the *Day of Stones,* I walk through the tunnel that links Copacabana to the Botafogo neighborhood and pass a drunk openly urinating on the sidewalk. With the Rolling Stones concert tonight, Rio de Janeiro locals are keeping it classy. The Stones' rock-and-roll party is off to an early start. People are already arriving en masse. Walking through the tunnel dragging coolers and carrying beach towels. The early birds will claim a spot in front of the stage. They will happily wait there for 12 hours for a chance of being sprayed in the face by some of Mick Jagger's sweat.

Even with the Rolling Stones playing a free concert on Copacabana Beach, there is no need for the locals to do anything differently from their normal day at the beach. They simply need to change the direction of their beach chair at 8pm.

Today's English lesson, for the advanced conversation class at the Wise Up school, is idioms. English language expressions used in the figurative sense that confuse someone new to the language when they understand only the literal meaning of the words. There are over 25,000 turns of phrase in the English language, so learning idioms could be its own separate doctorate course.

I spend a great deal of time making sure my students have an exceptionally good pronunciation of English words. Especially the swear words. The words *fuck* and *fucking* lose all of their gravity when not pronounced sharply.

"Fook. That is fooking horrible."

"I don't know why you people have such a fucking hard time saying the word fuck. Just copy me."

"I don't know why you people have such a fooking hard time saying the word fook?"

"No Vito, that is fucking shithouse."

Idioms are less important, but still fun. *To go on a wild goose chase*, does not imply chasing after our non-domesticated feathered friends. So, I must carefully explain every idiom phrase by phrase to my students, or they quickly become lost. Mind you, seeing the expressions on their faces as they try to comprehend the meanings on their own is priceless.

Hit the nail on the head is another example of an idiom. On each occasion, I state the phrase, give its implied meaning, and then find examples of its use in conversation. This is my all-time favorite class of the semester.

Round around in circles.
Keep an ace up your sleeve.
Do not cry over spilled milk.

Not only am I teaching the students well known English expressions, I sneak in some less widely known Australian ones too. A two for one package deal.

It looked like a dog's breakfast.
I would not piss on someone if they were on fire.
He is a few stubbies short of a six-pack.

The students scribble away in their notepads at a furious pace. They all get a real kick out of my class, while I have been able to improve my ability to speak in front of an audience. Near the end of class, I open the floor to the students to ask me about the meaning of any other idioms they may have heard but could not understand.

"A penny for your thoughts?" Asks one student.

"That's too easy. You should be able to work it out. Next?"

"Elvis has left the building," asks another.

"Self-explanatory. Next?" I reply.

"What is a one hit wonder?"

"Ahh, perfect example of an idiom. It is the name given to a band or singer that bursts onto the music scene with one great song and then never have another hit," I explain.

"Like *El Gato Volador* by El Chombo?" One student throws out.

"Are you smoking crack, Vito?" I respond.

I can only assume El Chombo is someone, or something, considered famous to a Brazilian. But unheralded by the other 99% of the world.

"I have no idea who the fuck that is," I continue. "Can we keep this discussion in English. It is a fucking English class, for God's sake. Let me think. A one hit wonder is like that Norwegian group, A-ha. Remember their huge hit, *Take on Me?*"

The faces in the class register complete confusion. I thought A-ha was the perfect example to explain the term one hit wonder. Maybe they cannot remember the band or the song. It was 1984, twenty odd years ago. But I am desperate to have the students understand my point. While I do not have the courage to sing even in the shower, I take a slow deep breath, then belt out my best impersonation.

"You know. Take on me, take on me. Take me on, take on me. I'll beeeeee gooonee. Then there is a super high note where I have no idea what he is saying, and those are all the lyrics I know."

I glance around at the bemused faces in the room.

"What? Didn't A-ha make it to Brazil? They had a cool music video where the guy looks like he was drawn in a comic book and the band all had pseudo Flock of Seagulls hairdos." Still, nothing shows on the student's faces. "Wow. Not even one of you has never heard of A-ha?"

"A-ha, yes. We all know the band," one student answers.

"Right. Well, A-ha is a one hit wonder. They never did anything else after that one hit song," I proclaim.

I still get blank stares from all corners of the room. Why is this such a hard concept for them to grasp? Then one hand slowly goes up.

"Yes, Tiago," I acknowledge the student.

"Um, teacher. A-ha have been on tour to Brazil five times," he states. "They are very popular. They have lots of hit songs and seven albums."

I nearly choke. Seven albums? Are we talking about the same A-ha? Could there be another A-ha? And these guys made it huge in Brazil. Wow, I learn something new every day.

"Fuck me," I exclaim.

"Fuck me."

"Excellent, Vito."

I head home after class, still scratching my head that the English-speaking world somehow missed seven album releases by the Norwegian band. And that I took a slam dunk explanation of an idiom and ended up confusing the hell out of my students. I arrive home and the LMY1 suggests we go down to the water's edge to enjoy a pre-Stones midday swim. Then come back home and have our pre-Stones lunch, then a pre-Stones siesta.

Basking on the golden beaches of the Marvelous City, not only is it an acceptable practice for a person to ask the closest stranger lying next to them to watch their stuff when they go for a swim, it is an unwritten law. Rio de Janeiro is not the safest city in the world. *The Rolling Stones* built themselves an entire bridge just to allow them to walk 100 meters safely. Pickpockets and thieves roam the beaches day and night, looking for unsuspecting tourists. A person would be insane to leave their belongings out in the open.

When I am ready to have a swim, I turn to a lady sitting near me on the beach and ask if she would not mind looking after my wife and my clothes.

"Not at all," the lady replies in broken English.

My wife's mouth drops to the floor. An idiom I had just discussed with my class only this morning.

"Oh, my God. Oh, my God," my wife starts whispering under her breath.

"What is the matter?"

"Do you know who that woman is?"

"Should I?" I replied.

"That is Vera Gimenez."

"That means nothing to me."

"She is the mother of Luciana Gimenez," my wife tells me. She says it, like I am supposed to know who that is. I wonder if that is the actual name of the famed El Chombo, one hit wonder of the Brazilian music industry.

"Luciana Gimenez means even less."

"She is the mother of Mick Jagger's son."

I did not know Mick even had a child, let alone eight with five different women. But I keep on learning new things every day.

When I walk back up from the swim and thank the woman for watching my things while I went for a swim, I confirm whether she is Vera Gimenez.

"I was wondering. My wife tells me you are the mother of the lady who had Mick Jagger's kid. Is she pulling my leg?"

"What does it mean, pulling your leg?" The lady asks, looking perplexed. She needs to sign up for my advanced English conversation class and learn some common idioms.

"Is she telling me the truth?" I ask again.

"Yes, it is true," the lady answers.

Then Vera - all her closest friends call her Vera - stands up and shakes the speckles of sand off her body. "Excuse me. Would you mind watching my things while I go to the water?" She asks me.

"No worries. Anything for Mick Jagger's son's grandmother," I reply cheerfully.

I can now add our interaction to my growing list of close brushes with famous people. Angelina Jolie scratching my back and Wesley Snipes nearly running me over.

The Rolling Stones concert was out of this world, even if I only watched it on the furthest billboard from the stage. My good buddy Mick puts on a hell of a show. That night, I scribe out an email to my friends and proudly tell them of my brush with celebrity on the beach.

Shane, my mate from high school I ran into in Steamboat, replies the next day from Sydney, Australia with a startling revelation. His girlfriend's father had been dating Luciana until the moment she decided to trade up to get pregnant by Mick Jagger.

The world is not that big.

But what is the relevance of this story to anyone still wandering through life trying to decipher the meaning of it all?

Two things. *Life is a journey, not a destination.*

And Simon Van Booy wrote this unforgettable line that ties it all together. *Coincidences mean you are on the right track.*

41

My math teacher called me average. How mean!

Living in Rio, my side hustle was to rent out my condominium to international guests during the peak tourism times of the New Year and Carnival. This was a nice little money maker that helped pay the condominium fee for the year. My English school salary barely put food on the table. Thankfully, we already had a table, as I did not make enough to buy one.

Teaching English overseas is the perfect job a person for a young person fresh out of high school to give them a chance to explore the world for a year or two. Or it makes some nice bonus money for a retiree who is finally following his lifelong dream of spending a year in Macedonia.

But it will not pay for a person to update his furniture even once a decade.

So, I rented out my place. And then some friends of the LMY1 asked if I could rent out theirs as well. I developed a little business that made me no money, as none of the landlords would give me a cut of the rental price. But I did it anyway, as that is the type of person I am.

Stupid.

In April of 2006, I rented out someone's apartment to twin brothers from Salt Lake City. Two good Mormon boys. Both filled with love, happiness, and empowered by the protection from the Lord above, watching over them.

One day, the brothers naively asked me if it is safe to swim on the beach at night.

"Do you see anyone else swimming on the beach at night?"

"No," they responded.

"And that is your answer."

Many basic questions people may have while traveling can easily be answered by opening their eyes and observing what is going on around them. Do not drink the tap water if you see the locals drinking from water bottles. Is it always required to wear a shirt while driving in Thailand? Yes. There is a reason all the Thais do it. Is it safe to go to a dangerous place like Tijuana alone? It is not safe to go to a place like Tijuana with friends. Just do not go to Tijuana.

Coming from Utah, I wonder if they had ever seen the ocean before for them to ask such a strange question. Maybe they were not up to speed with the intricacies of visiting one of the most dangerous cities in the world. Still, better safe than sorry. They had the good sense to ask for advice before doing something stupid.

Despite the Church of Jesus Christ of Latter-Day Saints having a strict policy against devotees using drugs, alcohol, and caffeine, they apparently have no ban on irony. The next evening, there was a frantic knock at my door. It was one of the twins, soaking wet, dressed in his boxers.

"Can I use your internet phone?" He pleads. "I need to call my credit card company. I just had all my stuff stolen off the beach."

It was a watershed moment for me. I experienced the rare emotion of being absolutely flabbergasted. I have been surprised, stunned, even astounded on one occasion, but never flabbergasted.

"You went swimming?"

"Yes."

"At the beach?"

"Yes."

"At night?"

"Yes."

"And you had your clothes stolen?"

"Yes."

"Well, you are lucky that is all you had to take."

"No, they took all the other stuff as well."

"Other stuff?"

"I had just gone shopping for gifts for everyone back home."

Not only did he go swimming by himself at night. To put whipped cream on top of the milkshake of his foolhardiness, he also went shopping beforehand. He had left his wallet, clothes, and two bags filled with newly purchased items, unattended on the beach. There was no way to make it any more obvious to any prospective thief, other than to light a signal beacon.

I do not profess to know much about the Church of Latter-Day Saints, but I wonder if members of this church, apart from leaving themselves wide open to theft, would also try to light toilet paper on the side of a mountain. That way, I could claim a semblance of common-sense superiority.

42

My girlfriend dated a clown right before she met me. I have some big shoes to fill.

On **Christmas Day,** when I was four, instead of getting presents from Santa in my stocking, I received potatoes wrapped in aluminum foil. The Australian equivalent of getting lumps of coal. Whatever I had done that year, it had royally angered Santa. For that yuletide, Kris Kringle considered me the Stalin of the land Down Under.

This family story gets trotted out over every Christmas meal. As well as on Easter Sunday, the Show Day Holiday, and the Queen's birthday long weekend. This is the reason I followed the straight and narrow path in life. My rebellious streak peaked when I was four. But when I was bad, I was very, very bad. In my lifetime, I have never heard of any other person living on the continent of Australia who received potatoes in their stocking as a punishment at Christmas.

It is remembering these small moments when we are feeling down that lifts our spirits and keeps us going. This is why memories of trips, travels, excursions, getaways, tours, journeys, junkets, treks, and safaris bolster a person when they are sad. My recall of experiences has always been vital in helping me fend off the black dog, which is why my recollection of events is so vivid.

And on New Year's Day 2006, the black dog of depression was nipping at my heels. I was as sad as I had been bad in 1972 to incur the wrath of Santa and his elves. My mental health living in Brazil was falling apart. Culture shock is not only the expression of amazement at how expensive everything is at the store. It is also the feelings of anxiety, uncertainty, and confusion when in an unfamiliar environment. It did not help that my family-in-law were experts in emotional isolation and abuse. They also had zero ability to regulate their own emotions. Aside from that, they were all crazy.

On New Year's morning I am sitting on the kitchen floor of my wife's family's apartment, depressed and crying my eyes out.

As my mental health slowly circles the drain over the first months of 2006, the only thing I look forward to is Wednesday night rugby training. This is the case for the other ex-pats in Rio too. It is the only two or three hours of our week that makes any sense for many of us.

Travel tip. A key point for anyone planning to live overseas or even just taking a trip for a few weeks. Maintain some contact with elements of life with which you are familiar. Celebrate your National Days in the traditional manner, watch your sporting championships, hang out with others who are far from home too, so you have people to bond with.

This is a critical point. The world may not be as big as you think, but it will still swallow a person whole.

After our rugby sessions, most of us stay around for a beer and a talk. It is a very local affair. We drink at the little cabana beside the section of beach where we train at Posto 8 in Ipanema. They usually have plenty of cold beers on hand to satisfy the 20 to 25 guys who stay.

One Wednesday evening, our training session holds a little more exhilaration than usual. Running around the beach in one of the most exotic locales on the planet is usually enough. But this night, as we pass the ball around on the sand, a running gun battle is occurring in the Cantagalo favela a few blocks inland. This slum spreads itself up the sides of a Morro, or granite hillock, on the corner of Copacabana and Ipanema. The *Policia* are shooting at some drug dealers. Or some drug dealers are shooting at the *Policia*. It is hard to know from a kilometer away.

The rapid-fire ricochets of the heavy armaments tell me the weapons are more than powerful enough for stray bullets to cross the 1000 meters between the shanty town and our rugby practice on the beach. So, I cower behind the cement wall separating the street from the sand.

Being gunned down long range by an errant bullet from a high-powered magazine while standing on the beach in Rio de Janeiro. Now *that* is a once in a lifetime experience.

The battle rages for 15 minutes. The steep, narrow streets of the favela are constantly lit up by gunfire. It is like the Chinese New Year. I am shocked how clearly I can see the bursts of fire from the barrels of the fully automatic weapons engaged in the primal tug of war for drug turf. Gun battles occur daily in the poorest parts of the city. A never-ending testament to humanity's desire for power. I am anxious when looking in my stocking on Christmas Day. I would never want to have to wake up in the morning fretting over what percentage of my drug distribution control in the neighborhood might have been seized overnight by a rival gang faction.

After this training, everyone drinks more heavily than usual to calm our nerves, and the cabana runs out of beer. After watching a war unfold in front of us, the ex-pats feel compelled to continue their conversations about dealing with life in Brazil. A dozen of us cross the road and walk one block inland to Praca General Osorio, which houses a bar with a small outdoor beer garden. Here we continue our therapy session.

I am in great need of being in the company of fellow strugglers, and time gets away from me. It is close to 2am before I get up to go home. To get to my apartment, I just need to walk the four-kilometer length of Copacabana Beach by myself.

Copacabana Beach is not the scariest place in the world at night. The streets of Cantagalo favela rate slightly ahead of it in the rankings. Normally I walk home from training at 10.00pm. Half the city is still on the streets at that hour. At 2am, there is a much higher level of trepidation being alone on the sidewalk. The Ipanema end of Avenida Atlantica, which runs the length of Copacabana's beachfront, is lit until early morning by the lights of the night market held on the median strip. By 2am, the stalls of the market barely register any economic activity. It is almost closing time, as only a handful of tourists continue to shop. Under the misguided assumption they can score cheaper deals as it gets later.

Across the street from the night market is the enormous Club Help. This landmark building is the most recognizable facade along the Copacabana beachfront. It is a nightclub/brothel. Normally, there is a buzzing crowd lined up outside this oversized club at any hour. Tonight, there are no more than two white male tourists and a prostitute in fishnet stockings. Things are slow for a Wednesday night.

But that is all about to change.

43

Never date an apostrophe. They can be a little possessive.

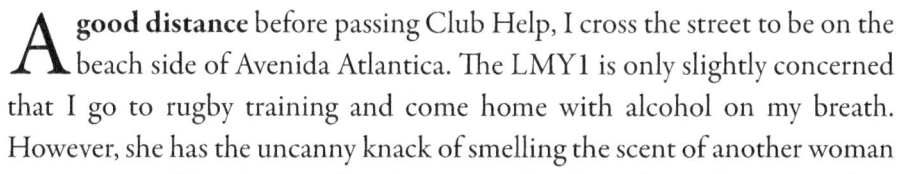

A **good distance** before passing Club Help, I cross the street to be on the beach side of Avenida Atlantica. The LMY1 is only slightly concerned that I go to rugby training and come home with alcohol on my breath. However, she has the uncanny knack of smelling the scent of another woman on me, even if I only passed within 50 yards of another girl. Great White Sharks have a weaker capacity to sense blood in the water.

Chanel #5 in a concentration of one part per million is enough for the LMY1 to get riled up. Prostitutes working the city of Rio bath in fragrance before going to work. I have zero sense of smell because I broke my nose playing rugby. But if I can detect the aroma of a woman in my vicinity, it is already far too late for me to avoid their scent attaching itself to me. So, I give the hookers of Rio as wide a berth as I can.

I cross the road 100 meters upwind of Club Help. I cannot be too careful. Now I am on the beach side of Avenida Atlantica. There is much less foot traffic at this hour of night here. None, to be precise. All the beachside cabana bars have closed. No nighttime parties winding up or winding down. It is not unheard of for people in Rio to be out celebrating life, music, and the joy of alcoholic drinks served in coconuts until sunrise. But not tonight.

Things are extremely slow for a Wednesday.

After the first mile of beachfront, I walk the rest of the three-mile journey in darkness. There are no lights in the hundreds of apartments facing the beach this time of the morning. There never seems to be at any hour. The nightly occupancy rate for this prime stretch of real estate always seems below 10%. The super wealthy people of this world love to own things they never use.

The air is calm and not too humid. A reasonable night to be out for a stroll. Even after having only three drinks in a four-hour period, I feel tipsy. The waves lap against the sand to my right. As long as that is the side I keep hearing the sound of the ocean, I know am headed in the right direction.

At the midpoint of the beach, I have a gut feeling I am being watched. A sense that there is an unseen group of people in the immediate area that is aware I am walking alone. The headlights of a random car passing by on Avenida Atlantica illuminate a huddle of silhouettes dashing across the road to my side, 200 meters in front of me. I stop walking and wait. Five minutes pass, and no one approaches me down the sidewalk. Whoever they are, they are waiting for me.

I know they are not going for a nighttime swim.

They are looking for a victim to mug.

Even if I were not slightly tipsy, I would have Buckley's chance in a fight. I could not defend myself against a kangaroo when I was seven, and my fighting abilities have only gone downhill since then.

If I cross to the other side of Avenida Atlantica, directly in front of all the unlit apartments, I might be in a safer position if attacked. However, I doubt my cries of help will get heard by anyone, as every wealthy condominium resident is apparently vacationing in Europe right now. I could go backwards, except it is now 2.30am and I am desperate to crash into my bed. I am badly in need of sleep.

In the grand scheme of life, everyone starts off with, then later returns to, an age where going to bed trumps every other concern.

Sippy cup - no, would rather go to bed.

Play with toys - no, would rather go to bed.

Late-night movie and a cuddle - no, would rather go to bed.

Taking a mile detour while walking home to avoid being assaulted - no, would rather go to bed.

I make a decision that could drastically shorten the course of my life.

Now I am not overly brave, but neither am I overly foolish. As I walk along the sidewalk, my mind races to the memories of moments when I have been in a pickle. The night in Madrid after three days of no sleep, when I was set on by the gang of kids looking to pickpocket me. I survived that. This helps me develop a plan to give me the greatest chance of survival. When I want to be a badass, I can be. My worldly travels have taken me around the block a time or two.

Plus, these muggers do not know they are dealing with a former nemesis of Santa's.

The very foundation of human existence is a battle for survival. A person has only three basic needs they must satisfy: food, shelter, and, if they are female, Louis Vuitton handbags. Writers have written endless pages about humanity's continuous struggle to attain these three items. Homer's *Iliad*, *War and Peace* by Tolstoy, *In Search of Lost Time* by Marcel Proust, *The Devil Wears Prada*.

However, an individual's survival is also predicated on the avoidance of pain. It is the balance between the need for food, shelter, and matching accessories, on the one hand, and our evasion of discomfort on the other that determines a person's action in any scenario. A starving man wants to feed himself. But he will not risk being shot to achieve that goal. If a proud person wants to come in from the cold, they will happily grovel before an innkeeper to receive help. If a stingy man does not want to deal with his wife's frustrations, he will readily agree to buy her a Hermès purse to stop her criticizing him in Macy's.

This is the way of the world.

The ocean side of Avenida Atlantica is lined alternatively with kiosks, open stretches of sand, and little groves of coconut trees. There is also a giant sand sculpture of a castle that seems to have existed for years. Apart from the open patches of beach, there are multiple structures giving a band of robbers plenty of opportunity to hide. They could jump out in front of me or jump me from behind.

Given that I saw at least three, they could even apply a two-pronged approach. Some of them jump out in front, while another comes at me from the rear. This approach would mimic General Douglas MacArthur and Admiral Nimitz's successful pattern of attack in the Pacific theater during World War II. And is the favored mode of attack for South American street gangs and thugs.

I pass the last deserted kiosk before a large open stretch of sidewalk finishing at a grove of trees and the Copacabana Beach Surf Lifesaving Clubhouse. Oh, the irony. To be robbed, beaten, then left for dead beside the Lifesaving club.

The robbers will come at me somewhere in the next 50 meters.

Thankfully, I know exactly what to do.

Security experts always try to impress on people the best weapon to have hidden on themselves for self-defense. A tactical knife, the Vipertek VTS-989 taser with snatch prevention technology, or a can of pepper spray concealed within a fluffy Beanie Baby key-chain attachment.

Any of that would be fine.

I only have my wits.

I have also spent a reasonable amount of my working life going into psych wards to treat patients that are certifiably nuts. And there is nothing that scares the beJesus out of a person more than dealing with someone who is crazy.

If Mike Tyson was walking on the sidewalk flanked by four seven-foot bodyguards and an insane baglady without any teeth steps in front of him and started cussing at the sky, Mike and his posse would all quietly tiptoe around her. No one, and I repeat, no one, on the face of the planet wants to deal with crazy.

It is never worth the effort.

So, I just need to act like a crazy person.

And what is the best way to do that?

Sing.

And sing annoyingly loudly.

Now the choice of a song is particularly important. There are plenty of rap and dance tracks by modern artists that are guaranteed to get a person killed rather than scare away an attacker. Anything by Rihanna is an immediate nonstarter.

Thankfully, I am a child of the greatest era of rock music composed for the purpose of self-preservation. And there is one particular song that stands out above all others to send out a Hannibal Lecter/Norman Bates/Taxi Driver vibe when under threat.

"Roxxxxxxxanne," I shrill at the top of my lungs with the highest pitch I can maintain for eight seconds. "You don't need to put on the red light. Tell you once, you don't need to..." it was important to really hit the ear-piercing note here, "... SELL your body tonight. Roxxxxxxx...... Anne. You don't need to put on the red light."

Sting would have been proud.

From this point on, I just continue with guns blazing, ignoring whatever is happening around me while maintaining my enthusiasm.

"Rox... Put on the red light. Rox... Put on the red light. Rox... put on the red light."

When Nero played the fiddle as Rome burned to the ground, all its citizens were like, okay, just let him finish and we can start the rebuild in the morning.

My stride lengthens as I determinedly hike up the Copacabana Beach sidewalk. I abruptly spin around every few meters and shrill at the empty air behind me, "Rox... put on the red light."

I do not let up my singing for a mile.

I am sure I look insane. It feels like I am insane.

The performance would rival Hitler giving his Nuremberg rally speech after freebasing crack.

It certainly gives my would-be assailants plenty to think about.

They are wondering if attacking me is worth the effort. Better to go home hungry than deal with this crazy idiot.

People, bad and good, leave me well and truly alone.

Every year tourists flock to Brazil in their thousands. Many to partake in the year-long celebration of the *Carioca* lifestyle showcased during Carnival. Visitors love the parties and the dancing till all hours. But every person I rent my apartment to gets robbed while they are in the city. Every single one.

I lived in Rio de Janeiro for 14 months. No one robbed me. No one ever tried to pull a knife on me. Very few people even spoke to me. I could have won the award for being the whitest person in the city every year I was there. That made me an obvious target for thieves.

But I always felt safe.

I put it down to my 80s collection of vinyl 45s.

I get home safely to my apartment with hardly any voice left. I try to slip into the bedroom without waking my wife.

Fail.

"What time is it?" She asks.

"It is still early. Go back to sleep." I say comfortingly.

"Are you okay?"

"You'll never guess what happened to me tonight."

"What is that I smell on you? Did you talk to a woman tonight?"

"I was nearly mugged."

"And this person who mugged you, was she female? Did she try to assault you with her lips? Where were your hands? Yes, I am asking you. It is a simple question. I bet she did not even have to chase you. Did she? Answer me. Do not give me any of your lame excuses about being out with your rugby mates at the bar. I am sure it was the waitress. No, do not answer me. I do not want your opinion. You know nothing about being a husband. Nothing."

I stand up, go into the living room, and fall asleep on the couch. As I was saying, nobody on the face of the earth wants to deal with crazy.

Nobody.

44

My boss is going to fire the employee with the worst posture. I have a hunch it might be me.

After 14 months of living in Rio de Janeiro, I moved back to San Francisco, then to Miami. My marriage to the LMY1 failed and as a result, my life was enveloped in an unimaginable world of hurt. I wrote a memoir about it, *My SECOND Life*, which will leave any reader huddling under their bedsheet shaking and wondering, why didn't I stick to nearly dying in plane crashes or boat disasters?

On some nights, the only thing that kept me going was the memories of the experiences I am sharing with you now. Nobody's life is an endless European summer vacation. There are always highs and lows. To survive our low periods, we all need something to sustain us. For me, combating my dark times, there was nothing more important to my well-being than being able to look back and think about what a crazy life I have lived!

I married the LMY2. A lovely lass from Spain with two beautiful kids I became a loving stepdad to. That marriage ended.

Behind every breakup, there is a grief that makes a person think that perhaps there is something wrong with them.

Then, one day, I randomly crossed paths with a girl I went out on two dates with while living in Los Angeles, who had moved to Belgium. We had completely lost contact for 20 years. She had recently moved back to the USA and was now living on the other side of Florida.

I left my job and moved in with her.

Go, go, gadget heart.

I thought I had rekindled a love with the one that got away.

I was wrong.

I was so wrong.

It was the least thought-out thing I have ever done. And I have done some mindless stupid things in my life.

Just as the relationship started to sour, the new neighbor, who had purchased the house next to my girlfriend's so he could move down South during COVID, asked me if I wanted to help his family drive their second car and campervan from Chicago down to Florida.

As a young man, I would have jumped at this opportunity. I had always wanted to go camping in a campervan.

I declined.

I was feeling so lost that even the adventure of going on a road trip did not appeal to me.

The girl I was living with ordered me to go. She wanted me out of the house for a week so she could reevaluate our relationship.

So, I flew to Chicago.

As I am standing on the sidewalk at Midway airport and the moment I see the mammoth campervan attached to the neighbor's truck, my beaten down spirits soar. A euphoria overtakes me. It is like a cover is being pulled off my body.

It has been a dream to take a road trip like this.

And life had made me forget about my dreams.

I smile for the first time in weeks. A wide, wide grin.

Maybe the hyperbole is a little intense, but that campervan symbolized freedom. It represented the reason we were put on this planet. To enjoy our lives. The hair on the back of my forearms prickles. This is the excitement I had forgotten in my heart. Giddy childish anticipation. An expectant elation that sends a heart racing. The feelings that I cherish more than anything else in life.

Within an hour of leaving Chicago, we are surrounded by boring cornfields, and I cannot wipe the smile off my face. Neither can my neighbor behind the wheel. It was only corn, for God's sake. But to us it is living gold. The neighbor introduces me to the song *Free* by the Zac Brown Band. This immediately became my anthem for life.

Every time I hear it, it reminds me of how I went from sadness to happiness in an instant. The song is a cue for me that no matter how bad a situation is, things will always get better. Everybody needs a trigger to help draw them back from the edge of darkness when they are down in the dumps. A spark. It can be a song. Or it can be an object like a life preserver or a plate of tacos.

Simple, simple things.

The first night we camp at an RV park in Louisville, Kentucky. The neighbor shows me the procedure of setting up the campervan. The sides of the vehicle expand out, turning it into a luxurious pad. There are knobs to twist and electricity and water lines to attach. Pilots spend less time running a pre-flight check. This thing has all the latest bells and whistles. Satellite TV. Full size fridge. Gas stove and microwave.

It is more comfortable than many hotels I have stayed in.

Later, I wander around the park and am delighted at the open friendliness of everyone I meet. Not a soul is unhappy. They are all enjoying themselves. The neighbor is heartily enjoying himself as well. He takes his two young children to the play area and is thrilled watching them play on a large inflatable bounce area with other kids.

The next day we drive South towards Atlanta but we are forced to have an unplanned overnight stay in Nashville, as one of the neighbor's kids feels sick. His wife has to take the boy to an urgent care. The neighbor takes it all in his stride.

"A road trip is never a straight line between two points," he tells me. "A person needs to let go and follow the flow sometimes."

The next morning, we are on the road again towards Stone Mountain Park Campground in Atlanta. At lunch we split up. The neighbor drives on ahead of the wife, kids, and me so we can spend some time in Chattanooga and drive to the top of Lookout Mountain to see the glorious views over this idyllically placed town. We discover that there is a waterfall deep inside a cave in Lookout Mountain, Ruby Falls, which is a must see. The tours for the day are all booked out, but I add it to my list of things to do if I am ever in the area again.

Three nights camping in the wooded site beside the lake at Stone Mountain, Georgia feels like bliss with lots of leaves. A decent author could write pages describing a single tree. And how the bracing breeze through its branches makes them speak. I am struck by the hanging mist of smoke and scent of barbeque at dinnertime. This is so relaxing. I am happy. I take a stab at writing some stories about my adventures in life that ended up being the basis of these memoirs. It is only a very special joy that inspires a man to share it on the page.

We reluctantly continue South into Florida and make it to a campground in the panhandle specifically designed for kids. And for adults who are kids at heart. We had decided that I would leave my traveling companions here and head to Orlando, where I would catch up with a mate I had not seen since our trip to Uruguay 28 years prior.

It felt like only yesterday that he watched me being dragged away by the immigration agent.

When I made it back to the house where I lived with the girl, I knew that it was over and I needed to leave. I stayed until the neighbor and his family arrived back so I could thank him for being a savior of sorts. He had done what my travel agent had years before, when he forced me to go on the trip to Hawaii. That trip inspired me to go to Japan. Which inspired me to go to Yosemite. Which inspired me to go to the Grand Canyon. Which inspired me to quit my job and take a six-month trip around the world, starting in Europe. And that is where the next book will pick up, with my slightly offbeat stories about the countries I visited over several trips.

My neighbor had reignited my soul to live life to the fullest.

That road trip also inspired me to write. And reminded me to find the spark that comes from looking for the funny, irreverent, and enjoyable aspects of life and travel. Not the distressing parts. Or if they are distressing, a person needs to find a way to make them funny.

But why would a book of silly stories be important to anyone? What do my stories have to offer apart from some mindless entertainment?

I am glad you asked.

A month after the road trip, I got some distressing news. The neighbor who had taken me on the drive had committed suicide.

I bet no one saw that coming.

I sure did not.

But it makes a person think.

In the opening chapter of Book 1, I posed the question: what is the measure of success? Now comes the question, can success be achieved in a vacuum? Can a person be wildly successful outwardly and yet, in their core, be unhappy? If so, are they still successful?

I do not profess to know very much about this world. I never know what tense to put my verbs in, I could not tell you what the current cost of a barrel of oil is. I know the last season of *Game of Thrones* was a massive letdown, but everyone knows that. But I like to think that all my travels and adventures have taught me what is most important in life.

And that is to be happy.

Oh, and of course, to always wear a life jacket when sailing.

Thank you for buying and reading the second book in my memoir travel series. If you enjoyed it and would like to leave a review on Amazon, then I thank you a second time.

You are now fully roped in. There is only one more book in this series to go, along with the memoir that is dearest to my heart: *My SECOND Life*. I hope you consider purchasing them.

How to Start a Riot in a Brothel in Thailand by Ordering a Beer, and Other Lesser Known Travel Tips.

How to Avoid Getting Mugged in Rio de Janeiro by Singing Songs by The Police, and Other Lesser Known Travel Tips.

How to Survive Making Yourself Look Silly While Dancing with the German Mafia at a Bavarian nightclub, and Other Lesser Known Travel Tips.

My SECOND Life.

Printed in Great Britain
by Amazon